IBM VERSION 2.0

Publish‹It!™

Tutorial and Applications

William R. Pasewark, Sr.
Professor Emeritus, Texas Tech University
Office Management Consultant

SOUTH-WESTERN PUBLISHING CO.

ISBN: 0-538-61763-2

1 2 3 4 5 6 DH 97 96 95 94 93 92

Printed in the United States of America

Managing/Acquisitions Editor: Bob First
Developmental Editor: Dave Lafferty
Production Editor: Carolyn Morgan
Associate Photo Editor/Stylist: Mike O'Donnell
Marketing Manager: Brian Taylor

Figure 1-1	Photo courtesy of Apple Computer, Inc.
Figure 1-2	Photo courtesy of Apple Computer, Inc.
Figure 1-3	Courtesy of International Business Machines Corporation
Figure 4-1	Wang Laboratories, Inc.
Figure 4-2	Courtesy of NEC Technologies, Inc., Printer Division
Figure 4-3	Photo Courtesy of Hewlett-Packard Company
Figure 4-4	Courtesy Epson America, Inc.
App. B Photo	Photo Courtesy of Hewlett-Packard Company

Publish It! and Publish It! Version 2.0 are trademarks of Timeworks, Inc.

PREFACE

TO THE STUDENT

Desktop Publishing and You

Desktop publishing is the process of combining text and graphics using a computer to create an attractive and stimulating publication. You will find desktop publishing experience an advantage in your school, personal, and career endeavors. With desktop publishing, you can design documents such as a newsletter for a student organization or a program for a relative's wedding.

Employers consider desktop publishing experience a valuable asset because many types of businesses use it to communicate information. Typical documents produced in the workplace using desktop publishing are letterheads, advertising brochures, newsletters, and annual financial reports. Business professionals who use desktop publishing include advertising executives, newspaper editors, publishers, and secretaries.

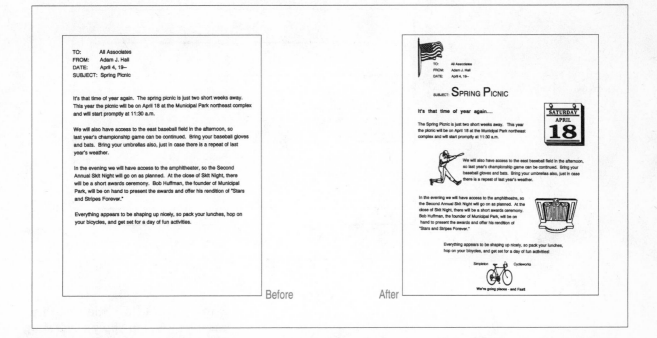

Figure 1
Desktop publishing can transform a plain document into a visually interesting publication.

Publish It!

Publish It!®,[1] the desktop publishing program you are about to study, has many features. With this single program, you can write, edit, and lay out a document. Publish It! provides dozens of clip art images and allows you to draw your own illustrations. You can also import text from word processing programs and import art from graphics programs.

      Publish It! can be used to create many types of documents. You can design a program for a school play, a personal notepad, or a greeting card.

Figure 2
A notepad is an example of a document created using desktop publishing.

The Tutorial and Applications—Learn and Apply

Publish It! Tutorial and Applications will teach you to use the program Publish It!, as well as give you general principles you can apply when you use other desktop publishing programs. The activities and applications are realistic projects that are practical and fun.

Note   1.   Publish It! and Publish It! Version 2.0 are registered trademarks of Timeworks, Inc.

Objectives listed at the beginning of each chapter give you an overview of the chapter. Short segments of text explain new information and tell why it is important. Then, activities with numbered steps guide you through the computer operation. These activities give you a chance to exercise the concepts you have just learned. This book includes many illustrations and activities to simplify complex concepts and operations. A summary, short-answer questions, and applications at the end of each chapter help you review the chapters.

TO THE TEACHER

Desktop Publishing and Your Students

Desktop publishing is the process of using a computer to merge text and graphics in an attractive and easily comprehensible format. Desktop publishing experience will benefit students as they prepare for their careers, as well as help them fulfill school and personal responsibilities.

Students enter computer classes with varying levels of computer expertise. *Publish It! Tutorial and Applications* helps overcome this teaching challenge by including applications that can be completed successfully by students with a wide range of computer abilities.

Publish It!

Features.   Publish It! is an inexpensive desktop publishing program that combines text, graphics, and page-layout features. Text can be keyed directly in Publish It! or imported from certain word processing programs. Editing commands allow cutting, copying, pasting, inserting, and deleting of text.

Publish It! includes drawing tools and over a hundred clip-art images for students to use to illustrate their documents. Graphics can also be imported from a number of other programs. Clip art and graphics can be cut, copied, pasted, resized, cropped, edited, and scaled.

Publish It! lets students design layouts with multiple columns, flow text around art, develop multipage documents, and design templates. A variety of fonts are included with which students can experiment.

Versions 2.0 and 1.2 Compatibility.   Publish It! Tutorial and Applications is 100% compatible with Publish It! Version 2.0. In addition, the template files are saved in a format compatible with both Publish It! Version 2.0 and Publish It! Version 1.2. Some of the features covered in the text–workbook are not available in Version 1.2.

System Requirements.   A minimum of an IBM PC® [2] with 640K of memory and a hard disk is necessary to run Publish It! Versions of Publish It! prior to Version 2.0 can be used without a hard drive as long as two floppy drives are available. The program supports and produces high-quality output with a wide variety of printers. A mouse is not required, but is recommended.

A Teaching Tool.   Publish It! is less sophisticated than some other desktop publishing programs, yet this simplicity makes the program an ideal introduction to desktop publishing. You will find Publish It! practical

---

2.   IBM is a registered trademark of International Business Machines Corporation.

for teaching your students to create many types of documents. Students can design documents such as a poster for school use, a party invitation for personal use, a student personal information form for classroom use, or a certificate of recognition for administrative use.

Distinguishing Features

Publish It! Tutorial and Applications is action oriented; it includes many practical activities and applications that students must complete with their hands on the keyboard.

The organization of each activity facilitates learning. Students are introduced to new information, informed why the information is pertinent, and instructed on how to complete the procedure.

Textual content is as important as strategic organization. The activities and applications relate to students' school, personal, and career lives. In addition, underlying themes of personal and societal responsibility, such as an obligation to the community, are incorporated within the book.

Teaching and Learning Aids

This instructional package is designed to simplify instruction and to enhance learning with the following learning and teaching aids:

- **Learning objectives** listed at the beginning of each chapter give students an overview of the chapter.

- **Enumerated step-by-step instructions** for specific operations allow students to progress independently while learning to use Publish It! When the same operations are repeated, instructions are "faded"; that is, fewer specific instructions are included, challenging the student gradually to perform the operations from memory without prompting.

- **Computer activities** immediately follow the presentation of new concepts and instructions. The activities give students the opportunity to apply what they have just learned.

- **Illustrations** explain complex concepts and serve as reference points as students complete activities.

- **Chapter summaries** provide quick reviews for each chapter, entrenching the main points in the students' minds.

- **Short-answer questions** and **computer applications** follow each chapter to gauge students' understanding of the chapter's information and operations. The applications offer minimal instruction so students must apply concepts previously introduced.

- The last two chapters present a **simulation** of a Desktop Publishing Center (DtPC) for a typical high school that operates after school hours and provides realistic work for students to complete. In Chapter 9, students generate publications to operate the DtPC such as business cards for student workers and job order forms. In Chapter 10, students prepare jobs brought to the DtPC by a school administrator, a teacher, students, and student organizations.

- **Appendices** include the following: A **glossary** of terms introduced in the book with their definitions. A **quick key reference** for menu shortcut keys. Fundamental **computer technology** information as a reference for students. A selection of **capstone projects**. These are projects of varying levels of difficulty that can expand the instruction for a longer course schedule. These projects can also be used by students who want additional practice or who want to obtain extra credit.

- A **comprehensive index** supplies quick and easy accessibility to specific parts of the tutorial.

Teacher's Manual

The complete teacher's manual includes a variety of aids for planning the course of study, presenting information, and managing the classroom. All are designed to ensure a successful and enjoyable teaching/learning experience. The manual includes the following features:

- **Course schedules** that suggest ways to use the tutorial for courses from 30 to 90 class meetings in length.
- **General teaching suggestions** that include strategies for efficient and effortless instruction throughout the course.
- **Specific teaching suggestions** that are presented for each chapter.
- Basic **computer technology** information on such subjects as microprocessor architecture, operating systems, expansion slots, and interface to help you understand and explain this information to students.
- **Reproducible testing materials** including end-of-chapter questions and applications as well as midterm and final exams. Answers are also provided.
- A desktop publishing **competency checklist**, created by the Computer Education Task Force of the National Business Education Association, that can be used to assess the proficiency level of students when they complete the course.

Template Disk

The template disk contains prekeyed text and selected graphics for activities and applications and may be copied for students. This disk allows students to use class time learning computer operations rather than keying text into the computer.

The Author's Commitment

In writing *Publish It! Tutorial and Applications*, the author dedicated himself to creating a complete and appealing instructional package to make teaching and learning desktop publishing an interesting, successful, and rewarding experience for both teachers and students. The author assembled in one resource all the materials and aids a teacher needs to create a learning environment in which students can successfully master skills that will serve them in their academic and career endeavors, as well as in their personal lives.

Acknowledgments

The author gratefully acknowledges the cooperative spirit and fine work of the following people who helped produce this book: Todd Knowlton, Angela Martin, and Kathy Schaefer.

CONTENTS

	Preface	**iii**
SECTION 1	**Introduction to Desktop Publishing**	**1**
	Chapter 1 Welcome to Desktop Publishing	**3**
	Learning Objectives	3
	Introduction to Desktop Publishing	3
	Starting Publish It!	7
	Publish It! Features and Capabilities	8
	The Publish It! Screen	9
	Basic Operating Procedures	11
	Summary	20
	Review	21
	Chapter 2 Working with Text and Fonts	**25**
	Learning Objectives	25
	Text in Publish It!	25
	A Clean Slate	25
	Creating Text	27
	Moving Around in Text	30
	Editing Text	32
	Reliving the Past	37
	Importing Text	38
	Find and Replace	39
	Exporting Text	42
	Fonts	43

Typeface Terminology 45

Summary 48

Review 49

Chapter 3 Graphics 55

Learning Objectives 55

Why Use Graphics? 55

Two Sources of Graphics 56

Graphic Frames and Rulers 56

Importing Graphics 58

Drawing Graphics in Publish It! 68

Enhancing Graphics 71

Positioning Graphics 75

Cutting, Copying, and Pasting Graphics 77

Summary 79

Review 81

SECTION 2   Publishing Design Concepts and Principles 85

Chapter 4 Printing Documents 87

Learning Objectives 87

Delivering the Message 87

Types of Printers 87

How Print Quality is Measured 90

Printer Setup 91

The Basics of Printing 91

Print Options 92

Getting a Preview of Your Document 94

Printing to a Disk 95

Summary 96

Review 97

Chapter 5 Using Style Sheets   **101**

Learning Objectives   101

Style Sheets   101

Page Format   101

Using Paragraph Styles   104

Modifying Paragraph Styles   105

Creating Paragraph Styles   109

Deleting Paragraph Styes   110

Tables and Tabs   111

Saving Style Sheets   114

Loading Style Sheets   115

Summary   116

Review   117

Chapter 6 Creating a Page Layout   **121**

Learning Objectives   121

Designing a Readable and Appealing Layout   121

Column Guides   124

Linking Frames   127

Text Runaround   129

Other Formatting Features   134

Summary   136

Review   139

SECTION 3   Advanced Desktop Publishing   143

Chapter 7 Advanced Publication Layout   **145**

Learning Objectives   145

Layout Strategies   145

Working with Multipage Documents   147

Master Pages   151

Headers and Footers   154

Page Numbers   155

Naming Text 157

Autoflowing Text 159

Frame Options 160

Summary 163

Review 165

Chapter 8 Working with Template Files 169

Learning Objectives 169

Templates 169

Using Templates 169

Creating Templates 171

Summary 175

Review 177

Chapter 9 Desktop Publishing Center Simulation 181

Learning Objectives 181

A Desktop Publishing Center Simulation 181

DtPC Documents 181

Chapter 10 Desktop Publishing Center Applications 189

Learning Objective 189

Customer Documents 189

Desktop Publishing in Your Future 190

Appendix A Quick Keys 205

Appendix B Desktop Publishing Technology 208

Appendix C Capstone Projects 214

Appendix D Proofreaders' Symbols 216

Appendix E Hyphen Rules 219

Glossary 220

Index 225

SECTION

1

Introduction to Desktop Publishing

Chapter 1
Welcome to Desktop Publishing

Chapter 2
Working with Text and Fonts

Chapter 3
Graphics

CHAPTER

❶

Welcome to Desktop Publishing

LEARNING OBJECTIVES

When you complete this chapter, you will be able to:

1. Understand terms related to desktop publishing.
2. Start Publish It!
3. Recognize basic features and capabilities of Publish It!
4. Identify parts of the Publish It! screen.
5. Use a mouse or keyboard to access menus and tools.
6. Open and save a document.
7. Change document view.
8. Use Help.
9. Exit Publish It!

INTRODUCTION TO DESKTOP PUBLISHING

The term **desktop publishing** is perhaps one of the most popular terms within the microcomputer-user community today. Desktop publishing is the production of professional quality documents, such as newsletters, pamphlets, journals, or business reports using a personal computer. With the advent of *relatively* inexpensive, yet powerful microcomputers and software, desktop publishing has become one of the fastest-growing microcomputer applications. What does all this mean to you, the student? This question can be answered by first taking a brief look at the history of desktop publishing.

Desktop publishing is a recent development in the microcomputer industry. This is because microcomputer hardware, such as laser printers and fast and powerful central processing units, were not easily affordable until recent years. However, desktop publishing is not a new concept. People have been practicing a form of desktop publishing for as long as typewriters, scissors, glue, and tape have been around. Some people use terms like *revolution* when describing the rapid growth of desktop publishing. The microcomputer has indeed revolutionized the desktop publishing process.

In the past, publishing involved several separate, yet interdependent jobs and was considered a complex and lengthy task. As someone who uses desktop publishing, you may be called upon to fill the roles of author, editor, layout designer, **typographer**, artist, and printer. Desktop publishing has brought the many jobs of the publishing process together and has placed them on the desktop of the computer user.

One of the first computer manufacturers on the desktop publishing scene in 1984 was Apple Computer, Inc. Apple produced a computer called the Macintosh, shown in Figure 1-1. This new computer was quite different from the other personal computers that existed at the time, and its text and graphics capabilities aided the growth of desktop publishing.

Figure 1-1
In 1984, Apple computer introduced the Macintosh, a computer that helped revolutionize the desktop publishing industry.

In 1985, Apple introduced the laser printer shown in Figure 1-2. The addition of the laser printer completed the desktop publishing package, and computer users could easily lay out and print publications that approached typeset quality.

After the Macintosh captured the interest of computer users, desktop publishing software and hardware were developed for other computers, resulting in competition. This competition has given computer users a variety of desktop publishing software and hardware. Figure 1-3 illustrates an IBM computer and laser printer used for desktop publishing.

Desktop publishing allows the production of high-quality publications that in the past was prohibited by high costs. Figure 1-4 illustrates how materials that were once typed on a typewriter or keyed into a word processor and printed with a letter-quality printer can now be easily produced with a professionally published look.

Figure 1-2
The introduction of Apple's LaserWriter printer completed the desktop publishing package.

Prior to the advent of desktop publishing technology, producing a memo similar to the "After" publication pictured in Figure 1-4 involved sending the typewritten "Before" copy to a printer and paying the printer to design, lay out, and print the publication.

Figure 1-3
A wide variety of computers, such as this model from IBM, is now used for desktop publishing.

TO: All Associates
FROM: Adam J. Hall
DATE: April 4, 19--
SUBJECT: Spring Picnic

It's that time of year again. The spring picnic is just two short weeks away. This year the picnic will be on April 18 at the Municipal Park northeast complex and will start promptly at 11:30 a.m.

We will also have access to the east baseball field in the afternoon, so last year's championship game can be continued. Bring your baseball gloves and bats. Bring your umbrellas also, just in case there is a repeat of last year's weather.

In the evening we will have access to the amphitheater, so the Second Annual Skit Night will go on as planned. At the close of Skit Night, there will be a short awards ceremony. Bob Huffman, the founder of Municipal Park, will be on hand to present the awards and offer his rendition of "Stars and Stripes Forever."

Everything appears to be shaping up nicely, so pack your lunches, hop on your bicycles, and get set for a day of fun activities.

Before

After

TO: All Associates
FROM: Adam J. Hall
DATE: April 4, 19--

SUBJECT: SPRING PICNIC

It's that time of year again....

The Spring Picnic is just two short weeks away. This year the picnic will be on April 18 at the Municipal Park northeast complex and will start promptly at 11:30 a.m.

We will also have access to the east baseball field in the afternoon, so last year's championship game can be continued. Bring your baseball gloves and bats. Bring your umbrellas also, just in case there is a repeat of last year's weather.

In the evening we will have access to the amphitheatre, so the Second Annual Skit Night will go on as planned. At the close of Skit Night, there will be a short awards ceremony. Bob Huffman, the founder of Municipal Park, will be on hand to present the awards and offer his rendition of "Stars and Stripes Forever."

Everything appears to be shaping up nicely, so pack your lunches, hop on your bicycles, and get set for a day of fun activities!

Simpleton Cycleworks

We're going places - and Fast!

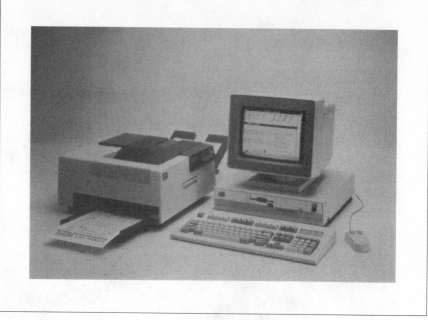

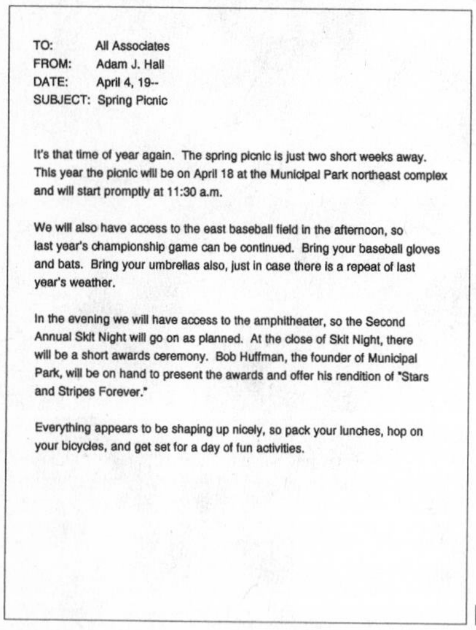

Figure 1-4
Advances in desktop publishing technology make the production of attractive and effective publications easy and inexpensive.

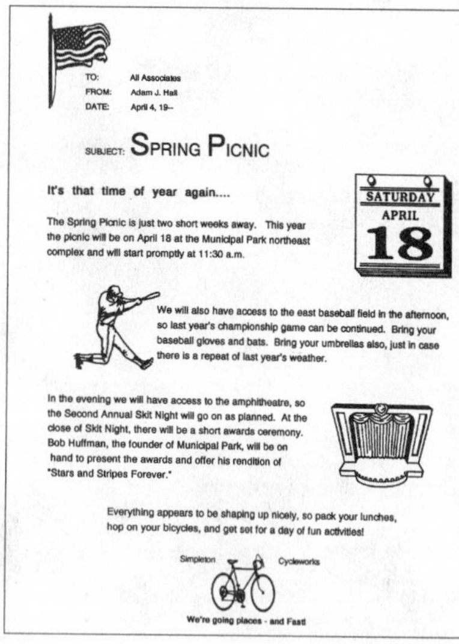

Desktop publishing technology, however, does not totally eliminate reliance on a professional printer in the publishing process. Desktop publishing software and personal computers normally are not used to produce multiple copies of a finished publication, mainly due to the high cost of printing.

You will find that users of desktop publishing most often create **camera-ready masters**. Camera-ready masters are the final copies of a publication with which the commercial printer makes the printing plates for printing the publication. Most often it costs less to supply a commercial printer with camera-ready copy than to print thousands of copies on your laser printer.

With the help of this text–workbook, the computer, and your teacher, you will learn about desktop publishing. You will also get a chance to practice the art of desktop publishing, using software called **Publish It!** and create some interesting publications of your own. Let's begin by starting Publish It! on your computer.

STARTING PUBLISH IT!

You will need the template disk that came with this text–workbook and a data disk for storing your own publications. Your teacher should provide you with these disks or give you instructions on how to obtain them. The template disk has samples and activities that you will use throughout this book. The data disk should be a blank, formatted disk. You will routinely open files on the template disk and save them to your data disk.

These instructions assume that the Publish It! software has been installed on a hard disk. If Publish It! has not been installed, refer to the Publish It! user's manual in the section called Installing Publish It!, or ask your teacher for assistance.

1. Turn on the computer monitor. The power switch may be located on the front or side of the monitor.
2. Turn on the central processing unit (CPU). The power switch may be located on the front or side of the unit. When the computer has completed its self-tests and DOS has booted, the C:\> prompt appears on the screen.
3. Key publish and press Enter. The Publish It! opening screen should flash on your monitor. After a few moments, a new, blank document, similar to Figure 1-5, appears.

Figure 1-5
A new, blank document appears on your monitor, and Publish It! is ready for you to create a document.

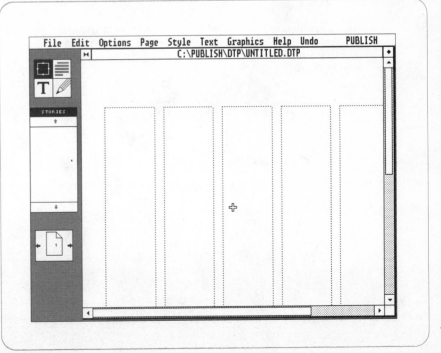

PUBLISH IT! FEATURES AND CAPABILITIES

Desktop publishing software offers a wide range of features and capabilities. Expensive programs such as Aldus PageMaker and Xerox Ventura Publisher are very powerful packages. It is possible to produce large publications, such as books or magazines, with these high-end desktop publishing packages.

Publish It! was not designed to produce books or magazines. If you attempted to produce a book or complex magazine with Publish It!, you would probably be somewhat discouraged. However, Publish It! works well for what it was designed to do: produce newsletters, flyers, and other simple documents. Even though Publish It! is considered to be a low-end desktop publishing package, it can produce professional-looking documents.

Publish It! allows you to format text in an almost unlimited number of layouts. These range from a single column layout to a complex, multicolumn layout. You can choose from many different typefaces to dress up the text, making it attractive and easy to read. If you have created text in a word processor, the text can be imported into a Publish It! document. Or you can create and edit text in Publish It!

Publish It! allows you to insert art into your publications. Publish It! includes more than a hundred pieces of clip art. If you desire, art can also be imported from other programs. If you want to create your own art from scratch or modify an existing piece of art, Publish It! allows you to do that as well. As you can see, Publish It! gives you a certain level of flexibility in your documents. Figure 1-6 illustrates some of the different documents you can create using Publish It!

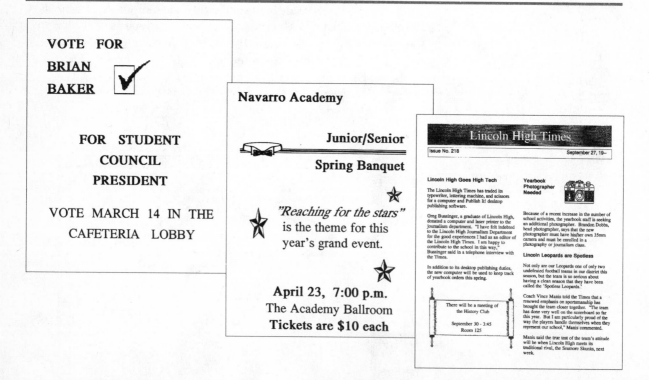

Figure 1-6
These three publications are just a few examples of what you can do with Publish It!

THE PUBLISH IT! SCREEN

The Publish It! screen could be called an electronic work table. On this "table" are your document and the tools necessary to work with text and art. Figure 1-7 illustrates the Publish It! screen and its components. The screens you see illustrated in this text–workbook were created with a VGA graphics card. If your computer uses a different graphics card, such as a Hercules, CGA, or EGA card, the Publish It! screen may look slightly different on your monitor. However, everything you need will be available.

Figure 1-7
The Publish It! screen is your electronic work table.

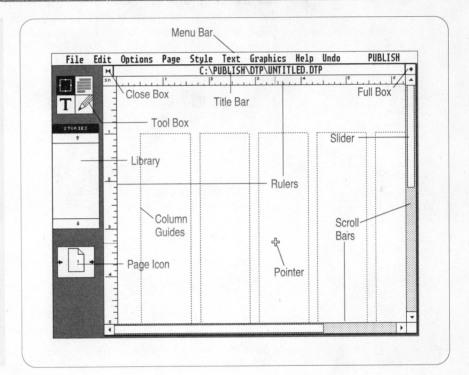

Work Area

The **work area** is where your document is displayed. The work area appears as a "window" on the screen. Surrounding the work area are the tools necessary to create a document.

Menu Bar

The **menu bar** is located across the top of the screen. It contains ten names which represent **pull-down menus**. Each menu includes a list of commands for you to use to create a document. Also, an on-line Help feature allows you to receive help while you are working with Publish It!

Title Bar

The **title bar** is located directly below the menu bar. It contains the name of the current document. The name includes the directory in which the document is saved. If the document has never been saved, the name is displayed as *UNTITLED*.

Close Box

Bordering the title bar on the left is the close box. The **close box** allows you to stop work on the current document without saving the changes.

Full Box

Bordering the title bar on the right is the full box. The **full box** expands the work area to fill the entire screen.

Scroll Bars

At the right side and at the bottom of the screen you will notice partially shaded columns called **scroll bars**. Frequently, you will work on a document that is larger than the window through which you are viewing it. On each end of a scroll bar are arrows you can use to move the document in the window to make different parts of it visible. Each scroll bar contains a rectangular box called a **slider**. You can move the slider to view different parts of the page on the screen.

Tool Box

At the top left of the screen is the **tool box**. The tool box contains tools you use to create and alter art and text. They are the Frame, Paragraph, Text, and Pencil tools.

Library

The **library** helps you keep track of what text and art have been included in your document. In addition, the library makes certain features more accessible.

Page Icon

The **page icon** tells you the page number that is currently displayed in the work area.

Pointer

You use the **pointer** to indicate where you want to work on the screen. It has a different shape for each of its functions in different areas of the screen. When you open a page, the pointer is shaped like an open cross (✛). The pointer is shaped like an arrow (↖) when you point outside the work area. When you are entering text, the pointer is shaped like an I-beam (Ⅰ). Other variations of the pointer will be discussed in later chapters. If you do not have a mouse, the pointer can be moved with the arrow keys.

Sometimes the pointer will transform into a small spinning wheel (✤) or an hour glass (⧖). These symbols usually appear when you issue a command. It is the software's way of asking you to wait while it completes the task.

Text Cursor

The **text cursor** is a thin, solid, vertical bar, which shows where text is to be inserted next.

Rulers

You can use the **rulers** to help you size objects, as well as to see your position on the page. The unit of measure can be changed from inches to centimeters or picas. The rulers are visible only when turned on from the Options menu.

Column Guides

Column guides appear as dotted lines in the work area. These do not print with your document. They are to help you line up the parts of your document.

BASIC OPERATING PROCEDURES

The next sections outline some basic operating procedures you will use when you are working with Publish It! You will practice some of these procedures by completing the activities provided, giving you some hands-on experience before you actually sit down to create a document. This book includes instructions for using both the mouse and the keyboard. As in the first activity that follows, the instructions are separated into columns with mouse instructions on the left (identified by a small mouse symbol at the top of the column) and keyboard instructions on the right (identified by a small keyboard symbol at the top of the column). If you do not have a mouse to use as you are working through the activities, follow the keyboard instructions.

Using the Mouse

A mouse is essential for the operation of some computers. Although not usually essential for the IBM and IBM-compatible computers, mice are now becoming quite popular among all computer users. If you have used a mouse, you are well aware of how it simplifies certain operations. Even though it is possible to use Publish It! without a mouse, some operations can be accomplished more efficiently with one.

The three skills you need in order to use the mouse are click, double-click, and drag.

- To **click**, place the pointer on an object then press and release the mouse button once.
- To **double-click**, place the pointer on an object and click twice quickly.
- To **drag**, move the mouse across the desk while pressing and holding the mouse button down.

Using the Keyboard

Publish It! can be used even if you do not have a mouse. Although some operations can be accomplished faster with a mouse, Publish It! allows you to operate with the keyboard only. In fact, some veteran computer users elect to use the mouse only for certain operations, completing most tasks using keyboard shortcuts, or **quick keys**. To the right of many of the commands in the pull-down menus, a diamond and a letter or a numeral are displayed. The diamond and the letter tell you to press Alt and the symbol to access the command. You will practice using the quick keys in the activities in later chapters.

When you're using the keyboard in place of the mouse, you can choose between two keyboard modes. In normal mode, the arrow keys do not move the pointer. In pointer mode, the arrow keys and the Home and End keys perform the functions of a mouse. For more precise movement in pointer mode, hold down the Shift key while you press an arrow key. To switch between the modes, hold down the Ctrl key and press the Shift key on the right side of the keyboard. This action will be indicated by Crtl + Right Shift in the activities.

Another useful key combination to remember is Alt + M. Each time Alt + M is pressed, the next tool is selected. For instance, if the Frame tool is highlighted, pressing Alt + M twice will select the Text tool.

The click, double-click, and drag mouse functions can be duplicated on the keyboard. The following table illustrates the keyboard equivalents for mouse functions in pointer mode.

Mouse Function	Keyboard Equivalent
Click	Press the Home key once.
Double-click	Press the Home key twice rapidly.
Drag	Press the End key and then press the arrow keys to move the pointer.

It is possible to accomplish some tasks faster using the keyboard rather than the mouse. As you become proficient with Publish It!, you can elect to carry out certain operations using the keyboard even if you have a mouse available. You should determine which way works best for you.

Menus

As mentioned previously, the pull-down menus are located in the menu bar at the top of the screen. Each menu is accessible from the keyboard or by using a mouse. In the following activity you will practice pulling down several menus.

ACTIVITY 1-1 • Pulling Down Menus

In this activity you will practice pulling down Publish It! menus. If you have a mouse, follow the mouse instructions at the left. If you do not have a mouse, follow the keyboard instructions at the right.

1. Use the mouse to move the pointer to the word **File** in the menu bar. When the pointer reaches the File header, the File menu drops down, displaying its list of commands (see Figure 1-8).

2. Move the pointer down through the menu. The commands in the menu are highlighted as the pointer moves across them. Notice that the gray commands do not become highlighted when the pointer moves across them. These commands are inactive and are not currently available for use.

3. To put away the menu without choosing a command, move the pointer outside the menu. Notice that none of the commands is highlighted.

4. Click the mouse button and watch the menu disappear.

5. Repeat the above steps to pull down the **Text** menu and the **Graphics** menu.

1. Press **Ctrl + Right Shift** to enable you to move the pointer with the arrow keys. Then move the pointer with the arrow keys to the word **File** in the menu bar. The File menu drops down to display its list of commands (see Figure 1-8).

2. Using the Down Arrow key, move the pointer down through the menu. The commands in the menu are highlighted as the pointer moves across them. Notice that the gray commands do not become highlighted when the pointer moves across them. These commands are inactive and are not currently available for use.

3. To put away the menu without choosing a command, use the arrow keys to move the pointer outside the menu. Notice that none of the commands is highlighted.

4. Press **Home** to put away the menu without choosing a command.

5. Now pull down the **Text** menu and the **Graphics** menu using the same steps.

Figure 1-8
To pull down a menu, simply move the pointer to the menu's header.

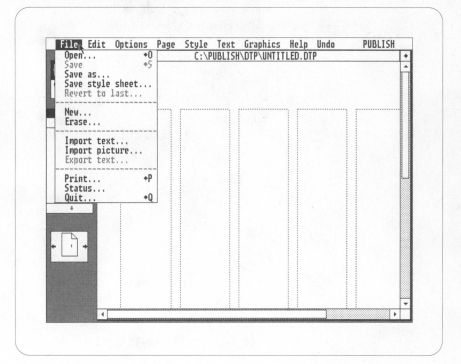

Dialog Boxes

One of the first things you will notice when you are working with Publish It! is that when you choose a command, the program often needs more information from you in order to continue. Dialog boxes are the way the program prompts you to provide this information. A **dialog box** usually contains several options. You choose the ones you need to complete the command. Figure 1-9 illustrates a typical dialog box, the Ruler Spacing dialog box.

Figure 1-9
The Ruler Spacing dialog box allows you to choose the unit of measure for the screen's rulers.

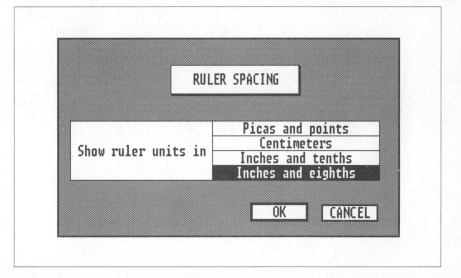

Filenames

Publish It! uses MS-DOS, the same **disk operating system** that most IBM programs use. Each file saved on an MS-DOS disk must have a unique filename. The filename can be up to eight characters long.

Documents should be given meaningful names. In addition to the name you assign, Publish It! adds a three-character extension. These specific filename extensions identify the file's type. Extensions make it easier for you to understand what types of data a file contains. The following is a list of the Publish It! filename extensions that are most often used.

Extension	Description
.DTP	*.DTP* files are documents created with Publish It!
.WPD	Files with a *.WPD* extension are WordPerfect 4 files that can be imported into a Publish It! document.
.IMG	*.IMG* files contain imported art that is packaged with Publish It! Some other art formats use extensions such as *.PCX* and *.PIC*.

File Management

Desktop publishing files are different from most word processor files because they generally take up more disk space. For that reason it is important that you manage your files and data disk properly. The following tips will help you manage your documents and their related files:

- Place a document and all related art and text files on the same data disk. Documents usually are composed of numerous files, and keeping them in one spot will ease the confusion that may result. If you have four or five disks floating around, the chances of losing something increase dramatically.

- Choose filenames for your documents and related files that are easy to understand. This point cannot be overemphasized. As an example, a filename like *STORY1.WPD for the first story in a newsletter is much easier to decipher than* NLFSTSTY.WPD.

- Save documents to your data disk, not your template disk. Your template disk already contains many files, and there may not be room to store your applications. By using a data disk, you reduce the chances of accidentally overwriting an important template file.

- Always keep a backup copy of your data disk. Update this backup copy daily. If your original data disk becomes damaged, you will always have a current backup available.

Opening a Document

The **Open command** in the File menu allows you to load a document from disk. Choosing the Open command brings up a dialog box known as the **Item Selector**. Figure 1-10 shows the Item Selector, which appears when the Open command is chosen. It contains a list of the files that are in the current directory of the disk from which you are running Publish It!

Near the top of the Item Selector is the **Directory line**. This line specifies the directory in which the Item Selector is to look. This directory line is commonly referred to as the **path** to a file, or **pathname**. To direct the Item

Selector to list the files in another directory, you simply key a new path into the Directory line. The following activity shows you how to change the Directory line and open a document.

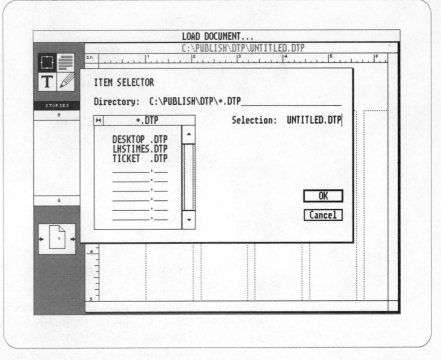

Figure 1-10
The Item Selector allows you to choose a file from any available disk and directory.

ACTIVITY 1-2 • Opening a Document

In this activity you will practice using menus and dialog boxes to open a document with the filename *ACT1-2.DTP from your template disk.*

1. Insert your template disk into drive A.	1. Insert your template disk into drive A.
2. Use the mouse to pull down the **File** menu.	2. Press **Ctrl + Right Shift** to enable the arrow keys. With the arrow keys, position the pointer on **File**, then position the pointer on **Open**, and then press **Home**. The Item Selector box appears on the screen. Since your template disk is located in drive A, you will need to tell Publish It! to look there. If the disk is in drive B, use this drive.
3. Move the pointer down until the **Open** command is highlighted.	
4. Click to choose the **Open** command. You now see the Item Selector dialog box on the screen. Since your template disk is located in drive A, you will need to tell Publish It! to look there. If the disk is in drive B, use this drive.	3. Move the pointer to the Directory line with the arrow

Continued

5. Click on the Directory line. Backspace over the pathname and in its place key **A:*.DTP**.

6. Press **Enter**. The disk drive whirs and a list of *.DTP* files appears in the Item Selector box. The file called *ACT1-2.DTP* is the one you want.

7. Click the mouse on *ACT1-2.DTP* to highlight it.

8. Click on **OK**. After a few moments Publish It! displays the contents of the file.

keys. Press **Home** to place the text cursor at the end of the pathname. Backspace over the pathname and in its place key **A:*.DTP**.

4. Press **Enter**. The disk drive whirs and a list of *.DTP* files appears in the Item Selector box. The file called *ACT1-2.DTP* is the one you want.

5. With the arrow keys, move the pointer to *ACT1-2.DTP*.

6. Press **Home** to select the file.

7. Press **Enter**. After a few moments Publish It! displays the contents of the file.

Changing Your Perspective

Publish It! allows you to view your document in several sizes. Normally, the view you see is the actual size of the document. However, the Page menu allows you to zoom in and out using the commands **Half size**, **3/4 size**, **Actual size**, **Double size**, and **Size to fit**.

Another way to change the view is by enlarging the work area using the full box. The full box is located to the right of the title bar. When you click on it, the full box expands the work area to fill the entire screen. The tool box and other elements around the work area are hidden. Clicking the full box again returns the work area to its original size.

ACTIVITY 1-3 • Zooming In and Out

1. Pull down the **Page** menu.

2. Choose **Half size**. The document will shrink to half its actual size. Think of it as taking a step back to get an overall view.

3. Pull down the **Page** menu again and this time choose **3/4 size**. The document is a bit larger now, but not quite actual size.

4. Pull down the **Page** menu and choose **Double size**. Now the document is twice its actual

1. Using the arrow keys, pull down the **Page** menu. Hint: Press **Ctrl + Right Shift**, if necessary, to enable the arrow keys.

2. Choose **Half size** by highlighting the command and pressing **Home**. The document will shrink to half its actual size. Think of it as taking a step back to get an overall view.

3. Pull down the **Page** menu again and this time choose **3/4 size**. The document is a bit larger now, but not quite actual size.

Continued

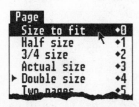

size. This view is good for aligning objects on the page when accuracy is important.

5. Choose **Size to fit** from the Page menu. The Size to fit command selects a view for you that will accommodate your entire document. Use this command to get an overview when you are not sure which view is best.

6. Choose **Actual size** from the **Page** menu. The Actual size command returns the document to its normal size.

7. Click on the **full box**. The work area expands to fill the screen.

8. Click on the **full box** again. The work area returns to its normal size.

4. Pull down the **Page** menu and choose **Double size**. Now the document is twice its actual size. This view is good for aligning objects on the page when accuracy is important.

5. Choose **Size to fit** from the **Page** menu. The Size to fit command selects a view for you that will accommodate your entire document. Use this command to get an overview when you are not sure which view is best.

6. Choose **Actual size** from the **Page** menu. The Actual size command returns the document to its normal size.

7. Using the arrow keys, move the pointer to the **full box**. Press **Home**. The work area expands to fill the screen.

8. Press **Home** on the **full box** again. The work area returns to its normal size.

Saving a Document

An important feature of most computer programs is that they allow you to save your work on disk. Publish It! provides two different save commands. The first is the Save as command and the second is the Save command. Use the **Save as command** the first time you save a document and any time you want to save the document with a new name. It allows you to assign a filename to the document. After the document is saved once, you can save again using the Save command. The **Save command** lets you quickly save the document without specifying a name.

ACTIVITY 1-4 • Using Save As

  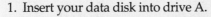

1. Insert your data disk into drive A.

2. Pull down the **File** menu and choose **Save as**. The Item Selector appears.

3. The Directory line should read A:*.DTP. If it does not, click on

1. Insert your data disk in drive A.

2. Move the pointer to the **File** menu and choose **Save as** by pressing **Home** while Save as is highlighted. The Item Selector appears.

Continued

the Directory line, backspace over the pathname, and key **A:*.DTP**.

4. Click on the **Selection** line.

5. Press **Esc** to clear the Selection line.

6. Key **JOINBAND.DTP** and press **Enter**. The file is saved to disk drive A.

3. The Directory line should read A:*.DTP. If it does not, move the pointer to the Directory line, press **Home**, backspace over the pathname, and key A:*.DTP.

4. Click on the Selection line.

5. Press **Esc** to clear the **Selection** line.

6. Key **JOINBAND.DTP** and press **Enter**. The file is saved to disk drive A.

Erasing Files

Publish It! allows you to erase files from your disks without exiting Publish It! This is done with the **Erase command** from the File menu. Use this command only if you are experienced with file management and only with the permission of your teacher. The Erase command can remove practically any file from your disk. Improper use of the Erase command could result in the loss of valuable or important data and programs.

Using Help

The Publish It! Help menu provides nine topics of assistance. The list of Help topics is displayed when you choose Help from the menu bar. When each window of information appears, you can choose a topic, move to the next window, return to the previous window, or cancel. Figure 1-11 illustrates a Help window.

Figure 1-11
Simply click the mouse on the Help menu, or position the pointer on Help and press Home. Help is on the way.

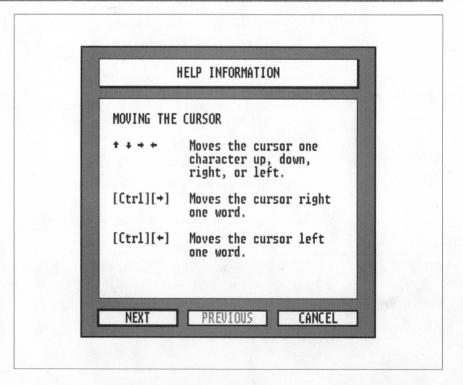

ACTIVITY 1-5 • Help Is on the Way

In this activity you will practice using the Help menu.

Help
Documents
Drawing tools
Frames
Keyboard
Pages
Paragraph styles
Pictures
Style sheets
Text

1. Pull down the **Help** menu.
2. Take some time to read the list of Help topics to familiarize yourself with what is available. Notice that the topics are organized alphabetically.
3. Position the pointer over the topic called **Keyboard** and click to select it. The Help window appears.
4. Click on the **Next** button. The next window of information appears.
5. Click on the **Previous** button to go back to the first window.
6. Click on the **Cancel** button to exit Help topics.

1. Point to the **Help** menu. The menu drops down.
2. Take some time to read the list of Help topics to familiarize yourself with what is available. Notice that the topics are organized alphabetically.
3. Position the pointer over the topic called **Keyboard** and press **Home**. The Help window appears.
4. Notice that the Next button has a heavy border. This indicates that the Next button can be chosen by simply pressing Enter. Press **Enter** to choose **Next**. The next window of information appears.
5. Position the pointer over the **Previous** button and press **Home**. The first window of information reappears.
6. Position the pointer over the **Cancel** button and press **Home**.

Combating That "I'm Not Finished" Feeling

Each chapter in this text–workbook contains several activities for you to complete as you sit at the computer. As you work through a chapter during class, there is the possibility that you will be in the middle of an activity as the end of the class approaches. If that happens, you can save your work on your data disk. The next time you work on the computer, simply open your file and continue where you left off.

How to Exit Publish It!

When you are finished working, it is important that you properly exit Publish It! and shut down the computer. This will reduce the chance of losing the document you have been working on or damaging the Publish It! software or the computer. While some computer systems have specific procedures for shutting down, the following activity contains steps that should apply to most computers. Ask your teacher if there are any specific differences that should be considered before you shut off your computer.

ACTIVITY 1-6 • Quitting for the Day

In this activity you will exit Publish It! using the **Quit command** and shut off your computer. Insert your data disk into drive A if it is not already there.

1. Pull down the **File** menu.
2. Choose the **Quit** command. You may see a message warning you to save changes. If such a message appears, click on **Abandon**.
3. Shut off your monitor and computer.

1. Pull down the **File** menu.
2. Choose the **Quit** command. The quick key for the Quit command is Alt + Q. Next time you exit Publish It!, you can use the quick key to save time and keystrokes. You may see a message warning you to save changes. If such a message appears, move the pointer to the **Abandon** button and press **Home**.
3. Shut off your monitor and computer.

SUMMARY

In recent years desktop publishing has become a household word among computer users. The advanced technology of desktop publishing has revolutionized the publishing and printing business. High-quality publications that were once quite expensive to produce are now affordable to most computer owners.

A variety of desktop publishing software is available with a wide range of capabilities. Publish It! allows the merging of text and graphics into a document to produce newsletters, flyers, reports, and a variety of other documents. Although Publish It! does not have as many features as some more expensive desktop publishing packages, it is capable of producing professional-looking documents.

The Publish It! screen is your electronic work table. The menu bar gives easy access to the pull-down menus. These pull-down menus contain the commands used to complete different tasks. The tool box contains tools used to create and modify text and art. The scroll bars allow the user to display different parts of a document on the screen.

Publish It! also contains an on-line Help feature. Help topics are available through the Help menu.

Although a mouse is sometimes helpful in desktop publishing, Publish It! can be operated from the keyboard without a mouse.

CHAPTER
❶
Review

Name _____ Date _____

TRUE OR FALSE

The following statements are either true or false. Circle T or F to indicate your answer.

1. Desktop publishing is a recent development in the micro-computer industry. (Obj. 1)

1. T F

2. You should not save your documents on your template disk. (Obj. 2)

2. T F

3. Publish It! has as many features as the most expensive desktop publishing programs. (Obj. 3.)

3. T F

4. The rulers on the Publish It! screen are always visible. (Obj. 4)

4. T F

5. The Tool Box is used to view different parts of a publication on a screen. (Obj. 4)

5. T F

6. A quick key is a keyboard shortcut used to save time when you're choosing a command. (Obj. 5)

6. T F

7. Filenames can be up to eight characters long with a three-character extension. (Obj. 6)

7. T F

8. The Size to fit command is identical to the Actual size command. (Obj. 7)

8. T F

9. Help is accessed by pressing Alt + F1. (Obj. 8)

9. T F

10. The quick key for the Quit command is Alt + Q. (Obj. 9)

10. T F

COMPLETION

Write your answers in the space provided.

11. Briefly define desktop publishing. (Obj. 1)

_____

12. List four of the seven roles someone who utilizes desktop publishing may be called upon to fill. (Obj. 1)

_____

_____

13. What are camera-ready masters? (Obj. 1)

_____

_____

14. What does the filename extension *.WPD* indicate? (Obj. 3)

_____

_____

15. Describe the use of the scroll bars. (Obj. 4)

_____

_____

16. What key is equivalent to clicking the mouse button? (Obj. 5)

_____

_____

17. Suppose you are working on a monthly newsletter for the computer science club in your school. Write a filename that accurately represents the contents of the file. (Obj. 6)

_____

_____

18. How often should a backup copy of your data disk be updated? (Obj. 6)

_____

_____

19. Give a reason why you might want to view a document at half size. (Obj. 7)

_____

_____

20. What are the three buttons available in a Help window? (Obj. 8)

_____

_____

_____

CHAPTER

Working with Text and Fonts

LEARNING OBJECTIVES

When you complete this chapter, you will be able to:

1. Create text.
2. Move around in text.
3. Edit text.
4. Use the undo features.
5. Import text.
6. Export text.
7. Understand terms describing fonts.
8. Change fonts.

TEXT IN PUBLISH IT!

In Chapter 1 you saw some examples of publications that can be created using desktop publishing technology. The examples show that the arrangement of text and the addition of illustrations can help a publication get the attention of the reader. However, once you have the reader's attention, it is up to the text to present the message. Therefore, it is important to be able to work with text effectively.

There are two ways to get text into your Publish It! documents: creating the text in Publish It!, and importing text from a word processor.

All text, regardless of where it comes from, is placed in an area called a text frame. A **text frame** is a box that holds text in your document. The job of a text frame is to keep your text "framed" in the area you define. Text frames are created using the **Frame tool**, located in the upper right corner of the tool box.

The **Text tool** allows you to work with text within a text frame. The Text tool is in the bottom left corner of the tool box. The text cursor indicates the position of the next character typed on the keyboard. When it's over the work area, the pointer appears as an I-beam and is used to reposition the text cursor. Figure 2-1 illustrates the Frame tool, the Text tool, the text cursor, and the pointer.

A CLEAN SLATE

When you start Publish It!, you have a new, blank document with which to work. If you want to start over with a "clean slate" without restarting the program, use the New command. The **New command** creates a new document just as if you had restarted the program. When you choose the New command, you will be asked if you want to load a style sheet. Style sheets will be discussed in Chapter 5.

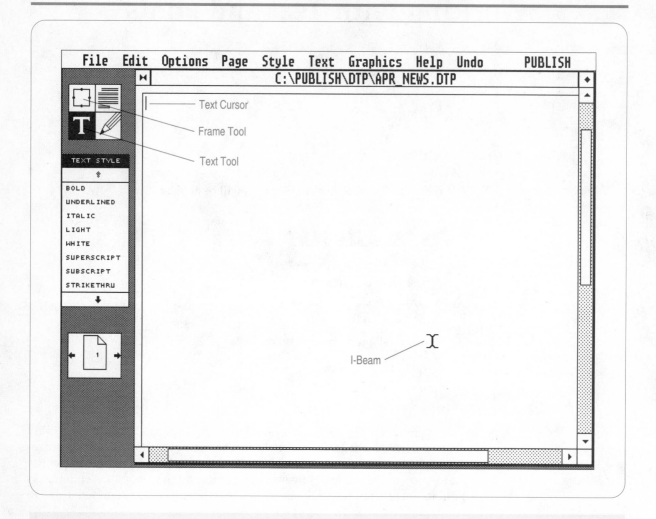

Figure 2-1
The Frame tool, Text tool, text cursor, and I-beam pointer are used to create and edit text.

ACTIVITY 2-1 • The New Command

In this activity you will practice using the New command.

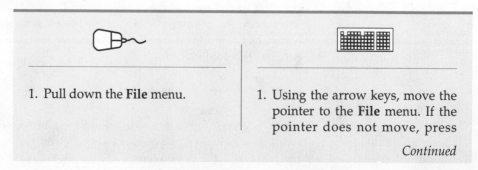

1. Pull down the **File** menu.

1. Using the arrow keys, move the pointer to the **File** menu. If the pointer does not move, press

Continued

2. Choose the **New** command. You may be asked if you want to save the current document. If you need to save the current document, click **Save**, otherwise click **Abandon**. Next, a dialog box appears asking if you want to load a style sheet.

3. Click on **No**. The Page Format dialog box appears. It allows you choose page dimensions, page orientation, and other format features.

4. Click on **OK** to accept the current settings. The new, blank document appears.

Ctrl + Right Shift to switch to pointer mode.

2. Choose the **New** command by moving the pointer down until the command is highlighted, then press **Home**. You may be asked if you want to save the current document. If you need to save the current document, choose **Save**, otherwise choose **Abandon**. Next, a dialog box appears asking if you want to load a style sheet.

3. Choose **No**. The Page Format dialog box appears. It allows you choose page dimensions, page orientation, and other format features.

4. Choose **OK** to accept the current settings. The new, blank document appears.

CREATING TEXT

To create text in Publish It!, you must first draw a text frame. Publish It! starts up in frame mode. The Frame tool is highlighted in the tool box in the top left corner of the screen. In frame mode, the pointer looks like an open cross when it's over the work area.

To draw a text frame:

1. Select the **Frame tool**.

2. Move the pointer to the upper left corner of the area in which you want the text frame.

3. Drag to where you want the lower right corner to be.

Text frames can be moved and resized if necessary. To select a frame, click on a text frame in frame mode. When a frame is selected, small boxes, called **handles**, appear on the border of the frame. To resize a frame, drag the handle of the corner or side you want to adjust. During resizing, the pointer looks like a hand with a pointing finger. To move a frame, drag the frame from within the border. While a frame is being moved, the pointer looks like a spread hand.

To begin keying the text, highlight the Text tool and click in the text frame. A cursor appears in the upper left corner of the text frame. The cursor may be hidden by the border of the frame. When you begin keying, you will see the characters appear and your cursor will become visible.

When keying directly into Publish It!, you have many of the editing features found in word processors. One of the important features to understand is word wrap. **Word wrap** allows you to key lines of text without having to press the Enter key at the end of each line. When the text reaches the right margin, any word that will not fit on the current line is automatically moved to the next line without interruption in keying. You do not have to pause while the word wrap feature takes the cursor to the next line. Press Enter only at the end of paragraphs or when you want to end a line. If you have used a word processor, this feature will be familiar to you.

ACTIVITY 2-2 • Keying Text Directly into Publish It!

In this activity you will key two short paragraphs into a text frame.

1. Place your data disk in drive A.
2. Choose **Size to fit** from the **Page** menu. An alternative is to press Alt + 0.
3. Position the pointer at the top left corner of the first column guide.
4. Drag right and down, creating a frame that covers the first four column guides. The dotted rectangular column guides disappear and are replaced with your frame (see Figure 2-2).
5. Choose **Actual size** from the Page menu. An alternative is to press Alt + 3.
6. Select the **Text tool** from the tool box. The pointer appears as an I-beam when it's positioned over the work area.
7. Click in the text frame. A cursor appears in this corner. The cursor may be so close to the left edge of the frame that it is not visible.
8. Key the two paragraphs of text shown in Figure 2-3. Press the **Space Bar** twice after the period at the end of each sentence. When you reach the end of the first paragraph, press **Enter** twice. If you make a mistake, do not correct it at this point. Just continue keying the text. You will have an opportunity to correct any errors in a later activity.
9. Choose **Save as** from the **File** menu.
10. Press **Escape**, then key **DEVELOP.DTP**.
11. Click on the Directory line. Press **Esc**, then key **A:*.DTP** for the path.
12. Click on **OK** to set the directory.
13. Click on **OK** to save the document.
14. Leave this file open for the next activity.

1. Place your data disk in drive A.
2. Choose **Size to fit** from the **Page** menu. An alternative is to press Alt + 0.
3. Position the pointer at the top left corner of the first column guide. Hold down the Shift key while you press an arrow key to move the pointer more precisely.
4. Press the **End** key. Then press the **Down Arrow** and the **Right Arrow** keys until the first four column guides are included in the box. Press the **Home** key when you are finished. The dotted rectangular column guides disappear and are replaced with your frame (see Figure 2-2).
5. Press **Alt + M** twice to enable text mode. The pointer appears as an I-beam when it's positioned over the work area.
6. Position the I-beam in the text frame. Press **Home**. A cursor appears in the top left corner. The cursor may be so close to the left edge of the frame that it is not visible.
7. Choose **Actual size** from the **Page** menu. An alternative is to press Alt + 3.
8. Key the two paragraphs of text shown in Figure 2-3. Press the **Space Bar** twice after the period at the end of each sentence. When you reach the end of the first paragraph, press **Enter** twice. If you make a mistake, do not correct it at this point. Just continue keying the text. You will have an opportunity to correct any errors in a later activity.
9. Pull down the **File** menu and choose **Save as**. The Item Selector appears.
10. Move the pointer to the Directory line and press **Home**. Press **Esc**. Key **A:*.DTP**.
11. Move the pointer to the Selection line and press **Home**. Press **Esc**, then key **DEVELOP.DTP**.
12. Press **Enter**.
13. Leave this file open for the next activity.

Figure 2-2
Before text can be keyed into Publish It!, a frame to hold the text must be created.

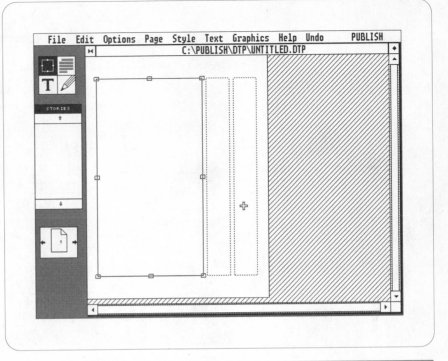

Figure 2-3
You can key text directly into Publish It!

Early computer designers did not foresee computers being used for desktop publishing. In fact, prior to the 1980s, most computers supported only upper-case letters. Because the developers had mathematical applications in mind, the lowercase letters were considered frivolous.

Now desktop publishing is an important part of computing. Now computers not only include lowercase letters, but they offer the desktop publisher a choice of type design. Without sacrificing any of the original capabilities, computers now work wonders with text as well as numbers.

THE STATUS COMMAND

The **Status command** presents a dialog box that shows information about your document and the computer itself. The Status command is located in the File menu. Through this command you can find out the number of words in your document, the amount of memory the document requires, the amount of storage space remaining on your hard drive, and more (see Figure 2-4).

Figure 2-4
The Status dialog box shows information about your document and the computer.

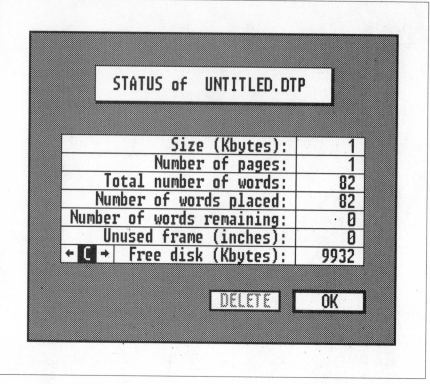

Size (Kbytes):	1
Number of pages:	1
Total number of words:	82
Number of words placed:	82
Number of words remaining:	0
Unused frame (inches):	0
Free disk (Kbytes):	9932

STATUS of UNTITLED.DTP

DELETE   OK

ACTIVITY 2-3 • The Status Command

In this activity you will use the Status command to see how many words you keyed into the text frame.

File
Open...   ◆O
Save   ◆S
Save as...
Save style sheet...
Revert to last...

New...
Erase...

Import text...
Import picture...
Export text...

Print...   ◆P
Status...
Quit...   ◆Q

1. Choose **Status** from the **File** menu. The Status box appears. Read the information to determine how many words you keyed into the document.

2. Click on **OK** when you're ready to close the window.

1. Move the pointer to the **File** menu and highlight the **Status** command. If the arrow keys do not move the pointer, change to the pointer mode by pressing **Ctrl + Right Shift**.

2. Press **Home**. The Status box appears. Read the information to determine how many words you keyed into the document.

3. Press **Enter** when you're ready to close the window.

MOVING AROUND IN TEXT

You can move around in the text using the mouse or the keyboard. Clicking the mouse moves the text cursor to the location of the I-beam pointer. You can also use the keyboard to move around in text—the keyboard can be used to move the pointer as well as the cursor. Recall from Chapter 1 that

Publish It! has two keyboard modes. Sometimes the arrow keys move the cursor in the text, and sometimes they move the pointer. To switch between modes, press Ctrl + Right Shift. The following table summarizes ways to move around in text.

Keyboard Action	Normal Mode	Pointer Mode
Left Arrow	Moves cursor to previous character	Moves pointer left
Right Arrow	Moves cursor to next character	Moves pointer right
Up Arrow	Moves cursor up one line	Moves pointer up
Down Arrow	Moves cursor down one line	Moves pointer down
Ctrl + Left Arrow	Moves cursor to previous word	Same as normal mode
Ctrl + Right Arrow	Moves cursor to next word	Same as normal mode
End	Moves cursor to end of line	Begins selection
Home	Moves cursor to beginning of line	Equivalent to click

You can determine which mode you are in by pressing an arrow key. If the pointer moves, you are in pointer mode. If the text cursor moves or there is no action, you are in normal mode.

ACTIVITY 2-4 • Moving Around in Text

In this activity you will practice moving the text cursor within the text.

1. Position the I-beam at the left of the word *mathematical* in the first paragraph. Click.

2. Try out the four arrow keys and return to the same position. If the I-beam moves instead of the cursor, press **Ctrl + Right Shift** to return to normal mode.

3. Press **Ctrl + Right Arrow** to move to the next word.

4. Press **Ctrl + Left Arrow** to move to the previous word.

5. Press **End** to move to the end of the line.

6. Press **Home** to move to the beginning of the line.

7. Leave the file open for the next activity.

1. In pointer mode, use the arrow keys to position the I-beam at the left of the word *mathematical* in the first paragraph. Press **Home**. The text cursor appears.

2. Press **Ctrl + Right Shift** to change to normal mode. Try out the four arrow keys and return to the same position.

3. Press **Ctrl + Right Arrow** to move to the next word.

4. Press **Ctrl + Left Arrow** to move to the previous word.

5. Press **End** to move to the end of the line.

6. Press **Home** to move to the beginning of the line.

7. Leave the file open for the next activity.

EDITING TEXT

One of the advantages of working with text on a computer is that you can make corrections and revisions without having to rekey all the text. Publish It! gives you the tools and functions necessary to modify text until you have the result you want.

Inserting Text

Text can be added in the middle of existing text. As new text is inserted, the existing text is spread apart. This makes room for the new text without loss of any existing text. To insert letters or words, simply position the text cursor where you want to insert the text and begin keying. The following activity demonstrates insertion.

ACTIVITY 2-5 • Inserting Text

In this activity you will insert a sentence into the existing text.

1. Position the pointer in the second paragraph after the word *design.* and before *Without*. Click.

2. Move the mouse to the right about an inch so that you can see the new position of the text cursor.

3. Press the **Right Arrow** key until the text cursor is on the right side of the *W* in *Without*.

4. Press the **Left Arrow** key once. This ensures that the text cursor is in the proper position for insertion.

5. Key the following sentence.

In addition, text can be revised directly on the screen using advanced text-editing features.

6. Press the **Space Bar** twice after the period at the end of the sentence.

7. Leave this file open for the next activity.

1. In pointer mode, position the I-beam in the second paragraph after the word *design* and before *Without*. Press **Home**.

2. Change to normal mode.

3. Press the **Right Arrow** key until the text cursor is on the right side of the *W* in *Without*.

4. Press the **Left Arrow** key once. This ensures that the text cursor is in the proper position for insertion.

5. Key the following sentence.

In addition, text can be revised directly on the screen using advanced text-editing features.

6. Press the **Space Bar** twice after the period at the end of the sentence.

7. Leave this file open for the next activity.

Selecting Text

Occasionally you will need to perform an operation on a word, sentence, or even a whole paragraph. Publish It! allows you to select some or all of the text on the screen. After text is selected, there are several operations you can apply to the selected area. To select text with a mouse, click and hold the mouse button down while you drag across the area you want to select. To select text with the keyboard, position the I-beam where the selection is to begin, press End, move to the end of the selection, and press Home. The selected text is highlighted to mark clearly the boundaries of the selection.

ACTIVITY 2-6 • Selecting Text

In this activity you will practice selecting portions of the text.

1. Make sure the Text tool is selected.
2. Click and hold the mouse button immediately at the left of the first word in the first paragraph.
3. Drag to the right and down until the entire first paragraph is highlighted.
4. Release the mouse button. The text is selected.
5. Select the second sentence in the second paragraph. The text already selected will unselect when you begin the new selection.
6. Select *1980* in the first paragraph. Do not include the *s*.
7. Select only the *8* in *1980s*.
8. Leave the file open for the next activity.

1. Make sure the Text tool is selected. Remember, Alt + M changes the selected tool.
2. Position the I-beam at the beginning of the text. Remember, using the Shift key with the arrow keys gives you more precise movement.
3. Press the **End** key.
4. Press the **Down Arrow** and **Right Arrow** keys until the first paragraph is highlighted. Press the **Home** key.
5. Select the second sentence in the second paragraph. The text already selected will unselect when you begin the new selection.
6. Select *1980* in the first paragraph. Do not include the *s*.
7. Select only the *8* in *1980s*.
8. Leave the file open for the next activity.

Deleting Text

Publish It! provides two methods for deleting text. You can delete a selected portion of text, or you can delete one character at a time using the Backspace key or the Delete key. To delete selected text, first select the text then press the Delete key. The Backspace key moves the cursor to the left and removes characters in its path one character at a time. The Delete key pulls text from the right, deleting characters one at a time. Be careful when deleting text. After text has been deleted, it cannot be recovered except by rekeying it.

ACTIVITY 2-7 • Deleting Text

In this activity you will practice deleting portions of the text.

1. Position the text cursor at the end of the first paragraph.
2. Press the **Backspace** key until the word *frivolous* is deleted.
3. Key the word **unimportant** and key a period at the end of the sentence.

1. Position the text cursor at the end of the first paragraph.
2. Press the **Backspace** key until the word *frivolous* is deleted.
3. Key the word **unimportant** and key a period at the end of the sentence.

Continued

4. Select the first sentence in the second paragraph, which reads, "Now desktop publishing is an important part of computing." Do not select the spaces that follow the sentence.

5. Press the **Delete** key once. The entire sentence disappears.

6. Press the **Delete** key twice to remove the spaces before the phrase *Now computers*. If you accidentally delete part of the phrase, rekey it now to correct it.

7. Leave the file open for the next activity.

4. Select the first sentence in the second paragraph, which reads, "Now desktop publishing is an important part of computing." Do not select the spaces that follow the sentence.

5. Press the **Delete** key once. The entire sentence disappears.

6. Press the **Delete** key twice to remove the spaces before the phrase *Now computers*. If you accidentally delete part of the phrase, rekey it now to correct it.

7. Leave the file open for the next activity.

Cutting Text

Just as you can cut text out of a newspaper, you can cut text out of your document using the Publish It! **Cut command** from the Edit menu. When you cut text or a picture from a document, the item that was cut is stored on the Clipboard. The **Clipboard** is an area in the computer's memory in which text or a picture can be held temporarily. A common use for the Clipboard is for moving text. Text is "cut" from your publication and stored on the Clipboard. After the text cursor is positioned in the desired location, the text can be "pasted" back into your document.

Pasting Text

The **Paste command** from the Edit menu allows you to paste text from the Clipboard back into your document. The text will be inserted at the location of the text cursor.

ACTIVITY 2-8 • Cut and Paste

In this activity you will practice cutting and pasting text.

1. Select the entire second paragraph.

2. Pull down the **Edit** menu.

3. Choose **Cut**. The second paragraph disappears. Pressing Alt + X or pressing the Delete key is an alternative to choosing Cut from the Edit menu.

4. Position the text cursor at the beginning of the first paragraph.

5. Press **Enter** twice. The paragraph moves down two lines.

1. Select the entire second paragraph.

2. Pull down the **Edit** menu.

3. Choose **Cut**. The second paragraph disappears. Pressing Alt + X or pressing the Delete key is an alternative to choosing Cut from the Edit menu.

4. Position the text cursor at the beginning of the first paragraph.

5. Press **Enter** twice. The paragraph moves down two lines.

Continued

6. Press the **Up Arrow** key twice. This and the previous step make room for the new paragraph.

7. Choose **Paste** from the **Edit** menu. The second paragraph reappears. Pressing Alt + V or pressing the Insert key is an alternative to choosing Paste from the Edit menu.

8. Leave the file open for the next activity.

6. Press the **Up Arrow** key twice. This and the previous step make room for the new paragraph.

7. Choose **Paste** from the **Edit** menu. The second paragraph reappears. Pressing Alt + V or pressing the Insert key is an alternative to choosing Paste from the Edit menu.

8. Leave the file open for the next activity.

Copying Text

The **Copy command** from the Edit menu allows you to place text on the Clipboard without removing the text from the document. The Copy command places a copy of the selected text on the Clipboard rather than cutting it from the document. In cases where the same text is repeated, copying text can avoid unnecessary keying.

ACTIVITY 2-9 • Copy and Paste

In this activity you will practice copying text using the Copy command.

1. Select the paragraph that begins with *Early computer*.

2. Choose **Copy** from the **Edit** menu. A copy of the paragraph has been placed on the Clipboard. Pressing Alt + C is an alternative to choosing Copy from the Edit menu.

3. Position the text cursor before the first paragraph.

4. Press **Enter** twice.

5. Press the **Up Arrow** key twice.

6. Press **Alt + V** to paste the text. The paragraph appears.

7. Leave the file open for the next activity.

1. Select the paragraph that begins with *Early computer*.

2. Choose **Copy** from the **Edit** menu. A copy of the paragraph has been placed on the Clipboard. Pressing Alt + C is an alternative to choosing Copy from the Edit menu.

3. Position the text cursor before the first paragraph.

4. Press **Ctrl + Right Shift** to change to normal mode.

5. Press **Enter** twice.

6. Press the **Up Arrow** key twice.

7. Press **Alt + V** to paste the text. The paragraph appears.

8. Leave the file open for the next activity.

ACTIVITY 2-10 • Cleaning Up

In this activity you will delete the extra paragraph on the screen and make any other corrections necessary to finalize your document.

Mouse	Keyboard
1. Select the second occurrence of the paragraph beginning with *Early computer*.	1. Select the second occurrence of the paragraph beginning with *Early computer*.
2. Press the **Delete** key to delete it.	2. Press the **Delete** key to delete it.
3. Compare the two paragraphs on your screen with Figure 2-5. Using the editing skills you have learned, correct any errors you made while keying the paragraphs. Also remove any extra lines that may now appear between the paragraphs.	3. Compare the two paragraphs on your screen with Figure 2-5. Using the editing skills you have learned, correct any errors you made while keying the paragraphs. Also remove any extra lines that may now appear between the paragraphs.
4. Choose **Save** from the **File** menu.	4. Press **Alt + S** to choose Save. You will get a message saying that the file already exists.
5. You will get a message saying that the file already exists. Click **Yes** to replace the old file with the new one.	5. Press **Enter** to replace the old file with the new one.
6. Leave the file open for the next activity.	6. Leave the file open for the next activity.

Figure 2-5
When the revisions are complete, your paragraphs should look similar to those shown here.

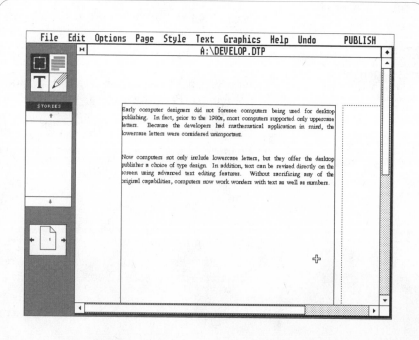

RELIVING THE PAST

There are two options that allow you to return to a previous step—these are called Undo and Revert to last, which are discussed in the following paragraphs.

Undo

The Undo menu has four options that allow you to recover frames, text, and graphics you have deleted. Anything deleted with the Delete key or by choosing Cut can be recovered with Undo. At the top of the Undo menu is the All command. The **All command** restores the document to the way it was last saved.

ACTIVITY 2-11 • The Undo Command

In this activity you will practice using the Undo command.

1. Select the second paragraph.	1. Select the second paragraph.
2. Press **Delete**. The paragraph is deleted.	2. Press **Delete**. The paragraph is deleted.
3. Pull down the **Undo** menu.	3. Pull down the **Undo** menu.
4. Choose **Text**. The paragraph reappears.	4. Choose **Text**. The paragraph reappears.
5. Leave the file open for the next activity.	5. Leave the file open for the next activity.

Revert to Last

If you make a mistake or make changes that you do not want to keep, you have the option of going back to the last version you saved. You could do this by closing the document you are working on without saving and opening the last saved version. To save steps, Publish It! includes the **Revert to last command** for returning to your last saved version. The All command from the Undo menu gives the same result.

ACTIVITY 2-12 • Reverting to the Last Saved Copy

In this activity you will practice reverting to the last saved copy of a document.

1. Select the first paragraph.	1. Select the first paragraph.
2. Press **Delete**. The paragraph is deleted.	2. Press **Delete**. The paragraph is deleted.

Continued

3. Pull down the **File** menu.

4. Choose **Revert to last**. You will be asked to verify that you want to return to the original copy.

5. Click on **OK**. The document returns to the way it was when it was last saved.

6. Leave the file open for the next activity.

3. Pull down the **File** menu.

4. Choose **Revert to last**. You will be asked to verify that you want to return to the original copy.

5. Choose **OK**. The document returns to the way it was when it was last saved.

6. Leave the file open for the next activity.

IMPORTING TEXT

Keying text directly into Publish It! is not always the most convenient way of including text in a publication. There are several reasons for this. First, some people key text faster than Publish It! can process it, resulting in lost characters. Second, the text may already have been keyed into another program. Last, you may prefer to key text into a word processor that offers such features as a spell checker. The process by which text is brought into Publish It! from another source is called **importing**.

Publish It! can import more than ten file formats from the Import Text dialog box (see Figure 2-6). Most popular word processors are supported. The most common file format used for importing text is called **ASCII** (pronounced *ask-e*). ASCII is an **acronym** for American Standard Code for Information Interchange. The ASCII format was developed to provide a standard for communication between programs and computers. It is a text-only format, meaning that only the text is imported. No type styles, tab settings, or margin settings are included in the file. ASCII files are sometimes referred to as text files. Although the ASCII format is commonly used in desktop publishing, it does not import into Publish It! well.

Figure 2-6
The Import Text dialog box allows you to choose a file format to import.

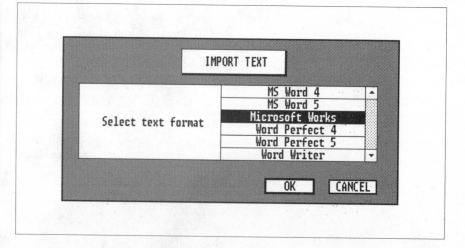

When you import text from an ASCII format file, Publish It! removes the hard returns from the text. A **hard return** is a code at the end of a paragraph of text that tells the computer to start a new line. Hard returns are generally inserted using the Enter key. When the hard returns are removed, all the paragraphs run together. Because of the extra work involved in separating the paragraphs, it is not recommended that you import ASCII files. If the text you need is already saved in an ASCII format, first load it into a word processor that is compatible with Publish It!, save it from the word processor, then import the word processor's file. The text files you will import from your template disk were created in WordPerfect 4.

ACTIVITY 2-13 • Importing Text

In this activity you will practice using the text import feature.

1. Choose **New** from the **File** menu. Click on **No** when asked if you want to load a style sheet. Click on **OK** to accept the default Page Format.	1. Choose **New** from the **File** menu. Choose **No** when asked if you want to load a style sheet. Press **Enter** to accept the default Page Format.
2. Press **Alt + 0** to choose Size to fit from the Page menu.	2. Press **Alt + 0** to choose Size to fit from the Page menu.
3. Create a text frame that covers three column guides (see Figure 2-7). Leave the frame highlighted.	3. Create a text frame that covers three column guides (see Figure 2-7). Leave the frame highlighted.
4. Insert your template disk in drive A.	4. Insert your template disk in drive A.
5. Choose **Import text** from the **File** menu. The format selector appears.	5. Choose **Import text** from the **File** menu. The format selector appears.
6. Click on **WordPerfect 4**. Click on **OK**.	6. Choose **WordPerfect 4**. Press **Enter**.
7. Key **A:*.WPD** on the Directory line. Press **Enter**.	7. Key **A:*.WPD** on the Directory Line. Press **Enter**.
8. Click on *ACT2-13.WPD* for the selection. Click on **OK**. The imported text appears in your frame.	8. Choose *ACT2-13.WPD* for the selection. Press **Enter**. The imported text appears in your frame.

FIND AND REPLACE

There are times when you need to search the text of your document for a specific word or phrase. The **Find command** allows you to search for a key word or phrase. Figure 2-8 shows the Find dialog box. The **Find again command** continues the search after a match is found.

Figure 2-7
Column guides help you
create frames of the right
size.

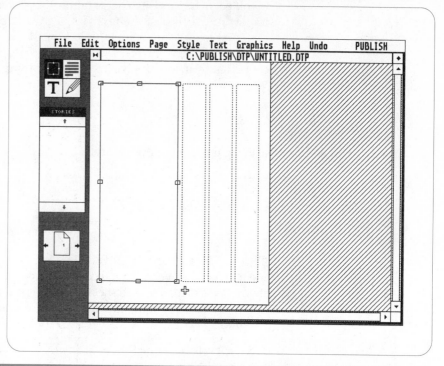

Figure 2-8
The Find command lets
you search text for a
specific word or phrase.

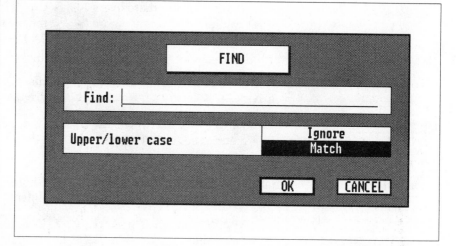

ACTIVITY 2-14 • Find

In this activity you will use the Find command to search for a specific word in your text.

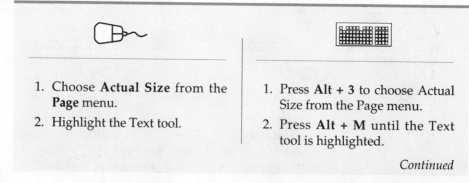

1. Choose **Actual Size** from the **Page** menu.
2. Highlight the Text tool.

1. Press **Alt + 3** to choose Actual Size from the Page menu.
2. Press **Alt + M** until the Text tool is highlighted.

Continued

3. Place the text cursor to the left of the heading at the top of the page.

4. Choose **Find** from the **Text** menu.

5. Key the word **text**

6. Click on **Match**. This tells the program that you want to find the word only when it is exactly as you keyed it. For instance, *Text* would not be found, but *text* would.

7. Click on **OK**. The first occurrence of the word is highlighted.

8. Choose **Find again** from the Text menu. The second occurrence of the word *text* is highlighted. Alt + A is the quick key for the Find again command.

9. Press **Alt + A** to choose Find again. Press **Alt + A** repeatedly until an alert box appears telling you that there are no more occurrences of the word.

10. Click on **Cancel**.

11. Leave the file open for the next activity.

3. Place the text cursor to the left of the heading at the top of the page.

4. Choose **Find** from the **Text** menu.

5. Key the word **text**

6. Position the pointer over the word Match. Press **Home**. This tells the program that you want to find the word only when it is exactly as you keyed it. For instance, *Text* would not be found, but *text* would.

7. Choose **OK**. The first occurrence of the word is highlighted.

8. Choose **Find again** from the **Text** menu. The second occurrence of the word text is highlighted. Alt + A is the quick key for the Find again command.

9. Press **Alt + A** to choose Find again. Press **Alt + A** repeatedly until an alert box appears telling you that there are no more occurrences of the word.

10. Choose **Cancel**.

11. Leave the file open for the next activity.

The **Find & replace command** not only finds the key word or phrase, but allows you to replace it automatically with another phrase. An example of a use for Find & replace is changing a name used throughout your document. Figure 2-9 shows the Find and replace dialog box. The Find again command works with Find & replace as well as with Find.

ACTIVITY 2-15 • Find and Replace

In this activity you will use the Find & replace command to search for a word and in some instances change it.

1. Position the text cursor at the top of the text.

2. Choose **Find & replace** from the **Text** menu. The Find and

1. Position the text cursor at the top of the text.

2. Choose **Find & replace** from the **Text** menu. The Find and

Continued

Replace dialog box appears (see Figure 2-9). Notice that the word *text* is still entered from the last activity.

3. Press **Tab**. Key the following: **words**

4. Click on **Some**.

5. Click on **OK**. The first occurrence of *text* is highlighted. Notice that the menu bar has been replaced with a question.

6. Press **Y** to replace. The word is changed. The next occurrence is highlighted.

7. Press **N** to ignore. The word is not changed. The next occurrence is highlighted.

8. Press **Esc**. The operation is canceled.

9. Leave the file open for the next activity.

Replace dialog box appears (see Figure 2-9). Notice that the word *text* is still entered from the last activity.

3. Press **Tab**. Key the following: **words**

4. Choose **Some**.

5. Choose **OK**. The first occurrence of *text* is highlighted. Notice that the menu bar has been replaced with a question.

6. Press **Y** to replace. The word is changed. The next occurrence is highlighted.

7. Press **N** to ignore. The word is not changed. The next occurrence is highlighted.

8. Press **Esc**. The operation is canceled.

9. Leave the file open for the next activity.

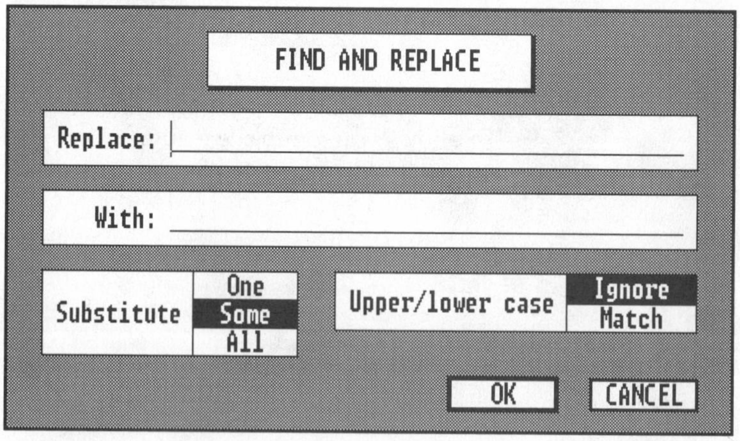

Figure 2-9
The Find and replace command allows you to search for a word or phrase and replace it with another word or phrase.

```
         FIND AND REPLACE

Replace: |_____

With: _____

                        One              Ignore
Substitute              Some    Upper/lower case
                        All              Match

                                   OK      CANCEL
```

EXPORTING TEXT

There may be times when saving the text from a publication to a text file may be useful. Suppose that a national magazine is interested in an article from your school newspaper. The editors of the magazine are requesting an ASCII file of the article's text. Publish It! will allow you to save the text from a publication as an ASCII text file.

ACTIVITY 2-16 • Saving Text in ASCII Format

In this activity you will practice saving the text from a publication.

1. Insert your data disk in drive A.
2. Select the text frame using the Frame tool.
3. Choose **Export text** from the **File** menu.
4. Key **EXPORT.ASC** for the filename. Press **Enter**.
5. If it is not already entered, key **A:*.ASC** for the pathname.
6. Click on **OK**.

1. Insert your data disk in drive A.
2. Select the text frame using the Frame tool.
3. Choose **Export text** from the File menu.
4. Key **EXPORT.ASC** for the filename. Press **Enter**.
5. If it is not already entered, key **A:*.ASC** for the pathname.
6. Choose **OK**.

FONTS

The term *font* refers to the type used in a publication. Desktop publishing gives you a wide selection of type designs. Fonts give flexibility in publication design. Careful font selection can make a document more visually appealing.

Fonts Explained

An understanding of fonts is important to your success as a desktop publisher. The best way to understand fonts is to understand the terms typeface, style, and size.

Typeface.   There are different designs of type just as there are different designs of clothing. Text can be dressy or casual. Type from a desktop publishing program can look like it came from a typewriter or it can be much fancier. These different designs of type are called **typefaces**. The differences between typefaces can be very obvious or very subtle. Figure 2-10 illustrates three different typefaces.

Figure 2-10
Desktop publishing allows text to be presented in different designs called typefaces.

This typeface is called Madison.

This typeface is called Ravinia.

This typeface is called Rockface.

Style. The **style** of a typeface can be changed to provide emphasis. Styles of typefaces are typically bold, italic, and normal. Publish It! provides a wide selection of text styles in addition to the typical ones. You will have an opportunity to experiment with them in an application at the end of this chapter. Figure 2-11 illustrates the Rockface typeface in normal, bold, and italic.

Figure 2-11
Typefaces can appear in different styles, such as normal, bold, and italic.

This is Rockface normal

This is Rockface bold

This is Rockface italic

Size. The **size** of type is determined by measuring its height in units called **points**. There are 72 points per inch. A common size for type is 12 point because it is approximately the size of type from a typewriter. Figure 2-12 illustrates the Sans typeface in 12, 20, and 36 point.

This is Sans 12 point

This is Sans 20 point

This is Sans 36 point

Figure 2-12
Different sizes can be selected within the same typeface.

Font. A **font** is a combination of typeface, style, and size. For example, in Figure 2-12, each of the three examples is a different font. Even though the typeface does not change, the size does. Sans typeface in a normal style and a size of 20 point is an example of a font description. Sometimes the words typeface and font are used interchangeably. People might say, "My favorite font is Sans," when they mean that their favorite typeface is Sans.

TYPEFACE TERMINOLOGY

Typefaces, like computers, are most easily described with a special set of terms. You have already learned the terms that describe the style and size of a typeface. Now let's discuss the terms that describe the design of the type itself.

Characters.   Each letter, number, and symbol in a typeface is called a **character**. Some typefaces include more characters than other typefaces. For example, some of the more unique typefaces may have only the uppercase letters as characters. The more common typefaces include most characters that can be keyed on a keyboard.

Baselines.   The **baseline** of a typeface is an invisible line on which the characters sit. The baseline serves the same purpose as the lines on notebook paper. The baseline is important for aligning the characters. In Figure 2-13, the bottom of most characters is on the baseline.

Figure 2-13
Special terms are used to describe typefaces.

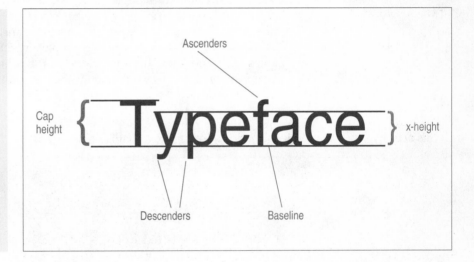

Descenders.   When a character extends below the baseline, the portion of the character below the baseline is called a **descender**. In Figure 2-13 the *y* and the *p* have descenders.

x-Height.   Another invisible line is drawn across the typeface at the level of the top of a lowercase *x*. This line is appropriately named the **x-height** (see Figure 2-13).

Ascenders.   When a character extends above the x-height, the portion of the character above the x-height is called an **ascender**. In Figure 2-13 the *f* has an ascender.

Cap Height.   The height from the baseline to the top of a capital letter is the **cap height** (see Figure 2-13).

Serifs.   Some typefaces have small lines added to the ends of the characters. These lines are called **serifs**. If a typeface has serifs, it is called a **serif typeface**. If a typeface does not have serifs, it is called a **sans serif typeface**, meaning "without serifs." Figure 2-14 illustrates a serif and a sans serif typeface.

Figure 2-14
Small lines added to the
ends of characters are
called serifs.

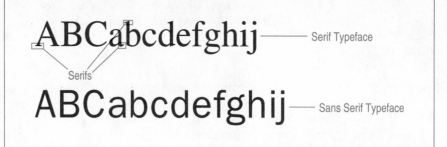

Selecting Fonts

If you intend to key text directly into Publish It!, it is a good idea to select a font before you begin keying. The two primary typefaces in Publish It! are a standard serif typeface and a standard sans serif typeface. These fonts will be identified by different names depending on your version of Publish It! and your printer type. On your computer, the serif typeface will be called Serif, Dutch, or Times. The sans serif typeface will be called Sans, Swiss, or Helvetica. This text–workbook will refer to the two primary typefaces with the two generic names Serif and Sans. If you see one of the other names on your screen, remember which typeface corresponds to Sans and Serif on your computer.

ACTIVITY 2-17 • Selecting Fonts

In this activity you will practice selecting a font for text that is being keyed.

1. Open a new, untitled document. Hint: Use the **New** command from the **File** menu.	1. Open a new, untitled document. Hint: Use the **New** command from the **File** menu.
2. Choose **Size to fit** from the **Page** menu.	2. Press **Alt + 0** to choose Size to Fit from the **Page** menu.
3. Using the Frame tool, create a text frame that covers four column guides.	3. Using the Frame tool, create a text frame that covers four column guides.
4. Choose the **Text tool**.	4. Choose the **Text tool**.
5. Choose **Actual size** from the **Page** menu.	5. Press **Alt + 3** to choose Actual Size from the Page menu.
6. Click in the text frame.	6. Position the I-beam pointer in the text frame and press **Home**.
7. Choose **Font/size** from the **Style** menu.	7. Choose **Font/Size** from the **Style** menu.
8. Click on **Sans** (or equivalent) in the typeface list.	8. Choose **Sans** (or equivalent) in the typeface list.
9. If it's not already selected, click on **10** point in the size list. Click on **OK**.	9. If it's not already chosen, choose **10** point in the size list. Press **Enter**.

Continued

10. Key **This is 10-point Sans serif normal**. Press **Enter**.
11. Choose **Bold** from the **Style** menu.
12. Key **This is 10-point Sans serif bold**. Press **Enter**.
13. Choose **Bold** from the **Style** menu to turn off the Bold style.
14. Choose **Font/Size** from the **Style** menu then choose **Serif** (or equivalent) and **20** point. Click on **OK**.
15. Key **This is 20-point Serif normal**. Press **Enter**.
16. Save the document as *FONTS.DTP* on your data disk.

10. Key **This is 10-point Sans serif normal**. Press **Enter**.
11. Choose **Bold** from the **Style** menu.
12. Key **This is 10-point Sans serif bold**. Press **Enter**.
13. Choose **Bold** from the **Style** menu to turn off the Bold style.
14. Choose **Font/size** from the **Style** menu then choose **Serif** (or equivalent) and **20** point. Press **Enter**.
15. Key **This is 20-point Serif normal**. Press **Enter**.
16. Save the document as *FONTS.DTP* on your data disk.

Text styles can also be chosen from the Library rather than the Style menu. You may find using the Library more convenient.

Changing Fonts

Often you will want to change the font of text that is already in a document. By selecting text, the font of the selected portion can be changed.

ACTIVITY 2-18 • Changing Fonts

In this activity you will import a text file and change the font of each line in the text.

1. Open a new, untitled document.
2. Insert your template disk in drive A.
3. Draw a text frame that covers four column guides. Hint: Zoom out to see the whole page, draw the text frame, and then return to actual size.
4. Choose **Import text** from the **File** menu.
5. Click on **WordPerfect 4**. Click on **OK**.
6. Import *ACT2-18.WPD*.
7. Highlight the Text tool.
8. Select the line that reads, "This is 12-point Sans normal." It may be easier to select the line from right to left rather than from left to right.
9. Choose **Font/size** from the **Style** menu.

1. Open a new, untitled document.
2. Insert your template disk in drive A.
3. Draw a text frame that covers four column guides. Hint: Zoom out to see the whole page, draw the text frame, and then return to actual size.
4. Choose **Import text** from the **File** menu.
5. Choose **WordPerfect 4**. Choose **OK**.
6. Import *ACT2-18.WPD*.
7. Select the line that reads, "This is 12-point Sans normal."
8. Choose **Font/size** from the **Style** menu.
9. Set the typeface to **Sans** (or equivalent) and the size to **12** point. Press **Enter**.
10. Select the next line.

Continued

10. Set the typeface to **Sans** (or equivalent) and the size to **12** point. Click on **OK**.
11. Select the next line.
12. Choose **Font/size** from the **Style** menu.
13. Set the typeface to **Sans** (or equivalent) and the size to **14** point. Click on **OK**.
14. Click on **Bold** in the Library to change the style from normal to bold.
15. Change the font of the remaining lines to the typeface, style, and size indicated by each line.
16. Save the file as FONTDOC.DTP on your data disk.

11. Choose **Font/size** from the **Style** menu.
12. Set the typeface to **Sans** (or equivalent) and the size to **14** point.
13. Position the pointer over the word **Bold** in the Library and press **Home**. The style will change from normal to bold.
14. Change the font of the remaining lines to the typeface, style, and size indicated by each line.
15. Save the file as FONTDOC.DTP on your data disk.

SUMMARY

It is important to be able to work with text effectively when you are creating documents in a desktop publishing program. All text is placed in text frames. Text frames provide a boundary for text.

Text can be entered directly into Publish It! using many of the editing features found in word processors. Text can be copied, inserted, moved, and deleted.

You can import text from another program, such as a word processor. Publish It! supports a wide variety of word processor files. You can export text by saving just the text from a document. The resulting file will be in ASCII format.

The term *font* refers to the type used in a publication. The design of the type is called the typeface. Typefaces come in one or more styles and sizes. A font is a combination of typeface, style, and size. Each letter, number, and symbol in a typeface is called a character. A typeface with small lines added to the ends of the characters is called a serif typeface. If the lines are not present, it is called a sans serif typeface.

When working with text, you can select a font before the text is keyed or imported. You can also change the font of existing text.

CHAPTER

Review

Name _____ Date _____

TRUE OR FALSE

The following statements are either true or false. Circle T or F to indicate your answer.

1. All text in Publish It! is placed in an area called a word frame. (Obj. 1)

    1. T F

2. The text cursor marks the end of each paragraph. (Obj. 1)

    2. T F

3. Word wrap allows you to press Enter at the end of each paragraph rather than the end of each line. (Obj. 1)

    3. T F

4. Pressing the End key will take the text cursor to the end of the last paragraph of text. (Obj. 2)

    4. T F

5. Some operations require that text first be selected. (Obj. 3)

    5. T F

6. The Undo command will allow you to undo any command. (Obj. 4)

    6. T F

7. Publish It! can import text in more than ten file formats. (Obj. 5)

    7. T F

8. Text can be exported in any of the word processor formats used for importing. (Obj. 6)

    8. T F

9. Any part of a character extending above the x-height line is called a serif. (Obj. 7)

    9. T F

10. Once text is entered, the font cannot be changed. (Obj. 8)

    10. T F

COMPLETION

Write your answers in the space provided.

11. Describe the process necessary to prepare a new document to accept keyed text. (Obj. 1)

_____

_____

_____

_____

12. What is the function of Ctrl + Right Arrow? (Obj. 2)

_____

13. Explain how to select text with a mouse. (Obj. 3)

_____

_____

14. Explain how to select text with the keyboard. (Obj. 3)

_____

_____

15. Which commands would you use to move a paragraph: cut and paste or copy and paste? (Obj. 3)

_____

16. Describe the steps necessary to import text. (Obj. 5)

_____

_____

_____

17. Give two examples of characters with ascenders. (Obj. 7)

_____

18. How many points are in one inch?

_____

19. Describe the difference between a typeface and a font. (Obj. 7)

_____

_____

_____

_____

20. List all the type styles available in the Styles menu. (Obj. 8)

_____

_____

_____

APPLICATION 2-1

In this application you will practice importing text from a word processor file.

1. Open a new, untitled document.
2. Create a text frame that covers four column guides.
3. Choose Import text from the File menu.
4. Import *APP2-1.WPD* as a WordPerfect 4 file from your template disk. Three paragraphs will be imported.
5. Leave the file open for the next application.

APPLICATION 2-2

In this application you will practice inserting text by keying a sentence into a paragraph.

1. Position the text cursor before the word *Often* in the second paragraph.
2. Key the following sentence:
   However, it was impossible to see the page until it was printed.
3. Leave the file open for the next application.

APPLICATION 2-3

In this application you will correct errors in the text. Move around in the text using the mouse or keyboard commands and make the specified corrections.

1. Capitalize the first letter of each word in the phrase "what you see is what you get" in the first sentence of the first paragraph.
2. Change *computers* to *computer's* in the second sentence.
3. Correct the spelling of the word *publication* in the second sentence.
4. Insert two spaces after the first sentence in the second paragraph.
5. Delete the words *have to* in the third paragraph. Remove any extra spaces in the sentence.
6. Leave the file open for the next application.

APPLICATION 2-4

In this application you will use Cut, Copy, and Paste to rearrange two paragraphs and create a heading. You will select fonts for the text and save the publication.

1. Select the entire third paragraph.
2. Choose Cut from the Edit menu. The paragraph is cut from the document and placed on the Clipboard.
3. Position the text cursor between the first and second paragraphs. Press Enter.
4. Choose Paste from the Edit menu. The paragraph is copied from the Clipboard to the document in the new location.
5. Adjust paragraph spacing as necessary.

6. Select *WYSIWYG* in the first sentence of the first paragraph.

7. Choose Copy from the Edit menu.

8. Insert two blank lines above the first paragraph.

9. Position the text cursor on the top line. Choose Paste from the Edit menu. The word *WYSIWYG* appears on the top line as a heading.

10. Select all of the text except the heading.

11. Change the font to 12-point Serif (or equivalent) normal.

12. Select the heading at the top of the document.

13. Change the font to a large size font of your choice.

14. Save the file as *WYSIWYG.DTP* on your data disk.

APPLICATION 2-5

In this application you will experiment with each of the text styles in the Library.

1. Open a new, untitled document.

2. Create a large text frame that covers all the column guides.

3. Key the following words into the text frame in 20-point Sans (or equivalent):

Bold

Underlined

Italic

Light

White

H2O

E=mc2

Box

Rounded Box

Strikethru

4. Select the line that reads *Bold* and choose Bold from the Library.

5. Use the Library to set the other lines to the indicated text style. Some of the styles may not be visible in the Library. The Library will scroll if you click on the arrows above and below the list. Change the 2 in *H2O* to a subscript. Change the 2 in *E=mc2* to a superscript.

6. Choose Size to fit to see the whole text frame. Resize the text frame to frame the text more closely.

7. Save the document as *TEXTSTYL.DTP* on your data disk.

APPLICATION 2-6

In this application you will classify each of the typefaces available to you as serif or sans serif.

1. Open a new, untitled document.

2. Create a text frame that covers all the column guides.

3. Key **ABCDEFGHIJKLMNOPQRSTUVWXYZabcdefghijklmn opqrstuvwxyz** into the text frame.

4. Select the text you just keyed.

5. Change the typeface to the first available typeface in the Font/size dialog box. Set the size to the largest available size.

6. Look closely at the typeface to determine if it is a serif or sans serif typeface. Record the name of the typeface and whether it is serif or sans serif on a sheet of paper.

7. Change the typeface to the next available typeface in the Font/size dialog box. Set the size to the largest available size.

8. Again examine the typeface to determine if it is a serif or sans serif typeface. Record the name of the typeface and whether it is serif or sans serif on the same sheet of paper.

9. Repeat steps 6 and 7 for each typeface available. Some typefaces may be hard to classify. Some may be sets of symbols rather than alphabetic characters. Answer as best you can.

CHAPTER

Graphics

LEARNING OBJECTIVES

When you complete this chapter, you will be able to:

1. Display and use the rulers.
2. Import graphics into a document.
3. Crop, edit, scale, and hide imported graphics.
4. Create your own graphics using the graphics tools.
5. Resize graphics.
6. Change the line and fill style of a graphic that you create.
7. Position graphics.
8. Cut, copy, and paste graphics.

WHY USE GRAPHICS?

Art, commonly called graphics, is an important feature of a document. Without art, a document is just a gray sea of text through which a reader must wade. The term *graphics* is a broad classification. As you probably guessed, clip art and art that you create are categorized as graphics, but did you know that boxes, lines, and photographs are also considered graphics? The purposes of **graphics** are to:

- Illustrate the meaning of text.
- Provide a path for the eye to travel.
- "Bookmark" text so the reader knows where to find specific information.

Relaying information using a combination of text and graphics is more effective than relying on text alone. For example, suppose your biology teacher asks you to write a report about a tadpole's development into a frog. Using pictures to illustrate the tadpole's physical changes would help your audience understand the development process better than by using text alone.

Graphics guide the reader through text by providing a direction for the eye to follow. For instance, a line placed between two columns draws a reader's attention down toward the end of the columns. This encourages a reader to continue reading. Graphics can also help you find specific segments of text. Suppose you were paging through a magazine and wanted to return to an article about your favorite musician. A photograph of the musician next to the text would help you locate the article.

TWO SOURCES OF GRAPHICS

Publish It! uses two sources of graphics: imported graphics and graphics drawn in Publish It! **Imported graphics** are loaded into Publish It! from files created in other programs. Graphics drawn in Publish It! are created using the graphics tools. Both types of graphics can be used in the same document.

GRAPHIC FRAMES AND RULERS

Graphics, like text, are placed in frames. Graphic frames are created the same way text frames are created.

Before you begin importing and creating graphics, you should become familiar with the **Show rulers command** and the **Ruler spacing command**. These commands are located in the Options menu.

The Show rulers command displays the rulers that allow you to create an appropriately sized frame and place it in the correct position in your document. The rulers remain on the screen regardless of which tool is selected.

The Ruler spacing command allows you to choose the unit of measurement for the rulers. The unit of measurement options include inches and eighths, inches and tenths, picas and points, and centimeters. You should be familiar with inches and centimeters. **Picas** are a measurement used in **typography**. There are approximately 6 picas per inch. There are 12 points in a pica. Unless you specify otherwise, Publish It! will use a ruler spacing of inches and eighths, which is the **default** setting. A default setting is a setting that is used by Publish It! unless the user changes it.

ACTIVITY 3-1 • Using Rulers

In this activity you will display the rulers, change the ruler spacing, and create a square frame. You need to have Publish It! running on your computer.

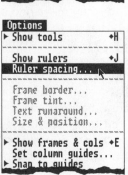

Mouse	Keyboard
1. Pull down the **Options** menu.	1. Pull down the **Options** menu.
2. Choose **Show rulers**. The rulers appear across the top and down the left side of the work area. Notice that the ruler spacing is in inches and eighths, the default setting.	2. Choose **Show rulers**. The rulers appear across the top and down the left side of the work area. Notice that the ruler spacing is in inches and eighths, the default setting.
3. Pull down the **Options** menu.	3. Pull down the **Options** menu.
4. Choose **Ruler spacing**. The Ruler Spacing dialog box appears, displaying the unit of measurement options, as shown in Figure 3-1.	4. Choose **Ruler spacing**. The Ruler Spacing dialog box appears, displaying the unit of measurement options, as shown in Figure 3-1.
5. Click on **Inches and tenths**. Click on **OK**. The rulers immediately reflect your choice.	5. Choose **Inches and tenths**. Press **Enter**. The rulers immediately reflect your choice.

Continued

6. Move the pointer across the screen. Note the movement of the lines on the rulers that shows the position of the pointer.

7. Select the **Frame tool**.

8. Position the pointer where both ruler lines are on the 1-inch mark.

9. Click and drag the pointer down and to the right until both ruler lines are on the 2-inch mark. Release the mouse button. You have created a perfect square frame. Your screen should look similar to Figure 3-2. You do not need to save this file.

6. Move the pointer using the arrow keys. Note the movement of the lines on the rulers that shows the position of the pointer.

7. Select the **Frame tool**.

8. Position the pointer where both ruler lines are on the 1-inch mark. Use the Shift key with the arrows for more precise movement.

9. Press the **End** key. Using the arrow keys, move the pointer down and to the right until both ruler lines are on the 2-inch mark. Press the **Home** key. You have created a perfect square frame. Your screen should look similar to Figure 3-2. You do not need to save this file.

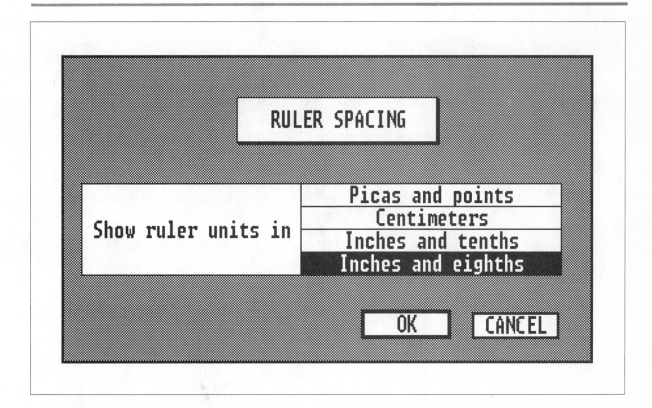

Figure 3-1
The Ruler Spacing dialog box allows you to choose among four units of measurement for the rulers. Inches and eighths is the default setting.

Figure 3-2
The rulers assist you when you create frames of specific sizes, such as this 1-inch square frame.

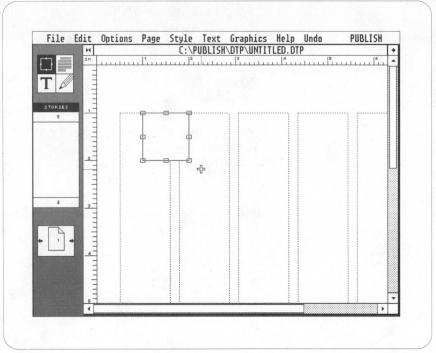

IMPORTING GRAPHICS

As mentioned earlier, graphics created in other programs can be used in Publish It! Graphics that originate in programs other than Publish It! are called imported graphics. Imported art is sometimes called **clip art**.

Sources of Imported Graphics

The sources of your imported graphics will vary. Different graphic programs save art in different file formats. Publish It! supports a wide variety of graphic file formats. File formats are generally indicated by the extension on the filename. For example, *DOG.PCX* would indicate a graphic of a dog in *.PCX* format. *.TIF*, *.PIC*, and *.IMG* are other popular formats. When importing graphics, you specify the file format from the Import Picture dialog box shown in Figure 3-3.

Figure 3-3
The Import Picture dialog box enables you to specify the file format of the graphic to be imported.

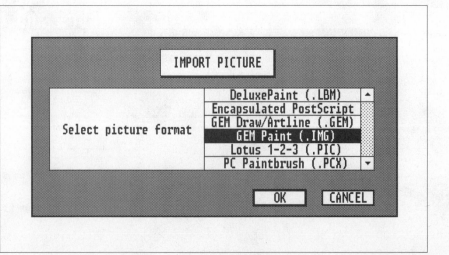

Using the Import Picture Command

Importing graphics is easy and fun. Publish It! provides the **Import picture command** in the File menu for importing graphics files. If a frame is drawn and selected when the Import picture command is chosen, the imported graphic appears in your document immediately.

ACTIVITY 3-2 • Importing Graphics

In this activity you will import a graphic into a new document. Be sure the rulers are visible on your screen.

1. Open a new, untitled document.	1. Open a new, untitled document.
2. Insert your template disk in drive A.	2. Insert your template disk in drive A.
3. Select the **Frame tool** from the tool box.	3. Select the **Frame tool** from the tool box.
4. Create a 3-inch square frame.	4. Create a 3-inch square frame.
5. Pull down the **File** menu.	5. Pull down the **File** menu.
6. Choose **Import picture**. The Import Picture dialog box appears.	6. Choose **Import picture**. The Import Picture dialog box appears.
7. Click on **PC Paintbrush (.PCX)**. Click on **OK**. The Item Selector box appears. Because your template disk is in drive A, you must tell Publish It! to look there.	7. Choose **PC Paintbrush (.PCX)**. Press **Enter**. The Item Selector box appears. Because your template disk is in drive A, you must tell Publish It! to look there.
8. Click the mouse button on the Directory line. A cursor appears after the *.PCX* extension.	8. Position the pointer on the Directory line. Press the **Home** key. A cursor appears after the *.PCX* extension.
9. Press **Esc** to delete the entire line.	9. Press **Esc** to delete the entire line.
10. Key **A:*.PCX** and press **Enter**. The *.PCX* files appear at the left of the Item Selector box.	10. Key **A:*.PCX** and press **Enter**. The *.PCX* files appear at the left of the Item Selector box.
11. Click on **ACT3-2.PCX**. If *ACT3-2.PCX* is not visible in the box, use the scroll bar to scroll through the filenames.	11. Choose **ACT3-2.PCX**. If *ACT3-2.PCX* is not visible in the box, use the scroll bar to scroll through the filenames.
12. Click on **OK**. A graphic of a tennis racket and tennis ball appears in the frame you created. Your screen should look similar to Figure 3-4.	12. Press **Enter**. A graphic of a tennis racket and tennis ball appears in the frame you created. Your screen should look similar to Figure 3-4.

Continued

13. Insert your data disk in drive A.

14. Save the document as **TENNIS.DTP** on your data disk.

15. Leave this file open for the next activity.

13. Insert your data disk in drive A.

14. Save the document as **TENNIS.DTP** on your data disk.

15. Leave this file open for the next activity.

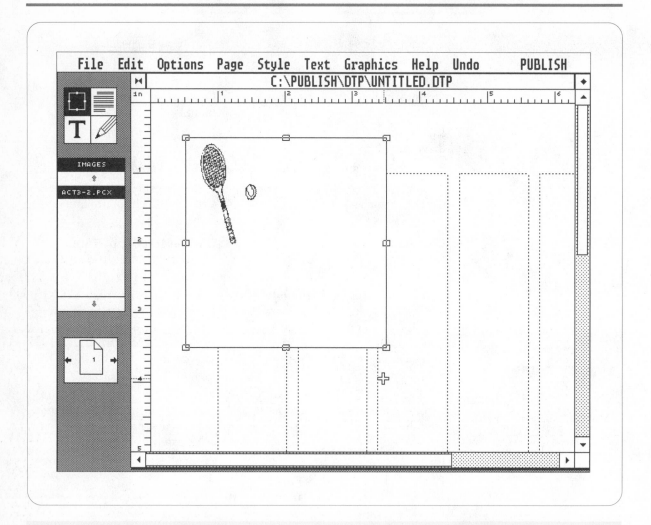

Figure 3-4

This imported graphic of a tennis racket and tennis ball would look great in a newsletter for a tennis club.

Importing Versus Placing

When a graphic is imported, the name of the graphic appears in the Library. The graphic is then available to be placed in your document. **Placing** a graphic refers to putting the graphic down on the page. Placing is not the same as importing, although importing and placing are often done at the same time. Importing only brings the graphic into the computer's memory to be included in your document. The distinction is important because you can place the same imported graphic twice in the same document and only import the graphic file once.

Two Types of Imported Graphics

An imported graphic can be classified as an image file or a line art file. **Image files** are created with a paint program or a scanner. **Line art files** are usually created with a drawing program. Publish It! treats the two types of files differently. The Library provides separate lists for image files and line art files.

ACTIVITY 3-3 • Placing Graphics from the Library

In this activity, you will import another graphic into your computer's memory once and place it on the page twice. You will also learn how to change the Library name to see the available lists.

1. Make sure the Frame tool is selected. Click on a vacant portion of the work area to deselect the frame that contains the tennis racket.

2. Choose **Import picture** from the File menu. Click on **OK**.

3. Import *ACT3-3.PCX* from your template disk. Because no frame was selected, the graphic does not appear in the work area. The name of the graphic, however, appears in the Library (on the left of the screen).

4. Create a frame, about 2-inches square, to the right of the frame already on the page.

5. With the frame selected, click on the name *ACT3-3.PCX* in the Library. The graphic is placed in the frame.

6. Scroll down to the bottom of the page. Create a 4-inch square frame.

7. With the frame selected, click on the name *ACT3-3.PCX* in the Library. The graphic is placed in the frame. You now have imported the same graphic once and placed it twice.

8. Click on the Library name (Images). The Library name changes to Stories. The Stories list is empty because you have no stories in your document.

9. Click on the Library name again. The Library name changes to Line Art. The Line Art list is empty because the two graphic files you imported are both image files.

1. Make sure the Frame tool is selected. In pointer mode, press **Home** on a vacant portion of the work area to deselect the frame that contains the tennis racket.

2. Choose **Import picture** from the **File** menu. Press **Enter**.

3. Import *ACT3-3.PCX* from your template disk. Because no frame was selected, the graphic does not appear in the work area. The name of the graphic, however, appears in the Library (on the left of the screen).

4. Create a frame, about 2-inches square, to the right of the frame already on the page.

5. With the frame selected, position the pointer on the name *ACT3-3.PCX* in the Library and press **Home**. The graphic is placed in the frame.

6. Scroll down to the bottom of the page. Create a 4-inch square frame.

7. With the frame selected, position the pointer on the name *ACT3-3.PCX* in the Library and press **Home**. The graphic is placed in the frame. You now have imported the same graphic once and placed it twice.

8. Position the pointer on the Library name (Images) and press **Home**. The Library name changes to Stories. The Stories list is empty because you have no stories in your document.

Continued

10. Click on the Library name again. You are back at the Images list.

11. Leave the file open for the next activity.

9. Press **Home** again. The Library name change to Line Art. The Line Art list is empty because the two graphic files you imported are both image files.

10. Press **Home** again. You are back at the Images list.

11. Leave the file open for the next activity.

Deleting Imported Graphics

Imported graphics can be deleted from a document. Deleting the frame in which your graphic was placed will only remove the graphic from your page, it will not remove the graphic from the Library. To delete a graphic from the Library, you must use the Status box. Double-clicking on the name of the graphic in the Library will cause the Status box to appear. In the Status box is the option to delete the graphic from the Library.

Additional Status Box Features

In addition to deleting graphics, the Status box allows you to rename the graphics in the Library and to see the size of the graphics in kilobytes. To rename the graphic, simply key a new name over the existing name in the Status box. When you exit the Status box, the name will be changed in the Library.

ACTIVITY 3-4 • Using the Status Box

In this activity, you will delete a graphic from the Library and rename a graphic in the Library. You will accomplish both of these tasks using the Status box.

1. Select the 4-inch frame at the bottom of the page. Press **Delete** to delete the frame.

2. Scroll up to the top of the page. Select the small frame containing the lightbulb graphic. Press **Delete** to delete the frame. Although the graphic no longer appears on the page, it has not been deleted from the Library.

3. Double-click on the file *ACT3-3.PCX* in the Library's Image list. The Status box appears.

4. Click on **Delete** to remove the graphic file from the Library.

5. Click on **OK** to verify. The graphic file is removed from the Library.

6. Double-click on the file *ACT3-2.PCX* in the Library's Image list. The Status box appears.

1. Select the 4-inch frame at the bottom of the page. Press **Delete** to delete the frame.

2. Scroll up to the top of the page. Select the small frame containing the lightbulb graphic. Press **Delete** to delete the frame. Although the graphic no longer appears on the page, it has not been deleted from the Library.

3. Position the pointer on the file *ACT3-3.PCX* in the Library's Image list and rapidly press **Home** twice. This is the keyboard equivalent of double-clicking a mouse. The Status box appears.

4. Choose **Delete** to remove the graphic file from the Library.

Continued

7. Backspace over the name *ACT3-2.PCX* and key **RACKET.PCX** in its place.

8. Click on **OK** to close the Status box. The name of the graphic is changed in the Library.

9. Leave this file open for the next activity.

5. Choose **OK** to verify. The graphic file is removed from the Library.

6. Position the pointer on the file *ACT3-2.PCX* in the Library's Image list and rapidly press **Home** twice. The Status Box appears.

7. Backspace over the name *ACT3-2.PCX* and key **RACKET.PCX** in its place.

8. Choose **OK** to close the Status box. The name of the graphic is changed in the Library.

9. Leave this file open for the next activity.

Altering the Appearance of Graphics

Although the graphics you import are already created, several features are available that enable you to alter the way the graphics appear on the page. These features include cropping, editing, and scaling. These commands are available for image files only.

Cropping Graphics. The **Crop picture command** allows you to cut down the size of a graphic to exclude all but the parts of the graphic that you need. **Cropping** also removes unwanted blank space surrounding a graphic and readjusts the graphic to fill the frame. Although the purpose of cropping is to remove unwanted space and objects, cropping has the effect of enlarging the graphic. If you make a mistake when cropping a picture, simply click on the graphic filename in the Library and Publish It! will restore the original graphic.

ACTIVITY 3-5 • Cropping Graphics

In this activity you will crop a graphic to remove the blank space and readjust the graphic within the screen. The tennis racket graphic should be on the screen.

1. Select the frame containing the tennis racket.

2. Pull down the **Graphics** menu.

3. Choose **Crop picture**. A pair of scissors appears in place of the pointer.

4. Using the mouse, move the scissors to the upper left corner of the graphic.

5. Click and drag the mouse down and to the right until a box sur-

1. Select the frame containing the tennis racket.

2. Pull down the **Graphics** menu.

3. Choose **Crop picture**. A pair of scissors appears in place of the pointer.

4. Using the arrow keys, move the scissors to the upper left corner of the graphic.

5. Press the **End** key. Use the Right Arrow key and the Down

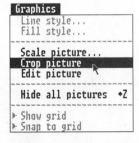

Continued

rounds only the tennis racket, as shown in Figure 3-5. Do not include the tennis ball or the blank space to the right of the graphic. Release the mouse button. Publish It! redraws the picture. The tennis racket appears larger and is better positioned within the frame.

6. Choose **Save** from the **File** menu. Publish It! tells you that *A:\TENNIS* already exists and asks if you want to overwrite the file.

7. Click on **Yes**.

8. Leave the file open for the next activity.

Arrow key to create a box around only the tennis racket, as shown in Figure 3-5. Do not include the tennis ball or the blank space to the right of the graphic. Press the **Home** key. Publish It! redraws the picture. The tennis racket appears larger and is better positioned within the frame.

6. Choose **Save** from the **File** menu. Publish It! tells you that *A:\TENNIS* already exists and asks if you want to overwrite the file.

7. Choose **Yes**.

8. Leave the file open for the next activity.

Figure 3-5
The Crop picture command allows you to remove the areas surrounding the part of the graphic you want to use.

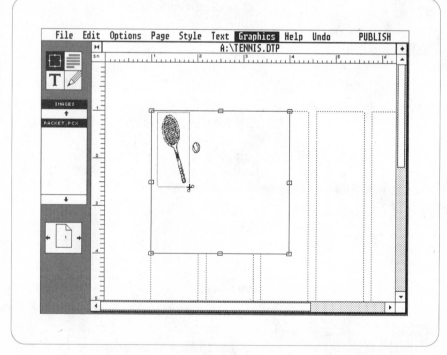

Editing Graphics. **Editing** magnifies a graphic to four times its original size so that you can work with the individual pixels. **Pixels** are the dots that make up a graphic. You can add and delete pixels by clicking on the mouse button. When clicked on, the white pixels become black, and the black pixels become white. If you click on a pixel and hold down the mouse button, the pointer continues to draw pixels of the opposite color.

ACTIVITY 3-6 • Editing Graphics

In this activity you will edit a graphic. The graphic you cropped in Activity 3-5 should be on your screen.

Graphics
Line style...
Fill style...

Scale picture...
Crop picture
Edit picture

Hide all pictures   ♦Z

▸ Show grid
▸ Snap to grid

Mouse column:

1. Pull down the **Graphics** menu.
2. Choose **Edit picture**. Publish It! magnifies the graphic to four times its size. The entire graphic will not fit on the screen. Use the scroll bars at the right and bottom of the screen to display different parts of the graphic.
3. Display the strings of the racket on the screen.
4. Position the pointer in the middle of the strings. Click on a black pixel and hold down the mouse button. Continue moving the pointer and holding the mouse button. Notice every pixel you pass over becomes white. If you change a pixel by mistake, simply click on the pixel again and it will change back.
5. Edit the tennis racket so that a hole appears in the strings, as shown in Figure 3-6.
6. Click on the close box in the upper left corner of the screen. A dialog box appears asking if you want to save the changes made to the graphic.
7. Click on **OK**. Publish It! redraws the tennis racket with the hole that you made in the strings.
8. Save the document on your data disk.
9. Leave the file open for the next activity.

Keyboard column:

1. Pull down the **Graphics** menu.
2. Choose **Edit picture**. Publish It! magnifies the graphic to four times its size. The entire graphic will not fit on the screen. Use the scroll bars at the right and bottom of the screen to display different parts of the graphic.
3. Display the strings of the racket on the screen.
4. Position the pointer in the middle of the strings. Press the **Home** key. Continue moving the pointer and pressing the Home key. Notice that the white pixels become black and the black pixels become white. If you change a pixel by mistake, position your pointer on the pixel and press the Home key to change it back.
5. Using the Home key and the arrow keys, edit the tennis racket so that a hole appears in the strings, as shown in Figure 3-6.
6. Position the pointer on the close box in the upper left corner of the screen and press **Home**. A dialog box appears asking if you want to save the changes made to the graphic.
7. Choose **OK**. Publish It! redraws the tennis racket with the hole in the strings.
8. Save the document on your data disk.
9. Leave the file open for the next activity.

Scaling Graphics. Cropping, editing, or modifying a graphic in any way can stretch the picture or alter its appearance. **Scaling** ensures that a graphic that has been modified is proportionally correct. When you select the **Scale picture command** from the Graphics menu, a dialog box appears, as shown in Figure 3-7.

Figure 3-6
Magnifying a graphic makes it possible to edit the individual pixels that make up the graphic.

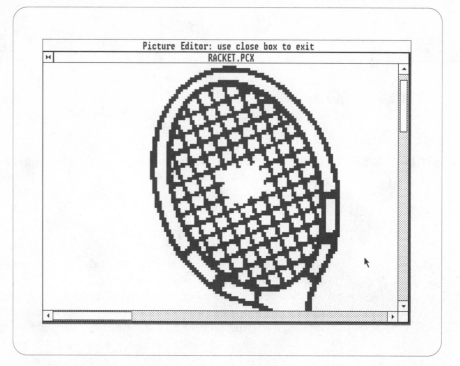

Figure 3-7
The options in the Scale Picture dialog box are used primarily to restore graphics that have been stretched out of proportion.

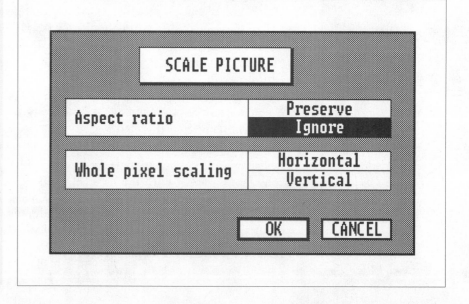

The **Preserve Aspect ratio** option shown in the dialog box restores original proportions to a graphic. The **Ignore Aspect ratio** option stretchs a graphic to fill the frame. **Whole pixel scaling** scales all pixels or dots equally, either horizontally, vertically, or both. Whole pixel scaling prevents the strange patterns that are sometimes produced when a graphic is reduced or enlarged by a fractional amount.

ACTIVITY 3-7 • Scaling Graphics

In this activity you will scale a graphic. The graphic that you edited in Activity 3-6 should be on the screen.

1. Pull down the **Graphics** menu.	1. Pull down the **Graphics** menu.
2. Choose **Scale picture**. The Scale Picture dialog box appears.	2. Choose **Scale picture**. The Scale Picture dialog box appears.
3. Click on **Preserve** in the Aspect ratio box.	3. Choose **Preserve** in the Aspect ratio box.
4. Click on **OK**. Publish It! redraws the graphic within the frame. The head of the racket and the handle are now proportionally balanced.	4. Press **Enter**. Publish It! redraws the graphic within the frame. The head of the racket and the handle are now proportionally balanced.
5. Save the document on your data disk.	5. Save the document on your data disk.
6. Leave the file open for the next activity.	6. Leave the file open for the next activity.

Hiding Graphics

The Hide all pictures command replaces all imported graphic images with an *X* and displays the graphic filenames in the middle of the frames. This is a temporary measure used for working on other parts of your document. Because graphics require a considerable amount of memory, redrawing the screen is sometimes a slow process. However, **hiding** a graphic reduces the time it takes Publish It! to redraw the screen. Although a hidden graphic cannot be seen on the screen, the graphic can be printed.

ACTIVITY 3-8 • Hiding Graphics

In this activity you will hide a graphic. The graphic you scaled in Activity 3-7 should be on the screen.

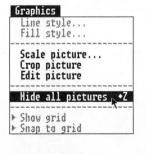

1. Pull down the **Graphics** menu.	1. Pull down the **Graphics** menu.
2. Choose **Hide all pictures**. The graphic is replaced by an *X* and the filename *RACKET.PCX*, as shown in Figure 3-8.	2. Choose **Hide all pictures**. The graphic is replaced by an *X* and the filename *RACKET.PCX*, as shown in Figure 3-8.
3. Pull down the **Graphics** menu.	3. Pull down the **Graphics** menu.
4. Choose **Hide all pictures** again. Publish It! restores your graphic. It is not necessary to save this document.	4. Choose **Hide all pictures** again. Publish It! restores your graphic. It is not necessary to save this document.

Figure 3-8
The Hide all pictures command replaces all imported graphics with *X*'s and the graphic filenames.

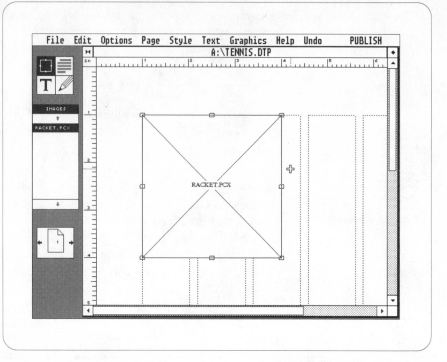

DRAWING GRAPHICS IN PUBLISH IT!

In addition to importing graphics from other graphic files, Publish It! allows you to draw your own graphics. A frame must be created and selected before you can create a graphic. When you create graphics, each circle, square, rectangle, or other shape that you draw appears within its own frame and has handles indicating that it is selected. The handles enable you to change the location and size of each graphic you create.

The Drawing Tools

The Pencil tool is used for drawing your own graphics. When the Pencil tool is selected, the Library contains eight drawing tools that you can use to create graphics, as shown in Figure 3-9.

Straight Line Tool.   The Straight Line tool allows you to draw straight lines horizontally, vertically, or diagonally. Lines are useful in documents because they lead the reader's eye to areas of the page that you want emphasized.

Graphics Pointer Tool.   The Graphics Pointer tool is used to select, move, and resize graphics that you have created.

Box Tool.   The Box tool allows you to draw squares and rectangles, which are referred to as boxes. Boxes can be used around text or graphics to catch a reader's attention. Boxes and lines may be combined to create charts and graphs.

Rounded Rectangle Tool.   The Rounded Rectangle tool lets you create squares and rectangles with rounded corners. A round-cornered box has a less rigid appearance and is sometimes more inviting to the eye than boxes with straight, sharp corners.

Figure 3-9.
When the Pencil tool is selected, the Library contains eight drawing tools for creating graphics.

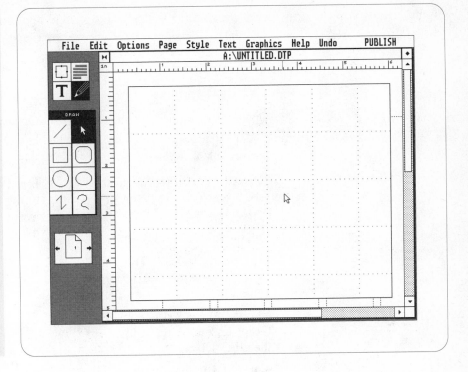

Circle Tool.   The Circle tool enables you to draw perfect circles. Circles can be used to enhance the appearance of a document. This tool is often used to create pie charts.

Ellipse Tool.   The Ellipse tool allows you to draw ovals. Ovals can be used to draw the reader's attention to a particular area of the page.

Polygon Tool.   The Polygon tool enables you to draw connected straight lines. You must anchor a line before attempting to draw in another direction. To anchor a line using the mouse, simply click the mouse button. To anchor a line using the keyboard, press the Home key. When you have completed your lines, double-click the mouse or quickly press the Home key twice.

Freehand Tool.   The Freehand tool lets you create a graphic as if you were drawing with a pen or pencil. You can draw curved lines and even write your name. Keyboard users must hold down the Shift key while pressing the arrow keys to create smooth curves.

Aligning Graphics

Two commands that will help you align graphics on the page are **Show grid** and **Snap to grid**. These commands are located in the Graphics menu and are displayed only when you are in graphics mode.

The Show grid command displays a **grid** within the frame, which enables you to draw straight lines and to align graphic elements. The Snap to grid command causes graphic objects to snap to the grid lines and helps align graphic objects. The Show grid and Snap to grid commands are always in effect unless you turn them off.

ACTIVITY 3-9 • Drawing Graphics

In this activity you will draw your own graphics using the Box, Circle, and Rounded Rectangle tools.

```
Graphics
  Line style...
  Fill style...

  Scale picture...
  Crop picture
  Edit picture

  Hide all pictures  ⬧Z

▶ Show grid
▶ Snap to grid
```

1. Open a new, untitled document.

2. Create a frame that covers most of the visible work area.

3. Select the **Pencil tool** from the tool box. Notice that the grid appears within the frame.

4. Pull down the **Graphics** menu.

5. Choose **Show grid**. The grid disappears and you have a blank frame.

6. Choose **Show grid** from the **Graphics** menu again to turn the grid back on.

7. Select the **Box tool** from the Library.

8. Move the pointer to the upper left corner of the frame you created.

9. Click and drag the pointer down and to the right to draw a rectangle. The rectangle should cover approximately half of the frame you created. Release the mouse button. Your screen will look similar to Figure 3-10.

10. Click outside the rectangle, but inside the frame, to deselect the rectangle.

11. Select the **Circle tool** from the Library.

12. Move the pointer to the center of the rectangle.

13. Click and drag the pointer down and to the right to draw a circle within the rectangle. Release the mouse button.

14. Select the **Rounded Rectangle tool** from the Library.

1. Open a new, untitled document.

2. Create a frame that covers most of the visible work area.

3. Select the **Pencil tool** from the tool box in the upper left corner of the screen. Press Alt + M to move from tool to tool.

4. Position the pointer in the frame and press **Home** to select it. Notice that the grid appears within the frame.

5. Pull down the **Graphics** menu.

6. Choose **Show grid**. The grid disappears and you have a blank frame.

7. Choose **Show grid** from the **Graphics** menu again to turn the grid back on.

8. Select the **Box tool** from the Library.

9. Move the pointer to the upper left corner of the frame you created.

10. Press the **End** key. Use the arrow keys to create a rectangle. Hold down the Shift key when using the arrow keys for more precise movement. The rectangle should cover approximately half of the frame you created. Press the **Home** key. Your screen should look similar to Figure 3-10.

11. Move the pointer outside of the rectangle. Press **Home** to deselect the rectangle.

12. Select the **Circle tool** from the Library.

Continued

15. Position the pointer below the rectangle.

16. Click and drag the pointer down and to the right to draw a rectangle with rounded corners. Release the mouse button.

17. Save this document as *DRAW.DTP* on your data disk.

18. Leave the file open for the next activity.

13. Move the pointer to the center of the rectangle.

14. Press the **End** key. Use the arrow keys to draw a circle within the rectangle. Press the **Home** key.

15. Select the **Rounded Rectangle tool** from the Library.

16. Position the pointer below the rectangle.

17. Press the **End** key. Use the arrow keys to draw a rectangle with rounded corners. Press the **Home** key.

18. Save this document as *DRAW.DTP* on your data disk.

19. Leave the file open for the next activity.

Figure 3-10
The Box tool allows you to draw squares and rectangles.

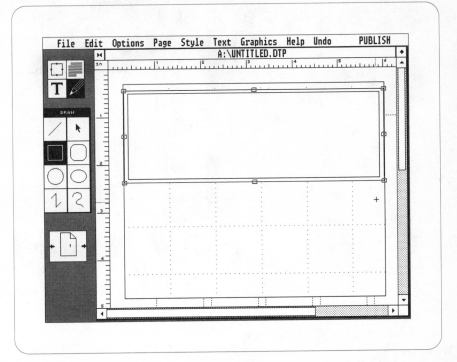

ENHANCING GRAPHICS

Although created graphics are seldom as picture-perfect as imported graphics, Publish It! offers several features that allow you to enhance the quality of the graphics you create. These features include resizing, line style, and fill style.

Resizing Graphics

Resizing enables you to change the size of an entire graphic or individual parts of a graphic. Just as with text frames, graphic frames are resized using the handles that are positioned around a selected frame. To resize an entire graphic, you must be in frame mode. To resize individual parts of a graphic you must be in graphics mode.

Line Style

As shown in Figure 3-11, the **Line Style command** allows you to choose the color of the lines in a graphic (black or white), the hairline style (dot, dot–dash, dash, and solid), and the width of the rules, or lines. You can also choose to put arrowheads at either or both ends of a line. The Line Style command is located in the Graphics menu and can be chosen before or after a graphic is created.

Figure 3-11
The Line Style dialog box offers several options for enhancing created graphics.

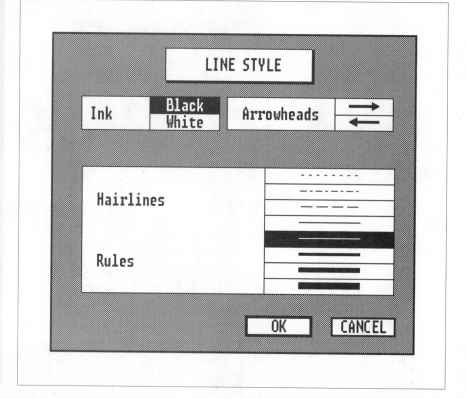

Fill Style

As shown in Figure 3-12, the **Fill Style command**, located in the Graphics menu, enables you to choose from a variety of patterns to fill a frame. You can choose the color of the pattern (black or white). You also can choose a clear or opaque fill pattern. A clear fill pattern lets other objects show through it; an opaque fill pattern hides other objects. You can choose whether to display the outer edge of an object. The Fill Style command can be chosen before or after a graphic is created.

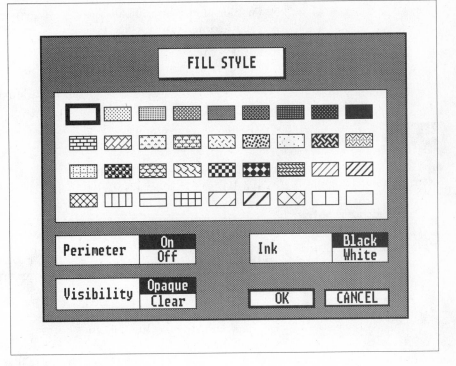

Figure 3-12
The Fill Style command offers additional methods of improving created graphics.

ACTIVITY 3-10 • Enhancing Graphics

In this activity you will resize a graphic and change the line style and fill style of a graphic. The graphic you created in Activity 3-9 should be on your screen.

1. Select the **Graphics Pointer tool** from the Library.

2. Position the pointer inside the circle you created.

3. Click the mouse button. Handles appear around the frame surrounding the circle, indicating that the frame is selected.

4. Position the pointer on the handle at the top left corner of the circle's frame. Click and drag the mouse up and to the left until the frame touches the top of the rectangle, as shown in Figure 3-13. Release the mouse button. The circle is resized.

1. Select the **Graphics Pointer tool** from the Library.

2. Position the pointer inside the circle you created.

3. Press the **Home** key. Handles appear around the frame surrounding the circle, indicating that the frame is selected.

4. Position the pointer on the handle at the top left corner of the circle's frame. Press the **End** key. Use the Left Arrow and Up Arrow keys to drag the frame until it touches the rectangle, as shown in Figure 3-13. Press the **Home** key. The circle is resized.

Continued

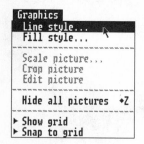

5. Position the pointer inside the round-cornered rectangle.

6. Click the mouse button to select the round-cornered rectangle.

7. Pull down the **Graphics** menu.

8. Choose **Line style**. The Line Style dialog box appears.

9. Click on the widest black line available. Click on **OK**. The Line Style dialog box disappears and the round-cornered rectangle is redrawn with the wide black line.

10. Position the pointer inside the rectangle, but outside the circle.

11. Click the mouse button to select the rectangle.

12. Pull down the **Graphics menu**.

13. Choose **Fill style**. The Fill Style dialog box appears.

14. Click on the pattern that is second from the right on the first line (it's black with white dots). Click on **OK**. The Fill Style dialog box disappears, and the rectangle is filled with the selected pattern.

15. Move the pointer outside the rectangle and click the mouse button to deselect the rectangle's frame.

16. Select the **Box tool** from the Library.

17. Create a rectangle within the circle. The rectangle has the fill pattern you chose in step 14. Your graphic will look similar to Figure 3-14.

18. Save the document on your data disk.

19. Leave the file open for the next activity.

5. Position the pointer inside the round-cornered rectangle.

6. Press the **Home** key to select the round-cornered rectangle.

7. Pull down the **Graphics** menu.

8. Choose **Line style**. The Line Style dialog box appears.

9. Choose the widest black line available. Choose **OK**. The Line Style dialog box disappears and the round-cornered rectangle is redrawn with the wide black line.

10. Position the pointer inside the rectangle, but outside the circle.

11. Press the **Home** key to select the rectangle.

12. Pull down the **Graphics** menu.

13. Choose **Fill style**. The Fill Style dialog box appears.

14. Choose the pattern that is second from the right on the first line (it's black with white dots). Press **Enter**. The Fill Style dialog box disappears and the rectangle is filled with the selected pattern.

15. Move the pointer outside the rectangle and press **Home** to deselect the rectangle's frame.

16. Select the **Box tool** from the Library.

17. Create a small rectangle inside the circle. The rectangle has the fill pattern you chose in step 14. Your graphic should look similar to Figure 3-14.

18. Save the document on your data disk.

19. Leave the file open for the next activity.

Figure 3-13
The Graphics Pointer tool is used to resize created graphics.

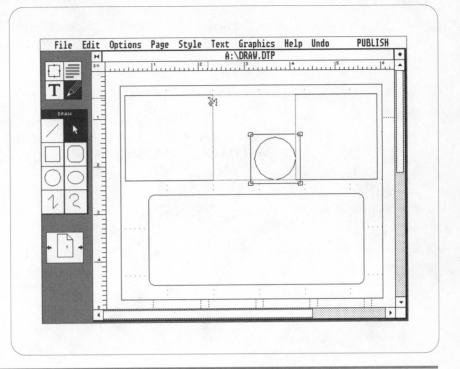

Figure 3-14
The resizing, line style, and fill style features allow you to enhance the quality of graphics.

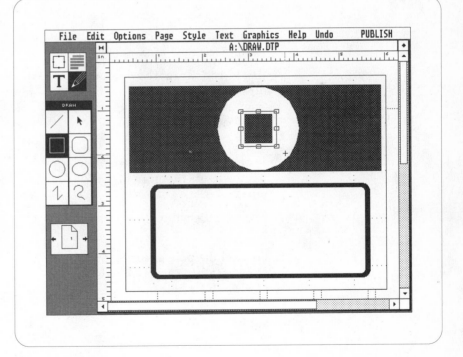

POSITIONING GRAPHICS

After graphics are created, you may want to move them within a document. The dragging method can be used to move both imported graphics and graphics drawn in Publish It! within a document. Imported graphics must be moved in frame mode. Graphics drawn in Publish It! may be moved in frame mode or Graphics mode. Frame mode lets you move an entire frame, whereas graphics mode allows you to move individual objects. However, individual objects cannot be moved outside their frames.

Graphics are placed in a document in layers. For example, in Activity 3-9 you drew a rectangle. Then you drew a circle within the rectangle. Because the rectangle was drawn first, it is in a layer behind the circle. Since the circle was drawn second, it is positioned in front of the rectangle. This layering effect makes it possible to move one graphic in front of or behind another graphic. The **Bring to front command** in the Options menu enables you to bring to the front a graphic that's in the back layer. The **Send to back command** enables you to send a graphic in the front layer to the back.

ACTIVITY 3-11 • Moving Graphics

In this activity you will move graphics by dragging. The graphics you enhanced in Activity 3-10 should be on the screen.

1. Select the **Frame tool** from the tool box.	1. Select the **Frame tool** from the tool box.
2. Position the pointer in the frame and click the mouse button to select the frame.	2. Position the pointer in the frame and press **Home** to select the frame.
3. Click and drag the mouse down until about half of the frame is visible on the screen. The entire frame is moved down the page.	3. Press the **End** key. Use the arrow keys to move the frame down until only about half of the frame is visible on the screen. Press **Home**. The entire frame is moved down the page.
4. Return the frame to its original position at the top of the screen.	4. Return the frame to its original position at the top of the screen.
5. Select the **Pencil tool** from the tool box.	5. Select the **Pencil tool** from the tool box.
6. Position the pointer inside the square, which is inside the circle, and click the mouse button to select the square. A frame appears around the square.	6. Position the pointer inside the square, which is inside the circle, and press **Home** twice to select the square. A frame appears around the square.
7. Click and drag the mouse down until the square is in the middle of the round-cornered rectangle, as shown in Figure 3-15. Release the mouse button.	7. Press **End**. Use the arrow keys to move the square into the round-cornered rectangle, as shown in Figure 3-15. Press **Home**.

Continued

8. Position the pointer inside the circle and click the mouse button to select the circle.

9. Pull down the **Page** menu.

10. Choose **Send to back**. The circle is placed behind the rectangle, but the frame remains visible.

11. Pull down the **Page** menu again.

12. Choose **Bring to front**. The circle reappears within the frame.

13. Save the document on your data disk.

14. Leave the file open for the next activity.

8. Position the pointer inside the circle and press **Home** to select the circle.

9. Pull down the **Page** menu.

10. Choose **Send to back**. The circle is placed behind the rectangle, but the frame remains visible.

11. Pull down the **Page** menu again.

12. Choose **Bring to front**. The circle reappears within the frame.

13. Save the document on your data disk.

14. Leave the file open for the next activity.

Figure 3-15
Graphics can easily be moved from one location to another using the dragging method.

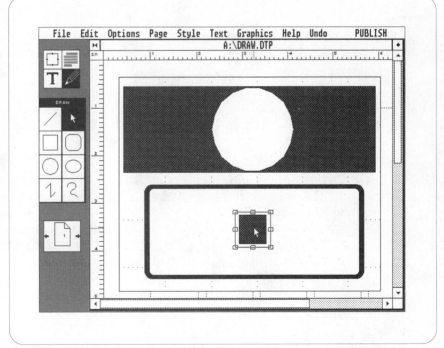

CUTTING, COPYING, AND PASTING GRAPHICS

The Cut, Copy, and Paste commands in the Edit menu are used to move or duplicate graphics. The Cut, Copy, and Paste commands are used in the same way for graphics as they are for text. They can be used within a document or between two documents. The Cut, Copy, and Paste commands can save you time by eliminating the need to recreate or import a graphic that has already been used in a document.

The **Cut command** cuts a graphic from a document and places it on the Clipboard. The **Copy command** places a copy of a graphic on the Clipboard, leaving the graphic in the document. The **Paste command** pastes a cut or copied graphic into a document. As an alternative to using the Cut and Paste commands, Publish It! allows you to use the **Delete key** for the Cut command and the **Insert key** for the Paste command.

Only one item can exist on the Clipboard at a time. An item remains on the Clipboard either until it is replaced by another item or until you quit Publish It!

Imported graphics are cut, copied, and pasted in frame mode. Graphics drawn in Publish It! may be cut, copied, and pasted in either graphics mode or frame mode. Graphics mode enables you to cut, copy, and paste individual parts of a graphic drawn in Publish It!, whereas frame mode lets you cut, copy, and paste the frame containing the graphic.

ACTIVITY 3-12 • Cutting, Copying, and Pasting Graphics

In this activity you will cut, copy, and paste graphics using the commands in the Edit menu and using the Delete and Insert keys.

1. Choose **Size to fit** from the **Page** menu.	1. Press **Alt + 0** to choose Size to fit from the Page menu.
2. Select the **Frame tool** from the tool box.	2. Select the **Frame tool** from the tool box.
3. Select the frame surrounding the graphic.	3. Select the frame surrounding the graphic.
4. Choose **Cut** from the **Edit** menu. The frame and the graphic are placed on the Clipboard.	4. Choose **Cut** from the **Edit** menu. The frame and the graphic are placed on the Clipboard.
5. Choose **Paste** from the **Edit** menu. The frame and the graphic reappear on the screen.	5. Choose **Paste** from the **Edit** menu. The frame and the graphic reappear on the screen.
6. Choose **Copy** from the **Edit** menu. The frame and the graphic remain on the screen, and a copy of the graphic is placed on the Clipboard.	6. Press **Alt + C** to choose **Copy** from the Edit menu. The frame and the graphic remain on the screen, and a copy of the graphic is placed on the Clipboard.
7. Choose **Paste** from the **Edit** menu. The copy overlaps the original graphic.	7. Press **Alt + V** to choose Paste from the Edit menu. The copy overlaps the original frame.
8. Using the mouse, click and drag the copied graphic to the bottom right corner of the screen. Release the mouse button.	8. Position the pointer over the newly pasted frame. Press **End**. Use the arrow keys to move the copied graphic to the bottom right corner of the screen. Press **Home**.
9. Create a small frame below the top graphic and to the left of the copied graphic.	9. Create a small frame below the top graphic and to the left of the copied graphic.
10. Select the **Pencil tool** from the tool box.	10. Select the **Pencil tool** from the tool box.
11. Select the small rectangle inside the lower frame.	11. Select the small rectangle inside the lower frame.
12. Press the **Delete** key. The square disappears and is placed on the Clipboard.	

Continued

13. Position the pointer inside the empty frame you created in step 9. Click the mouse button to select the frame.

14. Press the **Insert** key. The square appears in the frame.

15. Open a new, untitled document. It is not necessary to save this document.

12. Press the **Delete** key. The square disappears and is placed on the Clipboard.

13. Position the pointer inside the empty frame you created in step 9. Press **Home** to select the frame.

14. Press the **Insert** key. The square appears in the frame.

15. It is not necessary to save this document.

SUMMARY

Graphics are important to a document. They illustrate and explain text, making it easier to understand. Graphics also help guide a reader through a document. A graphic can help a reader find specific text, as well as contribute to the overall appearance of a document.

Publish It! uses two types of graphics: imported graphics and graphics drawn in Publish It! The rulers help you size and position graphics and frames. Cropping, editing, and scaling are features that alter the appearance of imported graphics. Publish It! has eight tools to assist you in creating your own graphics. Created graphics can be enhanced through the line style and fill style options.

Other graphics features include hiding graphics to allow Publish It! to redraw the screen more quickly and a grid for graphic alignment.

Graphics are placed into a document in layers, and they can be moved to different layers within the document. Graphics can also be moved to different locations on the page by dragging them. The cut, copy, and paste commands are used to move graphics within a document or from one document to another. All graphics can be cut, copied, and pasted, the way text is. Cut or copied graphics are placed on the Clipboard. Items remain on the clipboard until they are replaced with other items or until the program is turned off.

CHAPTER

③

Review

Name _____   Date _____

TRUE OR FALSE

The following statements are either true or false. Circle T or F to indicate your answer.

1. If you do not change the ruler spacing, Publish It! uses the inches and eighths unit of measurement. (Obj. 1)   1. T   F

2. You can import graphics created in other programs into Publish It! (Obj. 2)   2. T   F

3. A cropped graphic can be restored to its original condition. (Obj. 3)   3. T   F

4. Hiding a graphic increases the time it takes Publish It! to redraw the screen. (Obj. 3)   4. T   F

5. The Pencil tool must be selected in order to create your own graphics. (Obj. 4)   5. T   F

6. The Graphics Pointer tool is used to draw graphics. (Obj. 4)   6. T   F

7. A frame must be selected before it can be resized. (Obj. 5)   7. T   F

8. Publish It! allows some line and fill styles to be changed. (Obj. 6)   8. T   F

9. Graphics may not be moved once they are in a document. (Obj. 7)   9. T   F

10. The Cut, Copy, and Paste commands are located in the Graphics menu. (Obj. 8)   10. T   F

COMPLETION

Write your answers in the space provided.

11. Name the four units of measurement available for the rulers. (Obj. 1)

_____

_____

12. What are the two types of graphics that Publish It! uses? (Obj. 2)

_____

_____

13. What are two purposes of cropping an imported graphic? (Obj. 3)

_____

_____

14. What is the purpose of displaying a grid within a graphics frame? (Obj. 4)

_____

_____

15. List five of the eight drawing tools available in the tool box. (Obj. 4)

_____

_____

16. Which mode lets you resize individual graphic items? (Obj. 5)

_____

_____

17. The Line Style and Fill Style commands are used with which type of graphic? (Obj. 6)

_____

_____

18. Which command allows you to move one graphic in front of another graphic? (Obj. 7)

_____

_____

19. What are the keys that Publish It! recognizes as short cuts for the Cut and Paste commands? (Obj. 8)

_____

_____

20. How long does an item remain on the Clipboard? (Obj. 8)

_____

_____

APPLICATION 3-1

In this application you will display the rulers, then import, crop, and move a graphic.

1. Open a new, untitled document.
2. Display the rulers.
3. Change the ruler spacing to centimeters.
4. Create a 10-centimeter square frame at the top of the work area.
5. Import *APP3-1.PCX* from your template disk.
6. Crop the graphic to exclude any unwanted space surrounding the graphic.
7. Drag the graphic down and to the right until it appears centered on the screen.
8. Save this file as *GRADUATE.DTP* on your data disk.

APPLICATION 3-2

In this application you will move created graphics and change the line style and fill style.

1. Open *APP3-2.DTP* from your template disk.
2. Position the rectangle on top of the pencil.
3. Change the line style of the rectangle to the next-wider black line.
4. Change the fill style of the rectangle to the single horizontal line on the bottom row.
5. Use the Send to back command to position the rectangle behind the pencil.
6. Save this file as *PENCIL.DTP* on your data disk.

APPLICATION 3-3

In this application you will create a wagon by moving, copying, and pasting graphics.

1. Open *APP3-3.DTP* from your template disk.
2. Select the large circle at the top of the screen. Move the circle below the round-cornered rectangle and align it with the small circle.
3. Select the small circle.
4. Place a copy of the small circle on the Clipboard.
5. Paste the copy of the small circle into your document.
6. Move both small circles to the center of the large circle. Hint: Turn off Snap to grid from the Graphics menu to allow for more precise alignment.
7. Select the vertical line.
8. Move the vertical line until the bottom of the line is touching the right edge of the horizontal line.
9. Select the small rectangle.
10. Move the small rectangle down until the bottom left edge is aligned with the vertical line. You have created a simple wagon.
11. Save this document as *WAGON.DTP* on your data disk.

SECTION

Publishing Design Concepts and Principles

Chapter 4
Printing Documents

Chapter 5
Using Style Sheets

Chapter 6
Creating a Page Layout

CHAPTER

Printing Documents

LEARNING OBJECTIVES

When you complete this chapter, you will be able to:

1. Describe the differences among the various types of printers.
2. Understand how print quality is measured.
3. Print a document.
4. Use print options.
5. Preview a document.
6. Print to disk.

DELIVERING THE MESSAGE

The Gettysburg Address is recognized as one of the great speeches of all time. However, the speech was not recognized as great until Abraham Lincoln delivered it. Had he done no more than prepare it, you would never have heard of the Gettysburg Address. The goal of desktop publishing is communication. Although much time is spent preparing a document, communication does not take place until the message is delivered. Just as a speech must be spoken to deliver the message, a document must be printed to be complete.

Printing is the process that creates your document on paper. In desktop publishing, the term *printing* most often refers to the printing done by the computer. Occasionally the term refers to the mass production of a publication by a printing press or copier. To avoid confusion, this book refers to the mass production of a publication as **commercial printing**.

TYPES OF PRINTERS

There are many types of printers available to the desktop publisher. Let's look at four commonly used types of printers.

Letter-Quality Impact Printers

Most of the first computer printers were letter-quality impact printers such as **daisy wheel printers** (see Figure 4-1). These printers are basically computer-controlled typewriters. Like a typewriter, a character impacts the paper through an ink ribbon. These printers have no graphics or line-drawing capabilities, except for what can be drawn using the characters available. However, the text output is of the same quality as a typewriter. As a result, the letter-quality printer became popular for word processing.

Figure 4-1
A daisy-wheel printer is an example of a letter-quality impact printer.

Dot-Matrix Printers

Dot-matrix printers were developed as a relatively inexpensive, yet versatile, type of printer. **Dot-matrix printers** impact the paper through an ink ribbon like other impact printers. However, the dot-matrix printer forms letters, numbers, symbols, and graphics using pins. The printer pushes the appropriate pins into the ribbon to create an image of text or graphics. Figure 4-2 illustrates a typical dot-matrix printer.

Ink-jet Printers

Ink-jet printers are nonimpact printers that use tiny jets to spray ink on the page in the form of a character or graphic image. Ink-jet printers are faster and quieter than most impact printers. Figure 4-3 shows an ink-jet printer.

Laser Printers

Laser printers are the most commonly used desktop publishing printer. A laser printer operates much like a photocopier. A photocopier gets an image from light reflected off the page to be copied. A **laser printer** gets an image from the computer and uses a laser instead of the reflected light. Laser printers are quiet compared to dot-matrix, daisy wheel, or even ink-jet printers. The speed of a laser printer varies depending on the complexity of the image being printed. A typical laser printer is shown in Figure 4-4.

Figure 4-2
Dot-matrix printers are the most common type of impact printer.

Figure 4-3
Ink-jet printers offer quiet operation and quality output.

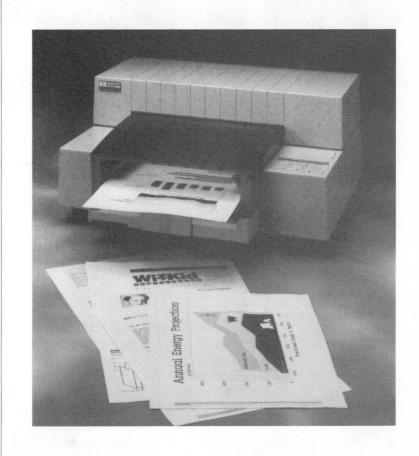

Figure 4-4
Laser printers are popular in desktop publishing.

HOW PRINT QUALITY IS MEASURED

For many desktop publishing tasks, the quality of print is important to the success of the publication. Print resolution and sharpness are terms used to describe print quality.

Print Resolution

Print resolution is a measure of the density of the dots that a printer creates on paper. For example, most laser printers have a print resolution of 300 dots per inch (dpi). This means that each dot on the page is only 1/300 of an inch in diameter. To draw a horizontal or vertical one-inch line on the paper, the printer would print 300 dots in a line. To draw a filled one-inch square like the one in Figure 4-5, a 300-dpi printer prints 90,000 dots! Resolution is the most commonly used measure of print quality because it can be specified numerically.

Sharpness

Sharpness is not as easily measured as resolution. **Sharpness** is judged by visual inspection of the printed product. Although a printer may print at

300 dpi or higher, sharp output is not guaranteed. The most effective way to see sharpness is to look closely at the edges of characters or graphics. If the edges of printed text are fuzzy, your reader may have to struggle to read the words. You do not want your reader to be distracted by poor-quality text. You want your reader to be free to concentrate on the message of your publication.

Except for very expensive printers used for commercial typesetting, laser printers are generally considered the best printers available for desktop publishing. Laser printers give very sharp and clean print at a resolution high enough for producing camera-ready artwork (see Figure 4-6). Most laser printers have a resolution of 300 dpi, although some offer much higher resolution. Some ink-jet printers print with a resolution greater than 300 dpi. However, the sharpness of ink-jet output varies. The ink tends to spread when it contacts the paper, sometimes creating fuzzy edges.

Figure 4-5
A one-inch square box, when printed on a printer with a resolution of 300 dots per inch, is created with 90,000 dots.

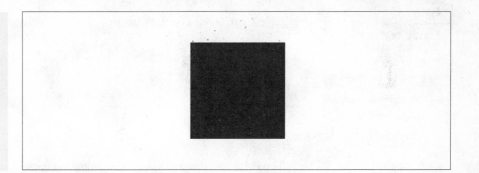

Figure 4-6
Laser printers produce characters with smooth curves and crisp edges.

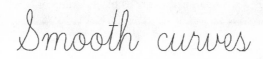

and crisp edges!

PRINTER SETUP

Before you can print a document, you must tell the computer the type of printer you will be using. This selection is made during the installation of Publish It! For more information of how to select a printer for use in Publish It!, see the Publish It! user's manual.

THE BASICS OF PRINTING

You use the **Print command** in the File menu to print a document. There are several options to consider when you print. In the next activity you will leave the options set at their defaults and learn the basics of printing with Publish It!

ACTIVITY 4-1 • Printing a Publication

In this activity you will open a document and print it.

Mouse	Keyboard
1. Open *ACT1-2.DTP* from your template disk.	1. Open *ACT1-2.DTP* from your template disk.
2. Choose **Print** from the **File** menu. The Print Document dialog box appears. There are several print options available on the screen. These will be explained later in the chapter.	2. Choose **Print** from the **File** menu. The Print Document dialog box appears. There are several print options available on the screen. These will be explained later in the chapter.
3. Click on **OK**. The document prints.	3. Choose **OK**. The document prints.
4. Leave the file open for the next activity.	4. Leave the file open for the next activity.

PRINT OPTIONS

The Print Document dialog box gives you control over all aspects of the printing of your document (see Figure 4-7). You select or deselect many of the options by clicking on the name of the option. If an option's name appears as white letters on a black background, the option is turned on. If the option's name appears as black letters on a white background, the option is turned off.

Figure 4-7
The Print Document dialog box lets you specify printing options before you send the document to the printer.

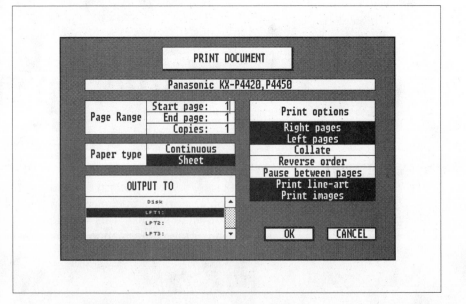

Page Range

In a document of more than one page, you may want to specify a **range** of pages to print, rather than print the entire document. To print a range of pages, key the number of the start page and end page in the spaces provided in the Page Range section of the Print Document dialog box.

Copies

The Page Range section of the Print Document dialog box also lets you specify the number of copies to print. In general, the computer's printer should not be used to make multiple copies of a document. Photocopiers are better suited for that purpose.

Paper Type

The Paper type section of the Print Document dialog box lets you choose between continuous paper and single sheets. **Continuous paper** is the type that is stacked in fan-fold fashion. Each sheet is attached to the next by a perforation. **Single sheet paper** is the type commonly found in photocopiers. The sheets are separate rather than hitched together. Laser printers and ink-jet printers use single sheet paper. Many dot-matrix printers can use either type of paper, although they are typically loaded with continuous paper. To select the paper type, click on the type of paper you are using.

Right Pages

If the Right pages option is highlighted, the right-hand pages of a multipage document are printed. This allows you to print on both sides of the paper. You can first print the right-hand pages of the document, then turn the pages over and run them through the printer again. On the second run through the printer, print the left-hand pages on the backs of the right-hand pages.

Left Pages

If the Left pages option is highlighted, the left-hand pages of a multipage document are printed.

Collate

When printing more than one copy of a multipage document, you have a choice of whether to collate the pages or not. To **collate** means to arrange the pages in their proper order. If the Collate option is highlighted, each document is printed with the pages in order. If the option is not highlighted, all copies of the first page are printed, followed by all copies of the second page, and so on, until the end of the document is reached.

Reverse Order

If the Reverse order option is highlighted, the last page is printed first and the first page last. Depending on the way your printer stacks the paper, you can use this option to make the pages come out in the correct order.

Pause between Pages

The Pause between pages option allows for hand feeding sheets of paper into the printer. When this option is on, the printer pauses after printing each page in a multipage document, allowing you to feed paper by hand.

Print Line Art and Print Images

When you are formatting text in a document, it may be helpful to print the document without imported graphics. Publish It! allows you to print without graphics, which speeds up printing. If the Print line art and Print images options are highlighted, the graphics are printed. If they are not highlighted, a box with an *X* through it appears on the printed page in the place of each graphic.

Output Destination

The Output To section of the Print Document dialog box allows you to specify the printer port to which you want to send the document. It also gives you the option of printing the document to disk. Printing to disk is discussed later in this chapter.

GETTING A PREVIEW OF YOUR DOCUMENT

Because Publish It! is a WYSIWYG program, what you see on your screen is very similar to what you see when you print. (WYSIWYG is an acronym for what you see is what you get.) Normally when you work on your document, there are column guides and frame borders visible on the screen. These items are helpful, but they can sometimes keep you from getting a clear picture of what your document looks like.

You can preview your document by removing items that will not be printed. The **Show frames & cols command** toggles the frames and column guides on and off, giving you an unobstructed view of your document. You can also use the **Show tools command** to hide the tool box, the library, and the page icon. With those items hidden, there is more room on the screen to display your document.

ACTIVITY 4-2 • Previewing a Document

In this activity you will preview the document printed in Activity 4-1, comparing the printed output to the image on the screen.

1. Choose **Size to fit** from the **Page** menu.	1. Press **Alt + 0** to choose Size to fit from the Page menu.
2. Choose **Show frames & cols** from the **Options** menu. Compare what you see on your screen to the document printed in Activity 4-1.	2. Choose **Show frames & cols** from the **Options** menu. Compare what you see on your screen to the document printed in Activity 4-1.
3. Choose **Actual size** from the **Page** menu.	3. Press **Alt + 3** to choose Actual size from the Page menu.
4. Choose **Show tools** from the **Options** menu. The tool box, library, and page icon disappear and the work area expands to fill the screen.	4. Choose **Show tools** from the **Options** menu. The tool box, library, and page icon disappear, and the work area expands to fill the screen.
5. Use the scroll bars to move around in the document and compare it to the printed copy.	5. Use the scroll bars to move around in the document and compare it to the printed copy.

Continued

6. Choose **Show tools** from the **Options** menu. The tools reappear.	6. Press **Alt + H** to choose Show tools from the Options menu. The tools reappear.
7. Choose **Show frames & cols** from the **Options** menu. The frames and column guides reappear.	7. Press **Alt + E** to choose Show frames & cols from the Options menu. The frames and column guides reappear.

PRINTING TO DISK

There are times when you do not have a printer available or when you want to print on a printer that is not connected to your computer. Suppose you are asked to design a flyer for a local charity event. The organization is requesting camera-ready copy to take to a commercial printer. You decide that the final copy should be printed on a laser printer. You have everything you need to do the job except the laser printer. What is the solution? The answer lies in a feature of Publish It! called printing to disk.

When you print your document to disk, a file is created that can be sent to a printer at a later time. The computer that does the final printing of the file does not even need to have Publish It! installed. The file that is saved when you print to disk is created for the specific printer you select.

Think of printing to disk as capturing the publication on its way to the printer and storing it on disk. You then transport the disk to the computer on which the printing will take place. The contents of the file are then released to continue the journey to the printer.

Printing to disk can also be used simply to delay printing. Sometimes printers must be shared by several computers and are not always available when needed. At such times, you can print your completed document to disk and then continue with other work until a printer becomes available. When you get your turn on the printer, you can print your file.

ACTIVITY 4-3 • PRINTING TO DISK

In this activity you will print to disk, exit Publish It!, and then send the file to the printer.

1. Open a new, untitled document.	1. Open a new, untitled document.
2. Create a text frame large enough to hold a short sentence.	2. Create a text frame large enough to hold a short sentence.
3. Key into the frame: **This document was printed to disk and then sent to the printer.** Choose any font at 14 or 18 point.	3. Key into the frame: **This document was printed to disk and then sent to the printer**. Choose any font at 14 or 18 point.
4. Choose **Print** from the **File** menu. Pressing Alt + P is an alternative to choosing Print from the File menu. The Print Document dialog box appears.	4. Choose **Print** from the **File** menu. Pressing Alt + P is an alternative to choosing Print from the File menu. The Print Document dialog box appears.

Continued

5. Choose **Disk** as the output destination.

6. Click on **OK**. The Item Selector appears.

7. Name the file *TESTPRT.PRT* and save it on your data disk.

8. Choose **Quit** from the **File** menu. It is not necessary to save the current document.

9. At the DOS prompt, key: **COPY A:\TESTPRT.PRT PRN/B**. The file is printed.

5. Choose **Disk** as the output destination.

6. Choose **OK**. The Item Selector appears.

7. Name the file *TESTPRT.PRT* and save it on your data disk.

8. Choose **Quit** from the **File** menu. It is not necessary to save the current document.

9. At the DOS prompt, key: **COPY A:\TESTPRT.PRT PRN/B**. The file is printed.

SUMMARY

The goal of desktop publishing is communication. Although much time is spent preparing a document, to deliver the message the document must be printed. There are four commonly used types of printers. Letter-quality impact printers were heavily used in years past for word processing. Dot-matrix printers are a relatively inexpensive and versatile alternative. Ink-jet printers have become popular in recent years because they demonstrate print quality near that of laser printers for less investment. Laser printers are the most commonly used desktop publishing printer.

Print quality is measured in resolution and sharpness. Resolution is a measure of the density of printed dots. The more dots per square inch the better the resolution. Sharpness is measured more by visual inspection than by mathematics. A sharp printout has clean edges and smooth curves.

When a publication is printed, several options are available. You can specify the number of copies you want, the range of pages to print, and the paper type. You can also choose whether or not to print right and left pages, collate the pages, print the pages in normal or reverse order, and pause between pages. You can specify whether or not you want to print imported graphics. Finally, you can choose the print destination (either a printer or disk).

CHAPTER

Review

Name _____ Date _____

TRUE OR FALSE

The following statements are either true or false. Circle T or F to indicate your answer.

1. Ink-jet printers provide near-laser-printer quality at less cost. (Obj. 1)   1. T F

2. Letter-quality impact printers are the most commonly used desktop publishing printers. (Obj. 1)   2. T F

3. The speed of a laser printer depends on the complexity of the image being printed. (Obj. 1)   3. T F

4. Print quality is measured in resolution and darkness. (Obj. 2)   4. T F

5. Higher resolution does not always mean higher quality. (Obj. 2)   5. T F

6. Printing is done with the Export text command. (Obj. 3)   6. T F

7. In a multipage document, you can select a range of pages to print. (Obj. 4)   7. T F

8. The Paper type selection allows you to choose between letter size and legal size paper. (Obj. 4)   8. T F

9. You can preview your document before printing with the Preview command. (Obj. 5)   9. T F

10. Printing to disk can be used to delay printing until a later time. (Obj. 6)   10. T F

COMPLETION

Write your answers in the space provided.

11. Name two printers that employ an ink ribbon in the printing process. (Obj. 1)

_____

12. In what way is a laser printer similar to a photocopier? (Obj. 1)

_____

_____

13. Explain how a printer with a resolution of 300 dpi could have higher quality output than a printer with a resolution of 370 dpi. (Obj. 2)

_____

_____

14. Why does an ink-jet printer sometimes produce characters with fuzzy edges? (Obj. 2)

_____

_____

15. What is the name of the printer port to which your printer is attached? (Obj. 3)

_____

16. Which print option would you use if you needed to print only page three of a four-page document? (Obj. 4)

_____

17. Explain the process you would use to print a multipage document on both sides of the paper. (Obj. 4)

_____

_____

_____

18. What does the Show frames & cols command do? (Obj. 5)

_____

_____

19. What does the Show tools command do? (Obj. 5)

_____

20. Explain the process of printing to disk. (Obj. 6)

_____

_____

_____

APPLICATION 4-1

For this application, locate a current source of computer advertisements such as a computer magazine or computer shopping periodical. Find examples of currently available printers. Record the print resolution and price for at least one dot-matrix, ink-jet, and laser printer. Record any other pertinent information you can find, such as print speed and included fonts. After you have compiled your information, compare the abilities and price of the printers in a chart or brief report.

CHAPTER

Using Style Sheets

LEARNING OBJECTIVES

When you complete this chapter, you will be able to:

1. Explain the function of a style sheet.
2. Change the page format of a document.
3. Use paragraph styles.
4. Create, modify, and delete paragraph styles.
5. Create tables.
6. Create, save, and load style sheets.

STYLE SHEETS

Every document you create in Publish It! is formatted using a style sheet. A **style sheet** is a set of format specifications for a document. These format specifications include page dimensions, orientation, and paragraph styles. Style sheets cannot be printed, but they can be saved and used with future documents. Style sheets are created for documents, such as newsletters, that must remain consistent in format and style.

PAGE FORMAT

The **page format** of a document specifies the page dimensions, orientation, and master pages. The page format can be changed only when a document is created. The Page Format dialog box appears when you choose the New command from the File menu.

Page dimensions refer to the size of the page on which your document is to be printed. The most common page dimensions are *Letter* (8.5 by 11 inches), *Note* (5.5 by 8.5 inches), and *Legal* (8.5 by 14 inches). You can also create a custom page dimension. The Custom size option allows you to specify page dimensions by keying the desired height and width of the page. The maximum page size recognized is 22.5 by 22.5 inches.

The **Orientation** of a document can be either vertical (portrait orientation) or horizontal (landscape orientation). A page is in **portrait orientation** when the long side of the paper is vertical, like a sheet of notebook paper (see Figure 5-1). A page is in **landscape orientation** when the long side of the paper is horizontal, as shown in Figure 5-2. If you have a 9-pin dot-matrix printer, Publish It! will not print in landscape orientation.

Master pages are used only for documents that have more than one page. They will be discussed in Chapter 7.

Figure 5-1
Portrait orientation is the most common orientation and is used with such documents as letters, memorandums, and reports.

FOURTH ANNUAL SCHOOL PICNIC

Soft drinks, iced tea, and lemonade will be provided by the Freshman class. Small drinks will be $.50 and large drinks $.75.

Ice cream and candy will be provided by the Sophomore class. Vanilla, chocolate, and strawberry ice cream and a variety of candy bars will be available. Ice cream will be $1.00 and candy $.50.

Hamburgers will be provided by the Junior and Senior classes and will be $1.75.

Come join the fun on April 30 at the park.

Figure 5-2
Some documents are more appealing when printed in landscape orientation.

OPEN HOUSE

Mountain Cabin

This beautiful mountain cabin features three bedrooms, two bathrooms, a wood burning fireplace, and a hot tub.

Located five miles south of Manytree, Colorado, on Old Elm Road, this cabin is just 20 miles from a ski resort.

Come see for yourself on November 19.

R.S.V.P. (845)555-0097

ACTIVITY 5-1 • Changing Page Format Specifications

In this activity you will change the page dimensions and orientation.

1. Choose **New** from the **File** menu.
2. Save the current document if necessary. Click on **No** when asked if you want to load a style sheet. The Page Format dialog box appears, as shown in Figure 5-3.
3. Choose **Note** for the page dimension. Choose **Portrait** for the orientation if it is not already selected. Click on **OK**. The page appears in note size and all columns are visible.
4. Choose **New** from the **File** menu.
5. Click on **No** when asked if you want to load a style sheet.
6. Choose **Organizer**.
7. Choose **Landscape** for the orientation. Click on **OK**. Only one column is visible, and the page is horizontal on the screen.
8. Choose **New** from the **File** menu.
9. Click on **No** when asked if you want to load a style sheet.
10. Choose **Letter** for the page dimension. Click on **OK**.
11. Choose **Size to fit** from the **Page** menu. Note the horizontal orientation of the page. This is because landscape orientation is still specified.
12. Choose **Actual size** from the **Page** menu.

1. Choose **New** from the **File** menu.
2. Save the current document if necessary. Choose **No** when asked if you want to load a style sheet. The Page Format dialog box appears, as shown in Figure 5-3.
3. Choose **Note** for the page dimension. Choose **Portrait** for the orientation if it is not already selected. Choose **OK**. The page appears in note size and all columns are visible.
4. Choose **New** from the **File** menu.
5. Choose **No** when asked if you want to load a style sheet.
6. Choose **Organizer**.
7. Choose **Landscape** for the orientation. Choose **OK**. Only one column is visible, and the page is horizontal on the screen.
8. Choose **New** from the **File** menu.
9. Choose **No** when asked if you want to load a style sheet.
10. Choose **Letter** for the page dimension. Choose **OK**.
11. Press **Alt + 0** for **Size to fit**. Note the horizontal orientation of the page. This is because landscape orientation is still specified.
12. Press **Alt + 3** to return to **Actual size**.

Figure 5-3
The Page Format dialog box enables you to change the page dimension and orientation of a document.

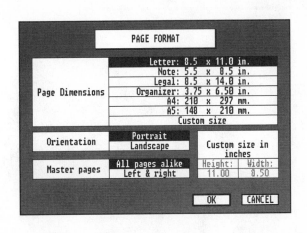

USING PARAGRAPH STYLES

The four paragraph styles created by Publish It! are Body Text, Bullet, Headline, and Subhead, and are illustrated in Figure 5-4. The Body Text paragraph style is simply normal text. The Bullet paragraph style is used to set off items in a bulleted list. In a bulleted list, a symbol (usually a filled circle called a bullet), precedes the text. A new bullet appears each time the Enter key is pressed. The Headline paragraph style is used for titles. Headlines are automatically centered and have a large type size. The Subhead paragraph style is a second-level heading and has a font size larger than the Body Text paragraph style but smaller than the Headline paragraph style. Unless you specify a different paragraph style, text keyed into a frame appears in the Body Text paragraph style.

Figure 5-4
Body Text, Bullet, Headline, and Subhead are the paragraph styles defined by Publish It!

Body Text Style

● Bullet Style

Headline Style

Subhead Style

ACTIVITY 5-2 • Using Paragraph Styles

In this activity you will use the four paragraph styles to improve the readability of a document.

Mouse	Keyboard
1. Open *ACT5-2.DTP* from your template disk.	1. Open *ACT5-2.DTP* from your template disk.
2. Select the **Paragraph tool** from the tool box. The four paragraph styles appear in the library, as shown in Figure 5-5.	2. Select the **Paragraph tool** from the tool box. The four paragraph styles appear in the library, as shown in Figure 5-5.
3. Position the paragraph pointer on the word *Exercise* at the top of the document. Click. *Exercise Means* is selected.	3. Position the paragraph pointer on the word *Exercise* at the top of the document. Press **Home**. *Exercise Means* is selected.

Continued

4. Position the Paragraph tool on the word *Headline* in the library. Click to choose the Headline style. The phrase *Exercise Means* is centered and appears in a large font.

5. Using what you learned in steps 3 and 4, change the word *Energy* to the Headline paragraph style.

6. Select *Why Exercise?* with the Paragraph tool.

7. Choose **Subhead** from the library. The phrase *Why Exercise?* appears larger, but remains left justified.

8. Change the headings *Benefits of Exercise* and *Activities* to the Subhead paragraph style.

9. Select **Tennis** under the *Activities* subhead.

10. Choose **Bullet** from the library.

11. Change each of the activities listed to the **Bullet** paragraph style.

12. Save this document as *HEALTH.DTP* on your data disk. Leave the file open for the next activity.

4. Choose **Headline** from the library. The phrase *Exercise Means* is centered and appears in a large font size.

5. Using what you learned in steps 3 and 4, change the word *Energy* to the Headline paragraph style.

6. Select *Why Exercise?* with the Paragraph tool.

7. Choose **Subhead** from the library. The phrase *Why Exercise?* appears larger, but remains left justified.

8. Change the headings *Benefits of Exercise* and *Activities* to the Subhead paragraph style.

9. Select **Tennis** under the *Activities* subhead.

10. Choose **Bullet** from the library.

11. Change each of the activities listed to the Bullet paragraph style.

12. Save this document as *HEALTH.DTP* on your data disk. Leave the file open for the next activity.

Figure 5-5
When the Paragraph tool is selected, the paragraph styles appear in the library.

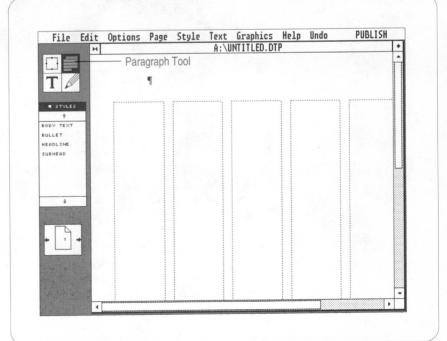

MODIFYING PARAGRAPH STYLES

The headline style that you used in the previous activity may not be what you need for all documents. Suppose you want to make the headline style smaller. To make the change you need to modify the paragraph style. Paragraph styles can be modified before or after text is keyed.

To modify a paragraph style, you first indicate which paragraph style you want to modify. There are two ways to do this.

1. Select the style name from the library.
2. Select a block of text that is set to the style you want to modify.

When you have indicated the paragraph style you want to modify, choose the **Paragraph style command** from the Text menu. The Paragraph Style dialog box appears, as shown in Figure 5-6. Each option in the Paragraph Style dialog box produces a secondary dialog box displaying the choices available for that option. The current setting is highlighted.

Figure 5-6
The Paragraph Style dialog box offers several text formatting options.

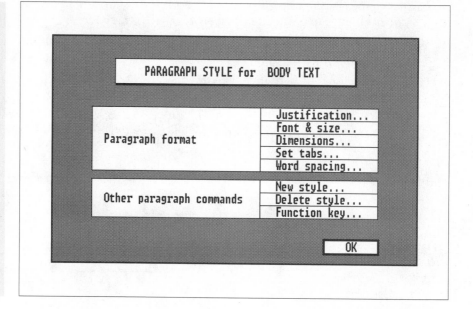

Justification

When the Justification option in the Paragraph Style dialog box is chosen, the Paragraph Options dialog box appears. Flushed left, Flushed right, Justified, Centered, and Table are the justification options. Examples of the Flushed left, Flushed right, Justified, and Centered justification options are shown in Figure 5-7. Flushed left is the most commonly used justification for business correspondence and produces a ragged or uneven right margin.

Flushed right justification produces a ragged left margin. When justification is set to justified, spaces are added between words so that text is aligned at the left and right margins. Articles in newspaper columns are usually justified. Centered justification centers each line of text within the margins. Document titles are usually created with centered justification. Table justification allows you to set tabs and is discussed later in this chapter.

Under the Justification option you have additional choices of Automatic hyphenation, Letter spacing, and Bullet style. Automatic hyphenation automatically hyphenates words at the ends of lines when they do not fit within the limits of the text column. Letter spacing lets you control the space between letters in individual words when you use justified text. When Letter spacing is on, Publish It! sometimes inserts space between letters in words. If you do not want extra space inserted between letters, turn Letter spacing off. When Bullet style is selected for body text, a bullet appears at the beginning of the next line each time the Enter key is pressed.

Figure 5-7
The justification options let you add variety to your documents.

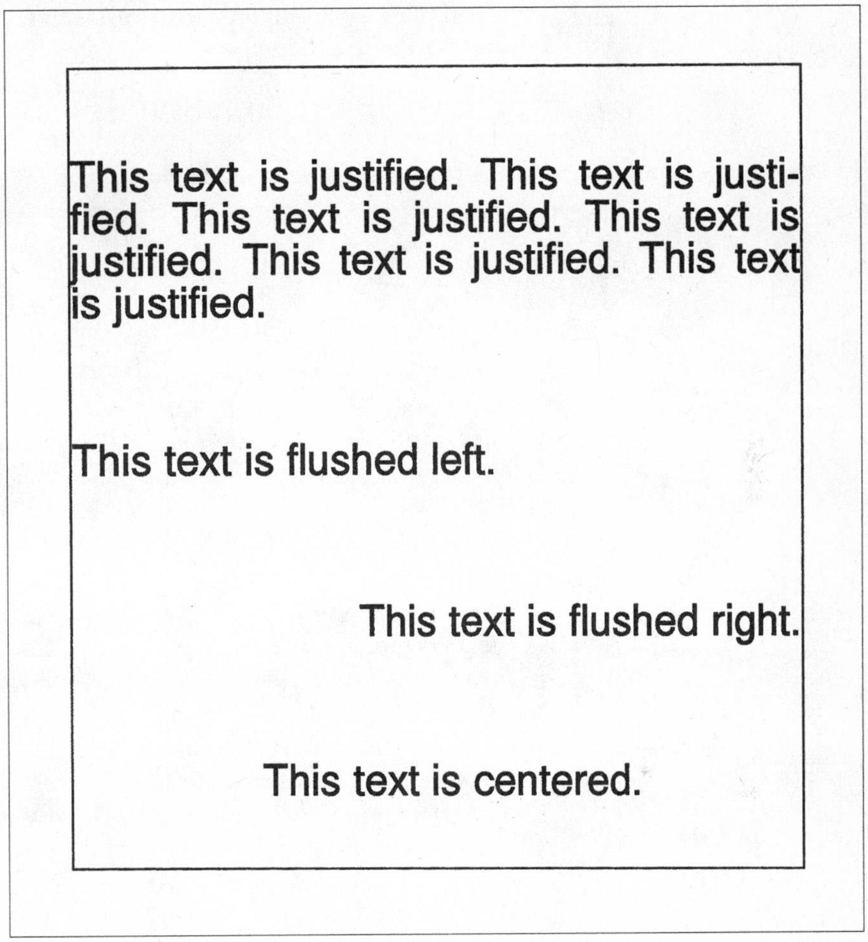

This text is justified. This text is justified. This text is justified. This text is justified. This text is justified. This text is justified.

This text is flushed left.

This text is flushed right.

This text is centered.

Font and Size

The Font & size option in the Paragraph Style dialog box lets you change the typeface and size of the characters. This option can be used, for example, to create a formal document with fancy lettering, such as a banquet invitation, or to call attention to various items in a newsletter.

Dimensions

The Dimensions option enables you to change the amount of white space above the paragraph, the size of any indent on the first line of the paragraph, the size of the left paragraph indent, and the size of the right paragraph indent. This option also controls the line spacing, or **leading** (rhymes with *heading*), which is the amount of space between lines of text.

Set Tabs

The Set tabs option is used to set tabular columns when Table justification is selected. With this option you can create informative tables and charts. Set tabs will be discussed later in this chapter.

Word Spacing

When Justified justification is selected, Publish It! adds spaces between words so that text is aligned at both margins. The Word spacing option allows you to set the maximum and minimum number of spaces that can be inserted between words. The Word spacing option also lets you set a suitable **hyphenation hot zone**. The hyphenation hot zone is an invisible area at the end of every line of text. If a word is too long to fit on a line and is in the hot zone, Publish It! hyphenates the word if Automatic hyphenation is on.

ACTIVITY 5-3 • Modifying Paragraph Styles

In this activity you will modify the paragraph styles used in *HEALTH.DTP*.

1. Select the **Text tool** from the tool box. Then select the **Paragraph** tool from the tool box. This ensures that no text is selected.

2. Choose **Subhead** from the library.

3. Choose **Paragraph style** from the **Text** menu. The Paragraph Style dialog box appears.

4. Choose **Font & size**. The Font and Size dialog box appears showing the choices available for font style and font size.

5. Choose **14** for the font size. Click on **OK**. Publish It! returns to the Paragraph Style dialog box.

6. Click on **OK**. Note the smaller size of the subheadings.

7. Click on **Body Text** in the library.

8. Choose **Paragraph style** from the **Text** menu.

9. Choose **Dimensions**.

10. Change the First line left indent, Left indent, and Right indent all to .50. Click on **OK**.

11. Choose **Justification**. The Paragraph Options dialog box appears.

12. Choose **Flushed left** justification. Click on **OK**. Click on **OK** again in the Paragraph Style

---

1. Select the **Text tool** from the tool box. Then select the **Paragraph** tool from the tool box. This ensures that no text is selected.

2. Choose **Subhead** from the library.

3. Choose **Paragraph style** from the **Text** menu. The Paragraph Style dialog box appears.

4. Choose **Font & size**. The Font and Size dialog box appears showing the choices available for font style and font size.

5. Choose **14** for the font size. Choose **OK**. Publish It! returns to the Paragraph Style dialog box.

6. Choose **OK**. Note the smaller size of the subheadings.

7. Choose **Body Text** from the library.

8. Choose **Paragraph style** from the **Text** menu.

9. Choose **Dimensions**.

10. Change the First line left indent, Left indent, and Right indent all to .50. Choose **OK**.

11. Choose **Justification**. The Paragraph Options dialog box appears.

12. Choose **Flushed left** justification. Choose **OK**. Choose **OK** again in the Paragraph Style

Continued

dialog box. The text is aligned only at the left margin.

13. Choose **Bullet** from the library.

14. Choose **Paragraph style** from the **Text** menu.

15. Choose **Justification**.

16. Choose the Bullet style that looks like an asterisk. The asterisk style is located at the bottom left corner of the Bullet style box. Click on **OK**. Click on **OK** again in the Paragraph Style dialog box.

17. Use the scroll bars to move to the end of the document. Note the change in the bullet style.

18. Save this document as *HEALTH.DTP* on your data disk. Leave the file open for the next activity.

dialog box. The text is aligned only at the left margin.

13. Choose **Bullet** from the library.

14. Choose **Paragraph style** from the **Text** menu.

15. Choose **Justification**.

16. Choose the Bullet style that looks like an asterisk. The asterisk style is located at the bottom left corner of the Bullet style box. Choose **OK**. Choose **OK** again in the Paragraph Style dialog box.

17. Using the scroll bars, move to the end of the document. Note the change in the bullet style.

18. Save this document as *HEALTH.DTP* on your data disk. Leave the file open for the next activity.

CREATING PARAGRAPH STYLES

With Publish It! not only can you modify existing paragraph styles, you can also create your own paragraph styles. The New style option in the Paragraph Style dialog box enables you to name the new paragraph style and assign a function key to that paragraph style. The new paragraph style name appears in the library with the other style names. If you assign a function key to a paragraph style, you can switch paragraph styles from text mode. The Function key option in the Paragraph Style dialog box enables you to assign function keys to the existing paragraph styles.

A new paragraph style has the same format (justification, font style, font size, dimensions, and so on), as the paragraph style you were using when you selected the New style option. Because of this, when you create a new paragraph style you should start with the style most similar to the new style you want. After the new style is named, you simply set the options that make the new paragraph style unique.

ACTIVITY 5-4 • Creating Paragraph Styles

In this activity you will create two paragraph styles to use in *HEALTH.DTP*. You should be in paragraph mode.

1. Choose **Body Text** from the library.

2. Choose **Paragraph style** from the **Text** menu.

1. Choose **Body Text** from the library.

2. Choose **Paragraph style** from the **Text** menu.

Continued

3. Choose **New style**. The Paragraph Style Name dialog box appears.

4. Press **Esc** and key **Center**.

5. Click on **F5** in the Function key box. The function key F5 is assigned to the Center paragraph style. Click on **OK**. Publish It! returns to the Paragraph Style dialog box.

6. Change the justification to **Centered**. Click on **OK.**

7. Change the font and size to **Sans 12** (or Helvetica 12). Click on **OK**.

8. Click on **OK** again to return to your document.

9. Scroll down to the activities listed at the end of the document.

10. Select **Tennis**.

11. Choose **Center** from the library. *Tennis* is automatically centered and has a different type size.

12. Select **Softball**. Press **F5**. Change the remaining activities to the Center paragraph style.

13. Save this document as *HEALTH.DTP* on your data disk. Leave the file open for the next activity.

3. Choose **New style**. The Paragraph Style Name dialog box appears.

4. Press **Esc** and key **Center**.

5. Position the pointer on F5 in the Function key box. Press **Home**. The function key F5 is assigned to the Center paragraph style. Choose **OK**. Publish It! returns to the Paragraph Style dialog box.

6. Change the justification to **Centered**. Choose **OK**.

7. Change the font and size to **Sans 12** (or Helvetica 12). Choose **OK**.

8. Choose **OK** again to return to your document.

9. Scroll down to the activities listed at the end of the document.

10. Select **Tennis**.

11. Choose **Center** from the library. *Tennis* is automatically centered and has a different type size.

12. Select **Softball**. Press **F5**. Change the remaining activities to the Center paragraph style.

13. Save this document as *HEALTH.DTP* on your data disk. Leave the file open for the next activity.

DELETING PARAGRAPH STYLES

Publish It! allows you to delete paragraph styles. In fact, you can delete any paragraph style except Body Text. When you select the Delete style option in the Paragraph Style dialog box, a warning box appears asking you to confirm that the style should be deleted. This warning prevents styles from being deleted accidentally. When a paragraph style is deleted, the style name disappears from the library and text created with that paragraph style becomes Body Text.

ACTIVITY 5-5 • Deleting Paragraph Styles

In this activity you will delete a paragraph style.

1. Select the **Text tool** from the tool box. Then select the **Paragraph tool** from the tool box. This ensures that no text is selected.

2. Choose **Headline** from the library.

1. Select the **Text tool** from the tool box. Then select the **Paragraph tool** from the tool box. This ensures that no text is selected.

2. Choose **Headline** from the library.

Continued

3. Choose **Paragraph style** from the **Text** menu.

4. Choose **Delete style**. Click on **OK** to confirm the deletion. Click on **OK** again to return to your document. The headline appears in the Body Text style.

5. Choose **Paragraph style** from the **Text** menu.

6. Choose **Delete style**. A warning box appears saying that the Body Text paragraph style cannot be deleted. Click on **Cancel**. Click on **OK** to return to the document.

7. Save the document as *HEALTH.DTP* on your data disk.

3. Choose **Paragraph style** from the **Text** menu.

4. Choose **Delete style**. Choose **OK** to confirm the deletion. Choose **OK** again to return to the document. The headline appears in the Body Text style.

5. Choose **Paragraph style** from the **Text** menu.

6. Choose **Delete style**. A warning box appears saying that the Body Text paragraph style cannot be deleted. Choose **Cancel**. Choose **OK** to return to your document.

7. Save the document as *HEALTH.DTP* on your data disk.

TABLES AND TABS

A **tab stop** (or simply *tab*) is a marker set at a specified position that is used for aligning text in columns. A typical use for tabs is in a table of contents (see Figure 5-8). A tab is set near the right margin to align the page numbers. The Tab key on the keyboard moves the cursor to the next tab stop.

Figure 5-8
A table of contents is a typical use for tab stops.

Table of Contents

Introduction...1

Getting Started...14

Basic Operation...22

Advanced Topics 38

Quick Reference..56

In Publish It!, tabs are part of a special justification setting, called *Table*. You should create a new paragraph style when you work with tabs to avoid disturbing the settings of existing paragraph styles. Tables can be created using the Set tabs option in the Paragraph Style dialog box. The justification must be set to Table before Publish It! will let you set tabs. If you select the Set tabs option while the justification is not set to Table, a dialog box appears asking if you want to change the justification to Table. Choosing the Set tabs option in the Paragraph Style dialog box displays the Set Tab Points dialog box, shown in Figure 5-9.

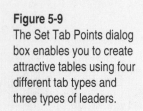

Figure 5-9
The Set Tab Points dialog box enables you to create attractive tables using four different tab types and three types of leaders.

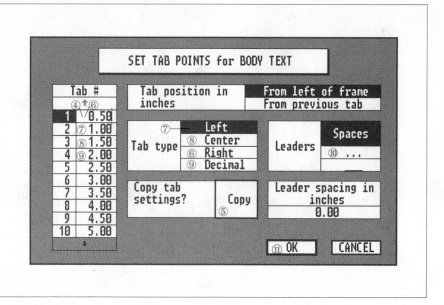

Setting Tabs

The Tab # option in the Set Tab Points dialog box lets you set up to fourteen tab stops. The tab stops are in a list at the left of the dialog box. By default, the tabs are set at ½-inch intervals. The tab stops use the same unit of measure as that of the rulers. For example, if you set the ruler unit of measure to centimeters, the tab stops must be specified in centimeters. You can key new values for any of the fourteen tab stops. The list scrolls to expose tab stops 11 through 14.

The Tab position option lets you specify whether the tabs will be set from the edge of the frame or from the previous tab. The most common way to measure tab stops is from the left of the frame.

Use the Copy tab settings? option as a shortcut when you want all of the tab settings to be the same. For example, if you want the tabs to be positioned 1½ inches apart, simply key 1.50 in the first tab setting box and select Copy tab settings. The tab settings will begin at 1.50 followed by 3.00, 4.50, and so on.

Tab Stop Options

Publish It! allows you to customize your tab stops to increase their effectiveness. There are four types of tab stops from which to choose. In addition, you can specify dotted lines or underscores, called **leaders** (pronounced *leeders*), to be inserted before tab stops.

The Tab type option offers you a choice of Left, Center, Right, and Decimal tabs. With these options, a tab stop can be used to line up text left justified against the tab stop, right justified against the tab stop, or centered over the tab stop. Decimal tabs let you line up numbers by their decimal points.

Leaders can improve the readability of a table especially when there are several columns of numbers. They ensure that the reader's eyes do not wander to the wrong line. You can specify dots or underscores for leaders. When you select leaders, they precede the tab for which they are chosen.

The Leader spacing option lets you specify the amount of space to appear between the leaders.

ACTIVITY 5-6 • Creating Tables

In this activity you will use the Set tabs option in the Paragraph Style dialog box to create a table. For help with this activity, refer to Figure 5-9. The labels on the figure indicate the step numbers in this activity.

Mouse	Keyboard
1. Open a new, untitled document. Use the standard letter size. Select the **Paragraph tool**. Click on **Body Text** in the library.	1. Open a new, untitled document. Use the standard letter size. Choose the **Paragraph tool**. Choose **Body Text** in the library.
2. Create a new paragraph style. Name the new style *TABLE*. Click on **OK**.	2. Create a new paragraph style. Name the new style *TABLE*. Press **Enter**.
3. Choose **Set tabs** from the Paragraph Style dialog box. A dialog box appears asking if you want to change the justification to Table. Click on **Yes**. The Set Tab Points dialog box appears.	3. Choose **Set tabs** from the Paragraph Style dialog box. A dialog box appears asking if you want to change the justification to Table. Choose **Yes**. The Set Tab Points dialog box appears.
4. Change tab 1 to **0.00**.	4. Change tab 1 to **0.00**.
5. Click on **Copy**. Notice that each of the tabs is cleared to zero.	5. Choose **Copy**. Notice that each of the tabs is cleared to zero.
6. Change tab 1 to **1.00**. Click on **Right** to change the tab type.	6. Change tab 1 to **1.00**. Choose **Right** to change the tab type.
7. Change tab 2 to **1.25**. The tab type should already be set to Left.	7. Change tab 2 to **1.25**. The tab type should already be set to Left.
8. Change tab 3 to **2.50**. Click on **Center** to change the tab type.	8. Change tab 3 to **2.50**. Choose **Center** to change the tab type.
9. Change tab 4 to **5.00**. Click on **Decimal** to change the tab type.	9. Change tab 4 to **5.00**. Choose **Decimal** to change the tab type.
10. Choose the dotted line as the leader for tab 4. Click on **OK**.	10. Choose the dotted line as the leader for tab 4. Press **Enter**.
11. Click on **OK** to return to your document.	11. Press **Enter** to return to the document.
12. Create a frame surrounding all the columns.	12. Create a frame surrounding all the columns.
13. Select the **Text tool** from the tool box.	13. Select the **Text tool** from the tool box.
14. Position the text cursor in the frame. Press the **Tab** key.	14. Position the text cursor in the frame. Press the **Tab** key.
15. Key **Trevor**. Select the **Paragraph tool** from the tool box. Select **Trevor** and change the paragraph style to **Table**.	15. Key **Trevor**. Select the **Paragraph tool** from the tool box. Select **Trevor** and change the paragraph style to **Table**.
16. Select the **Text tool** again.	16. Select the **Text tool** again.
17. Position the text cursor immediately after *Trevor*. Key the table shown in Figure 5-10. Do not key the headings above the columns. Remember to press Tab to move from one column to the next. Remember also to press Tab before you key the first name in each line.	17. Position the text cursor immediately after *Trevor*. Key the table shown in Figure 5-10. Do not key the headings above the columns. Remember to press Tab to move from one column to the next. Remember also to press Tab before you key the first name in each line.
18. Save the table as *TABLE.DTP* on your data disk.	18. Save the table as *TABLE.DTP* on your data disk.

Figure 5-10
You can create tables with a variety of tab types and leader styles.

First Name	Last Name	Award	Grade Point
Trevor	Allen	Business	3.9
Shelly	Buchanan	Math	4.33
Jay	Curtis	Literature	3.88
Melissa	Rendon	History	3.5
Pete	Zambrano	Athletic	3.66

SAVING STYLE SHEETS

As mentioned at the beginning of this chapter, the settings for page dimensions, orientation, and paragraph formats can be saved on a style sheet and used with documents you create in the future. For example, the editor of a monthly newsletter can save the format settings of the newsletter as a style sheet so that each newsletter is consistent in style and format. A style sheet is saved by selecting the **Save style sheet command** from the File menu. Style sheets are automatically assigned the *.STY* extension.

ACTIVITY 5-7 • Saving Style Sheets

In this activity you will create and save a style sheet.

1. Choose **New** from the **File** menu.
2. Click on **No** when asked if you want to load a style sheet. The Page Format dialog box appears.
3. Choose the **Note** page dimension. Click on **OK**.
4. Create a frame that covers a large portion of the work area.
5. Select the **Text tool** from the tool box.
6. Key the following sentence in the frame: **Graduation announcements may be picked up in Room 213 after 4:00 p.m. Thursday**.
7. Select the **Paragraph tool** from the tool box. Select the sentence you just keyed.

1. Choose **New** from the **File** menu.
2. Choose **No** when asked if you want to load a style sheet. The Page Format dialog box appears.
3. Choose the **Note** page dimension. Choose **OK**.
4. Create a frame that covers a large portion of the work area.
5. Select the **Text tool** from the tool box.
6. Key the following sentence in the frame: **Graduation announcements may be picked up in Room 213 after 4:00 p.m. Thursday**.
7. Select the **Paragraph tool** from the tool box. Select the sentence you just keyed.

Continued

8. Choose **Paragraph style** from the **Text** menu.

9. Change the justification to **Centered**.

10. Change the font style and size to **Sans 20** (or Helvetica 20). Click on **OK** twice to return to the document.

11. Choose **Save style sheet** from the **File** menu.

12. Change the Directory to **A:*.STY**. Key **NOTE.STY** on the Selection line. Press **Enter**.

13. Leave the file open for the next activity.

8. Choose **Paragraph style** from the **Text** menu.

9. Change the justification to **Centered**.

10. Change the font style and size to **Sans 20** (or Helvetica 20). Choose **OK** twice to return to the document.

11. Choose **Save style sheet** from the **File** menu.

12. Change the Directory to **A:*.STY**. Key **NOTE.STY** on the Selection line. Press **Enter**.

13. Leave the file open for the next activity.

```
File
 Open...            ◆O
 Save               ◆S
 Save as...
 Save style sheet...
 Revert to last...

 New...
 Erase...

 Import text...
 Import picture.
```

LOADING STYLE SHEETS

Once a style sheet is created and saved, you can load the style sheet by choosing New from the File menu and choosing Yes when asked if you want to load a style sheet. The *.STY* files will appear in the Item Selector box. A style sheet does not contain any frames or text, but does reflect the page dimensions, orientation, and paragraph styles of the document from which it originated.

ACTIVITY 5-8 • LOADING STYLE SHEETS

In this activity you will load the style sheet you saved in Activity 5-7.

1. Quit Publish It! and start it again. This is to ensure that the default styles are loaded.

2. Choose **New** from the **File** menu. Abandon the current document.

3. Click on **Yes** when asked if you want to load a style sheet.

4. Change the Directory line to **A:*.STY**. Choose *NOTE.STY* from the Item Selector box. Press **Enter**. The style sheet is loaded.

5. Choose **Size to fit** from the **Page** menu.

6. Create a frame that surrounds all the columns.

7. Choose **Actual Size** from the **Page** menu.

8. Key the text shown in Figure 5-11 into the frame. Note the font style and the centered text.

1. Quit Publish It! and start it again. This is to ensure that the default styles are loaded.

2. Choose **New** from the **File** menu. Abandon the current document.

3. Choose **Yes** when asked if you want to load a style sheet.

4. Change the Directory line to **A:*.STY**. Choose *NOTE.STY* from the Item Selector box. Press **Enter**. The style sheet is loaded.

5. Choose **Size to fit** from the **Page** menu.

6. Create a frame that surrounds all the columns.

7. Choose **Actual Size** from the **Page** menu.

8. Key the text shown in Figure 5-11 into the frame. Note the font style and the centered text.

Figure 5-11
Keyed text will reflect the format settings of selected style sheets.

> The Clayton High School Triathlon will be held next month. The race will consist of a 2-mile run, a 1-mile swim, and a 5-mile bicycle race. The triathlon will begin at the high school gym at 9:00 a.m. Get in shape and come join the fun.

SUMMARY

Each time you create a document, a style sheet is created. A style sheet contains the format specifications for a document, including the page dimensions, orientation, and paragraph styles.

The four default paragraph styles in Publish It! are Body Text, Bullet, Headline, and Subhead. A paragraph style can be designated before or after text is keyed. The Paragraph style command from the Text menu enables you to modify paragraph styles.

In addition to modifying existing paragraph styles, the paragraph style command can be used to create new paragraph styles, assign function keys to paragraph styles, delete paragraph styles, and set tabs.

When you create a document that will be produced periodically, such as a newsletter, you should save the style sheet for the document. This will enable you to produce future documents that are consistent in format and style.

CHAPTER
⑤
Review

Name _____ Date _____

TRUE OR FALSE

The following statements are either true or false. Circle T or F to indicate your answer.

1. Every document you create is formatted using a style sheet. (Obj. 1)

    1. T F

2. Landscape orientation is the most commonly used orientation. (Obj. 2)

    2. T F

3. The Headline paragraph style automatically centers text. (Obj. 3)

    3. T F

4. The Bullet paragraph style is assigned to all text unless you change the paragraph style. (Obj. 3)

    4. T F

5. The font size of a paragraph style cannot be changed. (Obj. 4)   5. T F

6. You can create your own paragraph styles. (Obj. 5)   6. T F

7. A warning box appears when you try to delete a paragraph style. (Obj. 6)

    7. T F

8. Before Publish It! will let you set tabs, the justification of the paragraph style must be set to Center. (Obj. 7)

    8. T F

9. Style sheets may be saved and used at a later time. (Obj. 8)   9. T F

10. The Load style sheet command is located in the Page menu. (Obj. 9)

    10. T F

COMPLETION

Write your answer in the space provided.

11. What is a style sheet? (Obj. 1)

    _____

    _____

12. Explain the difference between portrait and landscape orientation. (Obj. 2)

_____

_____

13. List the four paragraph styles defined by Publish It!. (Obj. 3)

_____

14. Which command allows you to modify a paragraph style? (Obj. 4)

_____

15. List the five justification options. (Obj. 4)

_____

_____

16. When a new paragraph style is created, where does the name of the new style appear? (Obj. 5)

_____

17. Which paragraph style cannot be deleted? (Obj. 6)

_____

18. List the four types of tabs. (Obj. 7)

_____

_____

19. What is the purpose of saving a style sheet? (Obj. 8)

_____

_____

20. When does Publish It! give you an opportunity to load a style sheet? (Obj. 9)

_____

_____

APPLICATION 5-1

In this application, you will use and modify the paragraph styles.

1. Open _APP5-1.DTP_ from your template disk. Be sure you are in paragraph mode.
2. Change the heading _What are the Academic Olympics?_ to the Subhead paragraph style.
3. Change the _Mathematical Baseball Game, Track History Contest,_ and _Block Spelling Contest_ headings to the Subhead paragraph style.

4. Assign the Bullet paragraph style to the events listed under the first subheading.

5. Change the justification for the Body Text paragraph style to Flushed left.

6. Reduce the Font size of the Subhead paragraph style to 14.

7. Change from bullets to open arrows.

8. Get into text mode.

9. Move the text cursor to the top left corner of the document.

10. Press F2. Key: Academic Olympics.

11. Save this document as *OLYMPICS.DTP* on your data disk. Leave the file open for the next application.

APPLICATION 5-2

In this application you will create and use paragraph styles.

1. Create a new paragraph style with the following specifications:
   Style name: *LEFT*
   Function key: F5
   Justification: Flushed left
   Font & size: Sans 10
   Dimensions: First line left indent .50
   Left indent: .50
   Right indent: .50

2. Change the paragraphs under the last three headings of the document to the Left paragraph style.

3. Create a new paragraph style with the following specifications:
   Style name: *MYSTYLE*
   Function key: F6
   Justification: Centered
   Font & size: Any font and size of your choice

4. Select the Text tool from the tool box. Move the text pointer to the end of the document.

5. Press F6. Key: Start Practicing for the Academic Olympics.

6. Leave this file open for the next application.

APPLICATION 5-3

In this application you will delete paragraph styles.

1. Delete the Left paragraph style.

2. Delete the Bullet paragraph style.

APPLICATION 5-4

In this application you will change page format settings and save and load a style sheet.

1. Choose New from the File menu. You do not need to save the current document. Do not load a style sheet.

2. Choose the Organizer page dimension.

3. Choose the Landscape orientation.

4. Create a frame surrounding the dotted-line rectangle.

5. Key the following sentence into the frame: I am creating a style sheet.

6. Change the Body Text paragraph style justification to Flushed left.

7. Change the font style and size to Sans 20 (or Helvetica 20).

8. Save the style sheet as *ORGANIZE.STY* on your data disk.

9. Choose New from the File menu. You do not need to save the current document. Do not load a style sheet.

10. Choose Custom size for the page dimension. Key 2.00 for the height and 4.00 for the width.

11. Change the orientation to Portrait. Choose OK.

12. Create a frame that surrounds all the columns.

13. Within the frame key: Jesse Hernandez.

14. Assign the Headline style to the text.

15. Save the style sheet as *NAMETAG.STY* on your data disk.

16. Choose New from the File menu. You do not need to save the current document.

17. Load the style sheet named *ORGANIZE.STY*.

18. Create a frame surrounding the dotted-line rectangle.

19. Key the following in the frame: Yearbook pictures will be taken on December 14 in Room 159. Senior pictures will be taken on December 17 in the auditorium.

20. Open a new, untitled document. You do not need to save the current document.

21. Load the style sheet named *NAMETAG.STY*.

22. Create a frame that surrounds all the columns.

23. Key your name within the frame using the Headline style. Your name will appear centered and large.

24. Save this document as *NAMETAG.DTP* on your data disk.

APPLICATION 5-5

In this application you will create a table.

1. Open a new, untitled document with Portrait orientation and Letter dimensions.

2. Create a frame surrounding all the columns.

3. Create a new paragraph style. Name the paragraph style *TABLE*.

4. Set the tabs as follows:
   Tab 1   0.50   Left
   Tab 2   3.00   Center
   Tab 3   5.50   Decimal

5. Enter the following table:

Polly Kitan	Biology	94.3
Cheyenne Black	Chemistry	87.0
Jorge Garza	Algebra	93.25
Marci Matthews	Data Processing	95.4
Estelle Myers	Spanish	79.7

6. Save this document as *GRADES.DTP* on your data disk.

CHAPTER

Creating a Page Layout

LEARNING OBJECTIVES

When you complete this chapter, you will be able to:

1. Design a readable and appealing layout.
2. Set the column guides.
3. Use the Snap to guides command.
4. Link frames.
5. Wrap text around graphics.
6. Create odd-shaped frames for text.
7. Use soft hyphens, fixed spaces, and kerning.

DESIGNING A READABLE AND APPEALING LAYOUT

The main objectives of a **layout** are readability and visual appeal. A document with a well-designed page layout can motivate the reader and keep the reader's interest. Follow these layout guidelines when you create a document:

- *Create asymmetrical layouts when possible.* (Refer to Figure 6-1 as you read about symmetry and asymmetry.) Imagine a page with a line drawn vertically down the center. On the page is a design composed of squares, rectangles, and circles. A **symmetrical** layout has objects of identical size, shape, and position on each side of the vertical line. In an **asymmetrical** layout, the objects do not mirror each other on each side of the vertical line. Asymmetrical layouts are more modern and eyecatching.

- *Consider the type of document you are creating.* Is it a report? A newsletter? The layout should support the material presented in the document. Reports, for example, traditionally are in a one-column layout. Two-column layouts, although symmetrical, are practical for long articles. Short newsletter articles are best presented in multicolumn layouts, which allow a reader to scan the page in search of an entertaining or informative article. Compare the newsletters in Figure 6-2a and Figure 6-2b and note the effectiveness of a multicolumn layout.

- *Allow sufficient space between columns so the document is easier to read.* The vertical strip of space between columns is called a **gutter**.

- *Enliven a document with graphics that relate to the text.* For example, use pictures of cars in an advertisement to sell a used car. Effective use of graphics enhance a document. Note in Figure 6-2a that the graphics do not relate to the text. The graphics are more meaningful when they relate to the text, as shown in Figure 6-2b.

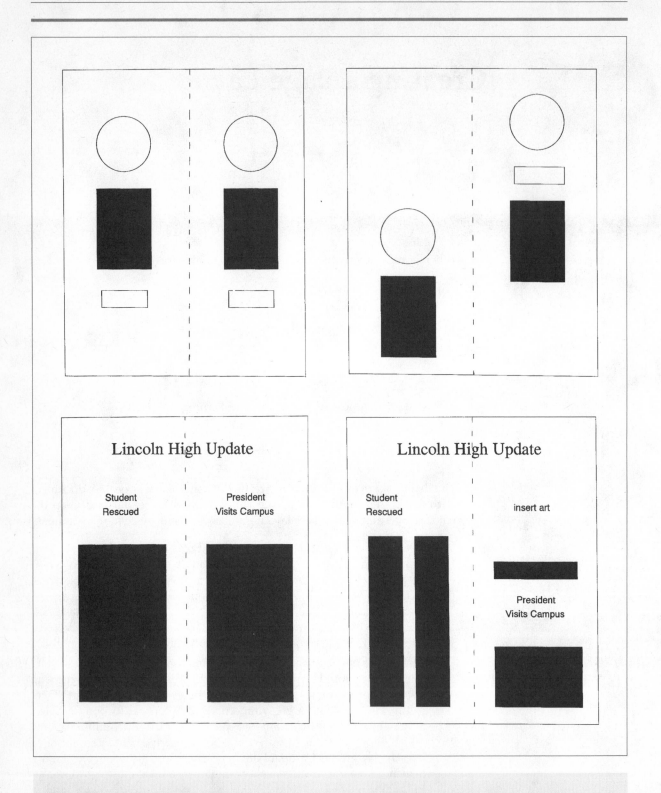

Figure 6-1
Where possible, create documents with asymmetrical layouts rather than symmetrical layouts.

- *Consider the position of a graphic on a page.* A graphic's placement should contribute to the overall visual appeal of a page.

- *Be generous with the use of white space, which is the area on a page that remains blank.* White space frames headings, columns of text, and art, and acts as a cushion for the eye against too much text. In Figure 6-2a, text fills the page, and the articles seem to run together. In Figure 6-2b, white space draws attention to and separates headings and columns of text, making the document easier to read.

- *Use fonts creatively to make the document more visually exciting.* Different typefaces can be used for headings and text to add interest, but don't overdo it, as in Figure 6-2a. The use of too many fonts is distracting to the reader. Limit yourself to two or three typefaces in a document, as in Figure 6-2b. For example, use a sans serif typeface for headings and a serif typeface for the body of text. This will unify a document.

- *Use boldface, italics, and underlining sparingly.* These add emphasis to the text, but are distracting and lose their effectiveness if used too often, as shown in Figure 6-2a. As with graphics and fonts, be certain your use of bold, italics, and underlining is relevant. For example, use bold for headings and italics to emphasize words.

Figure 6-2a
This newsletter is poorly designed: a one-column format with little white space does not separate the articles sufficiently, the art does not relate to the text, and typeface variation and bold are overused.

Lincoln High Update

Lincoln High School   Vol. XXI, No. 10   April 2, 19--

LHS TO GET NEW GYMNASIUM

A new gymnasium is planned for <u>Lincoln High School</u> according to the School Board announcement made on March 18. With so many athletic activities taking place at <u>LHS</u>, it was decided that an additional athletic facility was needed. The new gym will have *larger locker rooms and dressing rooms, a swimming pool, athletic offices, and seating for 700 on the main floor.* Additional parking will be made available on the west side of the tennis courts next to the new gym.

Construction is scheduled to begin as soon as the final school bell rings to release the students for their summer vacation. *The estimated cost of the new gym was not revealed.*

The architect for the 500,000-square-foot gymnasium is **Walsh & Boedecker, Inc.** They have provided <u>LHS</u> with a colorful sketch of how the gym will look once completed. The drawing is on the wall outside of Mr. Webb's office.

DEBATE TEAM WINS FINALS

<u>Lincoln High School's</u> debating team has returned from Bakerstown where they captured first place in the South State Debating Finals.

The team, composed of **Amy Everett, Tim Morrison,** and **Jennifer Knox,** will contend for the state honors on April 6th in Webster. If the team secures first place at the State Debating Contest, the team members will travel to Chicago, Illinois, to compete with the nation's finest debaters. **Debbie Tomlinson** is the debating team's coach.

PLEASE RETURN YOUR BOOKS

Mr. Copeland, a senior class English teacher, reports that his students are finding it difficult to obtain books they need for their senior theme research projects. **Miss Henderson,** Librarian, declares that many students have not responded to requests for return of the books. If you possess a library book that has been requested by the library, please show the consideration of returning the book immediately. Everyone should have equal access to these books.

Figure 6-2b
A well-designed newsletter makes use of a multicolumn layout and white space to draw attention to the articles. The art relates to the text, and the use of typeface and bold is consistent.

Lincoln High Update

Lincoln High School   Vol. XXI, No. 10   April 2, 19--

LHS TO GET NEW GYMNASIUM

A new gymnasium is planned for Lincoln High School according to the School Board announcement made on March 18. With so many athletic activities taking place at LHS, it was decided that an additional athletic facility was needed. The new gym will have larger locker rooms and dressing rooms, a swimming pool, athletic offices, and seating for 700 on the main floor. Additional parking will be made available on the west side of the tennis courts next to the new gym.

Construction is scheduled to begin as soon as the final school bell rings to release the students for their summer vacation. The estimated cost of the new gym was not revealed. The architect for the 500,000-square-foot gymnasium is Walsh & Boedecker, Inc. They have provided LHS with a colorful sketch of how the gym will look once completed. The drawing is on the wall outside of Mr. Webb's office.

DEBATE TEAM WINS FINALS

Lincoln High School's debating team has returned from Bakerstown where they captured first place in the South State Debating Finals.

The team, composed of Amy Everett, Tim Morrison, and Jennifer Knox, will contend for the state honors on April 6th in Webster. If the team secures first place at the State Debating Contest, the team members will travel to Chicago, Illinois, to compete with the nation's finest debaters. Debbie Tomlinson is the debating team's coach.

PLEASE RETURN YOUR BOOKS

Mr. Copeland, a senior class English teacher, reports that his students are finding it difficult to obtain books they need for their senior theme research projects. Miss Henderson, Librarian, declares that many students have not responded to requests for return of the books. If you possess a library book that has been requested by the library, please show the consideration of returning the book immediately. Everyone should have equal access to these books.

COLUMN GUIDES

Column guides are dotted lines that appear on the screen to help you position frames. The column guides are automatically displayed, but may be turned off by choosing the Show frames and columns command from the Options menu, as discussed in Chapter 4. Column guides are not printed.

Set Column Guides

The **Set column guides command** in the Options menu displays the Set Column Guides dialog box, as shown in Figure 6-3. The Set Column Guides dialog box lets you specify the number of columns to appear on the screen, the column dimensions, and the page offset.

Number of Columns. The number of columns that appear on a page can range from one to nine. Clicking on the left arrow decreases the number of columns, and clicking on the right arrow increases the number of columns. When determining the number of columns needed, consider the document you are creating. As discussed earlier, reports are usually created using a one-column layout, whereas newsletters are more effective in a multicolumn layout.

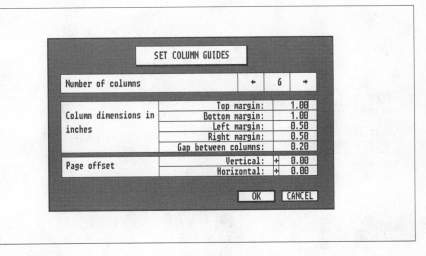

Figure 6-3
The Set Column Guides dialog box enables you to specify the number of columns, the column dimensions, and the page offset.

Column Dimensions. The Column dimensions in inches option enables you to change the top margin, bottom margin, left margin, right margin, and the gap or gutter between columns. If you do not change the column dimensions, Publish It! uses the default settings of 1-inch top and bottom margins, ½ inch left and right margins, and a .20 gutter.

Page Offset. The Page offset option shifts the image or document on the page. This is useful, for example, if the printer cannot print text along the right edge of a document. The Page offset option can shift the document to the left so that all the text prints on the page. A document can be shifted horizontally, vertically, or both. If a document is created in portrait orientation, choosing the plus sign (+) moves the document up vertically and to the left horizontally. Choosing the minus sign (–) moves the document down vertically and to the right horizontally.

If a document is created in landscape orientation, the plus sign (+) moves the document up horizontally and to the right vertically. The minus sign (–) moves the document down horizontally and to the left vertically. The plus sign can be changed to a minus sign and vice versa by clicking on the sign. The results of using the Page offset option will not appear on the screen. A summary chart of how documents are shifted follows:

		Portrait	*Landscape*
Vertical	+	Up	Right
	–	Down	Left
Horizontal	+	Left	Up
	–	Right	Down

ACTIVITY 6-1 • Setting Column Guides

In this activity you will change the number of columns, the column dimensions, and the page offset.

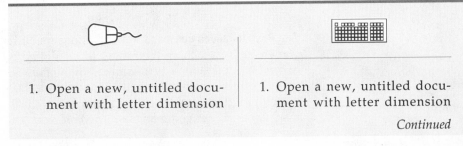

1. Open a new, untitled document with letter dimension

1. Open a new, untitled document with letter dimension

Continued

and portrait orientation. Note the amount of space around the columns.

2. Choose **Size to fit** from the **Page** menu.

3. Choose **Set column guides** from the **Options** menu.

4. Click on the right arrow until the number of columns is **nine**.

5. Change the top margin to **2.50**.

6. Click on **OK**. Note the amount of space above the columns compared to the amount of space below the columns.

7. Choose **New** from the **File** menu. You do not need to save the current document. Do not load a style sheet.

8. Change the page dimensions to **Note**. Change the orientation to **Landscape**. Click on **OK**.

9. Choose **Set column guides** from the **Options** menu.

10. Click on the left arrow until the number of columns is **two**.

11. Change the bottom margin to **2.00**.

12. Change the right margin to **1.00**.

13. Change the gap between columns to **0.50**.

14. Click on **OK**. Note the amount of space below the columns and between the columns.

15. You do not need to save this file.

and portrait orientation. Note the amount of space around the columns.

2. Press **Alt + 0** to choose **Size to fit** from the Page menu.

3. Choose **Set column guides** from the **Options** menu.

4. Position the pointer on the right arrow and press **Home** until the number of columns is **nine**.

5. Change the top margin to **2.50**.

6. Press **Enter**. Note the amount of space above the columns compared to the amount of space below the columns.

7. Choose **New** from the **File** menu. You do not need to save the current document. Do not load a style sheet.

8. Change the page dimensions to **Note**. Change the orientation to Landscape. Press **Enter**.

9. Choose **Set column guides** from the **Options** menu.

10. Position the pointer on the left arrow and press **Home** until the number of columns is **two**.

11. Change the bottom margin to **2.00**.

12. Change the right margin to **1.00**.

13. Change the gap between columns to **0.50**.

14. Press **Enter**. Note the amount of space below the columns and between the columns.

15. You do not need to save this file.

Snap to Guides

The **Snap to guides command** in the Options menu helps to align frames that you create by attaching the frames to the dotted column guides. The Snap to guides command is turned on as the default setting. Therefore, frames that you create snap to the column guides unless you turn the command off by selecting the Snap to guides command from the Options menu. When the Snap to guides command is turned off, you can create and move frames more freely.

ACTIVITY 6-2 • Using Snap to Guides

In this activity you will create frames with the Snap to guides command turned on and then turned off.

1. Choose **New** from the **File** menu.

2. Change the page dimensions to **Letter**. Change the orientation to **Portrait**. Click on **OK**.

3. Choose **Size to fit** from the **Page** menu if it's not already selected.

4. Create a frame around the first two columns. Notice how the frame snaps to the column guides.

5. Choose **Snap to guides** from the **Options** menu to turn the command off.

6. Create a frame around the last two columns. Try to place the frame on top of the column guides. Notice how it is more difficult with Snap to guides turned off.

7. Choose **Snap to guides** from the **Options** menu to turn the command back on.

8. Choose **Actual size** from the **Page** menu. You do not need to save this file.

1. Choose **New** from the **File** menu.

2. Change the page dimensions to **Letter**. Change the orientation to **Portrait**. Press **Enter**.

3. Press **Alt + 0** to choose **Size to fit** from the Page menu if it's not already selected.

4. Create a frame around the first two columns. Notice how the frame snaps to the column guides.

5. Choose **Snap to guides** from the **Options** menu to turn the command off.

6. Create a frame around the last two columns. Try to place the frame on top of the column guides. Notice how it is more difficult with Snap to guides turned off.

7. Choose **Snap to guides** from the **Options** menu to turn the command back on.

8. Press **Alt + 3** to choose **Actual size** from the Page menu. You do not need to save this file.

```
Options
▸ Show tools          ◆H

  Show rulers         ◆J
  Ruler spacing...

  Frame border...
  Frame tint...
  Text runaround...
  Size & position...

▸ Show frames & cols ◆E
  Set column guides...
▸ Snap to guides

  Set defaults...
  Automatic backup...
```

LINKING FRAMES

Text frames can be linked to allow imported text to flow from one text frame to the next. If an imported text file is too long for the selected frame, a broken line appears at the bottom of the frame, indicating that more text can be shown. To display the remaining text, you must create another frame and select the story name from the library.

Imported text files are called *stories*, and the story name appears in the library. The remaining text will flow into the frame you create. Frames can be linked in this manner until all the text is displayed. When several frames appear on one page, text flows into the frames in the order they are selected, regardless of where the frames appear on the page.

If you delete a frame, Publish It! readjusts the text within the existing frames. Suppose you have three frames containing text and you delete the second frame. Publish It! automatically moves the text that was in the second frame to the third frame. If you resize a frame, Publish It! reformats the text in each of the frames.

Double-clicking on the story name in the library displays the Status dialog box. The Status dialog box contains information about a story such as the number of frames the story occupies, the number of words in the story, and how much of the story does not fit in the frame. The Status dialog box also allows you to rename the story.

ACTIVITY 6-3 • Linking Frames

In this activity you will import text into a frame, link frames to accommodate the remaining text, and delete a frame.

<table>
<tr>
<td></td>
<td></td>
</tr>
<tr>
<td valign="top">

1. Open a new, untitled document.
2. Create three frames on the screen, as shown in Figure 6-4.
3. Select the frame at the top left corner of the column guides.
4. Choose **Import text** from the **File** menu.
5. Choose **WordPerfect 4** for the text format. Click on **OK**.
6. Change the directory to **A:*.WPD**. Choose *ACT6-3.WPD* from your template disk. Note the broken line at the bottom of the frame, indicating that more text can be shown.
7. Select the bottom frame.
8. Click on *ACT6-3.WPD* in the library. Another dashed line appears at the bottom of the frame.
9. Select the third frame.
10. Click on *ACT6-3.WPD* in the library. All of the text is displayed.
11. Save this document as *LINK.DTP* on your data disk.
12. Delete the bottom frame. The text that was in the bottom frame is moved to the third frame.
13. Double-click on *ACT6-3.WPD* in the library. The Status dialog box appears.
14. Click on **OK**. You do not need to save this document again.

</td>
<td valign="top">

1. Open a new, untitled document.
2. Create three frames on the screen, as shown in Figure 6-4.
3. Select the frame at the top left corner of the column guides.
4. Choose **Import text** from the **File** menu.
5. Choose **WordPerfect 4** for the Text format. Press **Enter**.
6. Change the directory to **A:*.WPD**. Choose *ACT6-3.WPD* from your template disk. Note the broken line at the bottom of the frame, indicating that more text can be shown.
7. Select the bottom frame.
8. Choose *ACT6-3.WPD* from the library. Another dashed line appears at the bottom of the frame.
9. Select the third frame.
10. Choose *ACT6-3.WPD* from the library. All of the text is displayed.
11. Save this document as *LINK.DTP* on your data disk.
12. Delete the bottom frame. The text that was in the bottom frame is moved to the third frame.
13. Position your pointer on *ACT6-3.WPD* in the library and press **Home** twice quickly. The Status dialog box appears.
14. Press **Enter**. You do not need to save this document again.

</td>
</tr>
</table>

Figure 6-4
Text flows into frames in the order in which they are selected.

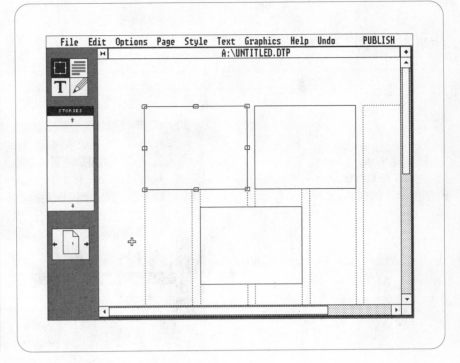

TEXT RUNAROUND

The **Text runaround command** is turned on as the default setting and causes text to run around the outline of an overlying frame, as shown in Figure 6-5.

Figure 6-5
Text automatically runs around the outline of an overlying frame unless you turn the Text runaround command off.

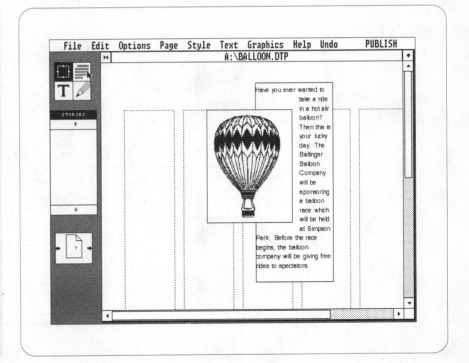

When you choose the Text runaround command from the Options menu, the Text Runaround dialog box appears, as shown in Figure 6-6. The Text Runaround dialog box allows you to choose if you want text to run around a frame and lets you determine how much blank space should appear around a frame.

Figure 6-6
The Text Runaround dialog box displays options available for wrapping text around the outline of an overlying frame.

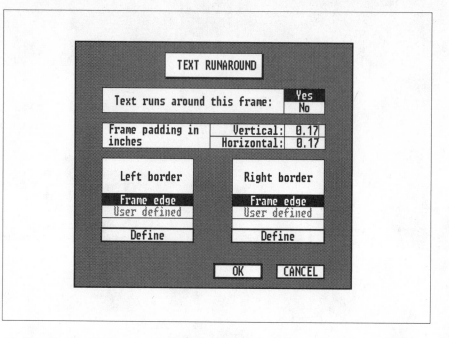

The Define option in the Text Runaround dialog box lets you define a border around a graphic so that text can flow around the graphic. The Define option is also used to create odd-shaped frames for text. Figures 6-7a and 6-7b illustrate documents that you can create using the Text runaround command.

Figure 6-7a
The Define option in the Text Runaround dialog box is used to create a border around a graphic for text to flow around.

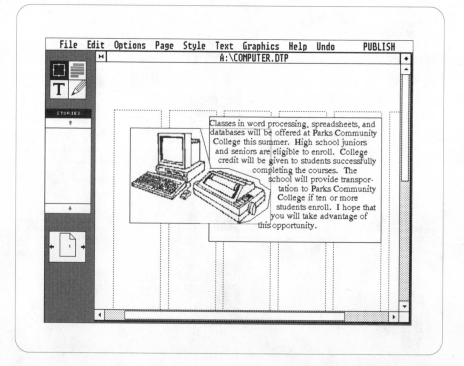

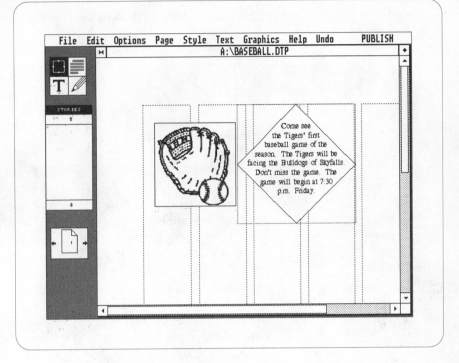

Figure 6-7b
The Define option is used to create an odd-shaped frame for text.

The Define option produces a broken line connected to the center handles at the top and bottom of the frame, as shown in Figure 6-8. You can move the line with the pointer and define a border for a graphic or text. The line is anchored by pressing the mouse button or the Home key. When you complete the border, a double-click returns you to the Text Runaround dialog box.

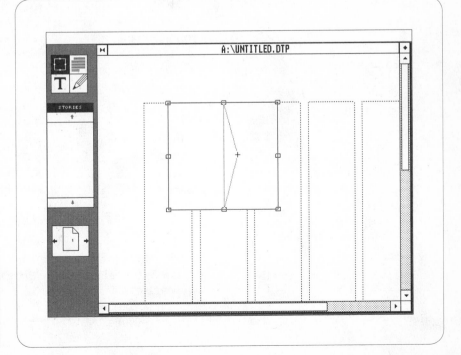

Figure 6-8.
The Define option produces a broken line that is used to create a border around a graphic or to create an odd-shaped frame for text.

ACTIVITY 6-4 • Using Text Runaround

In this activity you will use the Text runaround command to wrap text around a graphic and to place text in an odd-shaped frame.

```
Options
▶ Show tools          ◆H

  Show rulers         ◆J
  Ruler spacing...

  Frame border...
  Frame tint...
▶ Text runaround...   ⬎
  Size & position...

▶ Show frames & cols  ◆E
  Set column guides...
▶ Snap to guides

  Set defaults...
  Automatic backup...
```

1. Open *ACT6-4.DTP* from your template disk.
2. Select the frame containing the soccer ball.
3. Choose **Text runaround** from the **Options** menu. The Text Runaround dialog box appears.
4. Choose **Define** in the Right border box.
5. Move the pointer to the top of the soccer ball. Click the mouse button to anchor the line. Outline the right edge of the soccer ball by moving the pointer and clicking the mouse button, as shown in Figure 6-9. Double-click the mouse button to stop defining and return to the Text Runaround dialog box. Click on **OK**.
6. Create a 3-by-4-inch frame overlapping the right half of the soccer ball, as shown in Figure 6-10. Hint: Use the rulers.
7. Choose **Send to back** from the **Page** menu.
8. Import *ACT6-3.WPD* into the frame. Select **WordPerfect 4**. The text runs around the border of the soccer ball.
9. Choose **Text runaround** from the **Options** menu.
10. Change the frame padding to **0.05** for vertical and horizontal.
11. Choose **Define** in the Right border box.
12. Move the pointer to the middle handle on the right side of the frame, as shown in Figure 6-11. Double-click the mouse button. Click on **OK**. Some of the text does not fit in the new frame.

1. Open *ACT6-4.DTP* from your template disk.
2. Select the frame containing the soccer ball.
3. Choose **Text runaround** from the **Options** menu. The Text Runaround dialog box appears.
4. Choose **Define** in the Right border box.
5. Move the pointer to the top of the soccer ball. Press the **Home** key to anchor the line. Outline the right edge of the soccer ball by moving the pointer and pressing **Home**, as shown in Figure 6-9. Remember to use the shift key with the arrows for more precise movement. Press the **Home** key twice quickly to stop defining and return to the Text Runaround dialog box. Press **Enter**.
6. Create a 3-by-4-inch frame overlapping the right half of the soccer ball, as shown in Figure 6-10. Hint: Use the rulers.
7. Choose **Send to back** from the **Page** menu.
8. Import *ACT6-3.WPD* into the frame. Select **WordPerfect 4**. The text runs around the border of the soccer ball.
9. Choose **Text runaround** from the **Options** menu.
10. Change the frame padding to **0.05** for vertical and horizontal.
11. Choose **Define** in the Right border box.
12. Move the pointer to the middle handle on the right side of the frame, as shown in Figure 6-11. Press **Home**. Then press **Home**

Continued

13. Save this file as *TEXTRUN.DTP* on your data disk.

twice quickly. Some of the text does not fit in the new frame.

13. Save this file as *TEXTRUN.DTP* on your data disk.

Figure 6-9
The Define option in the Text Runaround dialog box allows you to define a border around a graphic.

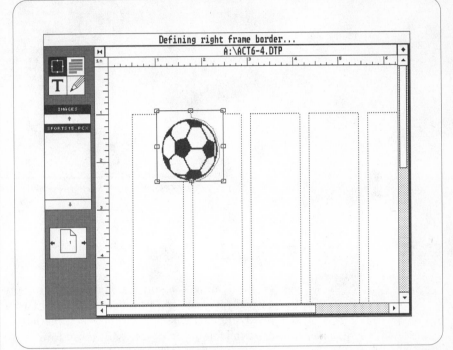

Figure 6-10
Defining a border around a graphic causes imported text to run around the graphic.

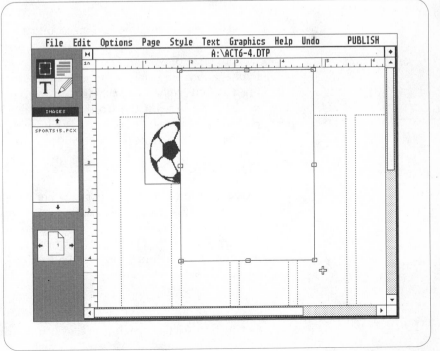

Figure 6-11
The Define option enables you to create different shapes of frames for text.

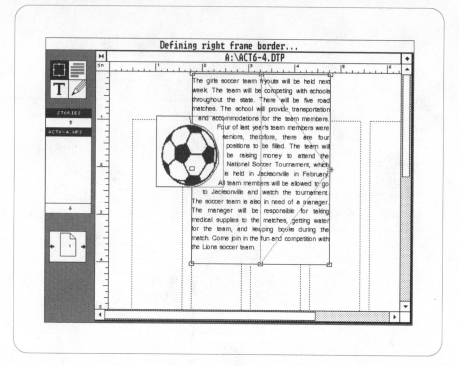

OTHER FORMATTING FEATURES

When creating a document, you want to be sure that words are hyphenated correctly, names and numbers that should appear on one line are not separated, and that the spacing between the letters is balanced. Three features are available to help you with these formatting issues: soft hyphens, fixed spaces, and kerning.

Soft Hyphens

A **soft hyphen** is a hyphen you insert into a word where you prefer the word to be broken. If a soft hyphen is placed at the beginning of a word, the word will not be hyphenated. The soft hyphen overrides the Publish It! automatic hyphenation and can be inserted by pressing Ctrl + - (hyphen) or by choosing the **Soft hyphen command** from the Text menu. Publish It! will not hyphenate a word if the word does not need to be broken. If text is reformatted and moves a hyphenated word with a soft hyphen away from the hyphenation hot zone, the hyphen does not appear.

Fixed Spaces

A **fixed space** holds related text together so that it is not split between lines. A fixed space is created by placing the text cursor between the words or numbers and pressing Ctrl + Spacebar. A normal word space width appears, but the space will not be affected by justification. A fixed space can be inserted, for example, between a first and last name so that the name is not split between two lines.

Kerning

Kerning adjusts the spacing between individual characters. You can kern characters by pressing Alt + K or by choosing the **Kern command** from the

Text menu. Each time you press Alt + K, the characters move 0.50 points closer. With the Kern command you can both increase and decrease space between letters. The Kern command also allows more precise kerning because the space between letters can be increased or decreased by as little as a tenth of a point. The Kern command displays the Kern Two Characters dialog box, as shown in Figure 6-12. The plus sign (+) increases the spacing between characters, and the minus sign (–) decreases the spacing between characters. You can change the sign by positioning your pointer on the sign and pressing Home or clicking the mouse button.

Figure 6-12
The Kern Two Characters dialog box enables you to increase or decrease the amount of space between characters.

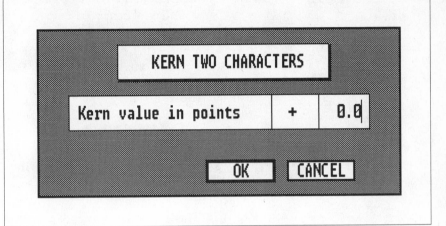

KERN TWO CHARACTERS

| Kern value in points | + | 0.0 |

OK CANCEL

ACTIVITY 6-5 • Using Soft Hyphens, Fixed Spaces, And Kerning

In this activity you will insert soft hyphens, insert fixed spaces, and kern two characters.

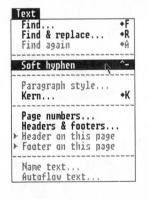

1. Open *ACT6-5.DTP* from your template disk.
2. Position the text pointer between the *i* and the *c* in *justification*.
3. Choose **Soft hyphen** from the **Text** menu. *Justification* is hyphenated after the second *i*.
4. Position the text pointer between the *s* and *d* in *eavesdropping*.
5. Press **Ctrl + -**. *Eaves-* moves to the first line.
6. Position the text pointer on the space immediately following *(808)*. Press the **Delete** key. *(808)* moves to the bottom line.
7. Press **Ctrl + Space Bar**. This inserts a space but does not

1. Open *ACT6-5.DTP* from your template disk.
2. Position the text pointer between the *i* and the *c* in *justification*.
3. Choose **Soft hyphen** from the **Text** menu. *Justification* is hyphenated after the second *i*.
4. Position the text pointer between the *s* and *d* in *eavesdropping*.
5. Press **Ctrl + -**. *Eaves-* moves to the first line.
6. Position the text pointer on the space immediately following *(808)*. Press the **Delete** key. *(808)* moves to the bottom line.
7. Press **Ctrl + Space Bar**. This inserts a space but does not

Continued

allow the phone number to be split between lines.

8. Position the text pointer on the space immediately following *Tim*. Press the **Delete key**.

9. Press **Ctrl + Space Bar**.

10. Position the text pointer between the *P* and *e* in *Pennsylvania*.

11. Choose **Kern** from the **Text** menu. The Kern Two Characters dialog box appears.

12. Enter **–3.5** and click on **OK**. Hint: Click on the plus sign to change it to a minus. If you clear the field completely, you will have to enter 03.5.

13. Position the text pointer between the two *n*'s in *Pennsylvania*.

14. Press **Alt + K** three times to decrease the space between the characters.

15. Position the text pointer between the *r* and *n* in *Kerning*.

16. Choose **Kern** from the **Text** menu.

17. Enter **+2.0** and click on **OK**. The characters move apart.

18. Save this document on your data disk as *FINETUNE.DTP*.

allow the phone number to be split between lines.

8. Position the text pointer on the space immediately following *Tim*. Press the **Delete** key.

9. Press **Ctrl + Space Bar**.

10. Position the text pointer between the *P* and *e* in *Pennsylvania*.

11. Choose **Kern** from the **Text** menu. The Kern Two Characters dialog box appears.

12. Enter **–3.5** and press **Enter**. Hint: Press Home with the pointer on the plus sign to change it to a minus. If you clear the field completely, you will have to enter 03.5.

13. Position the text pointer between the two *n*'s in *Pennsylvania*.

14. Press **Alt + K** three times to decrease the space between the characters.

15. Position the text pointer between the *r* and *n* in *Kerning*.

16. Choose **Kern** from the **Text** menu.

17. Enter **+2.0** and press **Enter**. The characters move apart.

18. Save this document on your data disk as *FINETUNE.DTP*.

SUMMARY

The effectiveness of a document often depends on the layout. The main objectives of the layout are readability and visual appeal. A layout should draw the reader's attention and motivate the reader to continue reading.

Column guides are dotted lines that appear on the screen to help you position frames. The Set column guides command lets you change the number of columns, the column dimensions, and the page offset. The Snap to guides command is activated as the default setting and causes frames to snap to the column guides. Turning off the Snap to guides command allows you to create and move frames more freely.

Frames can be linked to allow text to flow from one frame to another. If you import more text than will fit in a frame, a dashed line appears at the bottom of the frame to indicate that more text exists below the frame. You can then select another frame and click on the story name in the library to cause the text to flow from one frame to another. Text flows into frames in the order in which they are selected.

The Text runaround command allows you to run text around the outline of an overlying frame. The Define option in the Text Runaround dialog box is used to define a border around a graphic for text to flow around and to create an odd-shaped frame for text. The amount of padding or space that surrounds a graphic or frame can also be changed.

Three formatting features offered in Publish It! are soft hyphens, fixed spaces, and kerning. These features can refine the appearance of text. A soft hyphen is a hyphen you insert into text where you would prefer a word to be broken. Soft hyphens override the Publish It! automatic hyphenation. Fixed spaces connect words and numbers and keep them from being split between lines. Kerning is used to adjust the spacing between individual characters. You can kern characters by pressing Alt + K or by choosing the Kern command from the Text menu.

CHAPTER

⑥

Review

Name _____ Date _____

TRUE OR FALSE

The following statements are either true or false. Circle T or F to indicate your answer.

1. You should create symmetrical layouts when possible. (Obj. 1)   1. T F

2. Many different typefaces and font sizes should be used to create an interesting document. (Obj. 1)   2. T F

3. The maximum number of columns that can appear on a page is nine. (Obj. 2)   3. T F

4. The Snap to guides command is activated as the default setting. (Obj. 3)   4. T F

5. If you delete a linked frame, the text in that frame is also deleted. (Obj. 4)   5. T F

6. A border must be defined around a graphic before text will flow around that graphic. (Obj. 5)   6. T F

7. You cannot alter the shape of a text frame. (Obj. 6)   7. T F

8. A soft hyphen overrides the Publish It! automatic hyphenation. (Obj. 7)   8. T F

9. Pressing Alt + Space Bar creates a fixed space. (Obj. 7)   9. T F

10. Using the quick key method of kerning (Alt + K), characters can only be moved closer together. (Obj. 7)   10. T F

COMPLETION

Write your answer in the space provided.

11. What are the main objectives of a layout? (Obj. 1)

_____

_____

12. What are the three options available in the Set Column Guides dialog box? (Obj. 2)

_____

_____

13. What does the Page offset option do? (Obj. 2)

_____

_____

14. What is the purpose of the Snap to guides command? (Obj. 3)

_____

_____

15. Explain the process of linking frames. (Obj. 4)

_____

_____

_____

_____

16. What is the purpose of the Frame padding option in the Text Runaround dialog box? (Obj. 5)

_____

_____

17. When you define a border, how do you anchor the line and how do you stop defining the border? (Obj. 6)

_____

_____

18. What is a soft hyphen? (Obj. 7)

_____

_____

19. What is the purpose of a fixed space? (Obj. 7)

_____

_____

20. What is the difference between using Alt + K and the Kern command for kerning characters? (Obj. 7)

_____

_____

_____

APPLICATION 6-1

In this application you will change the number of columns, the column dimensions, and the page offset. You will also link frames to accommodate an imported text file.

1. Open a new, untitled document.
2. Change the number of columns to 4.
3. Change the left and right margins to 1 inch.
4. Turn off the Snap to guides command.
5. Using the rulers, create three 2-by-2-inch frames.
6. Import *APP6-1.WPD* into the first frame you created.
7. Link the frames to accommodate all of the text. You may not need to link the third frame, depending on your type size.
8. Save the document as *APP6-1.DTP* on your data disk.

APPLICATION 6-2

In this application you will use the Text runaround command to wrap text around a graphic and to create a different shape of frame for text.

1. Open *APP6-2.DTP* from your template disk.
2. Select the frame that holds a graphic of a key.
3. Change the Frame padding option to 0.00 horizontally and .10 vertically.
4. Define a border around the right edge of the key.
5. Select the frame containing the text.
6. Create a diamond-shaped frame for the text. Some of the text will not fit in the new frame.
7. Save the document as *KEY.DTP* on your data disk.

APPLICATION 6-3

In this application you will insert fixed spaces, insert soft hyphens, and kern characters.

1. Open *APP6-3.DTP* from your template disk.
2. Insert a soft hyphen between the *m* and *p* in *championship*.
3. Insert a fixed space between *Murray* and *High*. Even though the words are on the same line, inserting the fixed space now will prevent the words from becoming split later if text is added.
4. Insert a soft hyphen between the *n* and *g* in *congratulate*.
5. Insert a fixed space between *Sherry* and *Jones*.
6. Kern *GO TIGERS!* so that the spacing between the *R* and the *S* appears balanced.
7. Save the document as *TEAM.DTP* on your data disk.

SECTION

③

Advanced Desktop Publishing

Chapter 7
Advanced Publication Layout

Chapter 8
Working with Template Files

Chapter 9
Desktop Publishing Center Simulation

Chapter 10
Desktop Publishing Center Applications

CHAPTER

Advanced Publication Layout

LEARNING OBJECTIVES

When you complete this chapter you will be able to:

1. Apply guidelines to create an effective layout.
2. Plan a multipage document.
3. Add, insert, change, and delete pages.
4. Create single- and double-sided master pages.
5. Create headers and footers.
6. Change the page number format.
7. Name text.
8. Autoflow text.
9. Use the Frame border, Frame tint, and Size & position commands.

LAYOUT STRATEGIES

In Chapter 6 you became acquainted with several basic concepts about planning a layout. You discovered that asymmetrical layouts are more striking than symmetrical ones, that the information in a document should be reflected by the layout, that white space can be used as a design element, that graphics help communicate the text information to the reader, and that fonts can be used creatively to support the design of a document. These guidelines are important, but there are still others to consider in designing a layout. The following list will provide you with additional tips for designing a document.

- *Determine the purpose of the document.* Do you want it to explain, inform, or entertain? Knowing the purpose is the first step in designing an effective document.

- *Consider the type of image you want the document to project.* The typeface, paper quality, and paper color you use contribute to a document's character. For example, an elegant typeface on high-quality ivory paper is fitting for an invitation to a formal dinner. A modern typeface on medium-quality colored paper is suitable for an invitation to an informal birthday party.

- *Analyze your audience.* Who will be reading your document and why will they be reading it? Your document should be appropriate for the audience. For example, a newsletter to members of a student council could use a simpler language than a newsletter to members of an adult organization, such as the PTA. Consider that perhaps your intended audience will not even want to read your document. In this case, you will need to use strategies to grab the audience's interest. Lure readers into your document with a vivid graphic or a catchy heading.

- *Decide on the visual effects you will use.* As you learned in Chapter 3, graphics such as photos, clip art, graphs, and charts are useful in relaying information. Borders, boxes, and ruling lines are design elements that help organize a page and move the reader's eye through a page. The use of **sidebars**, boxes of related information set apart from the main body, also adds visual interest. A sidebar can contain highlights of an article for hurried readers. Or a sidebar can consist of a shorter, separate article that relates to a longer article. Make relationships among the pieces of information obvious with a hierarchy of headings, such as the headings in this book. For example, a main heading might consist of bold capital letters and a subheading of bold upper- and lower-case letters.

- *Watch for and remove distracting widows and orphans.* A **widow** is the final line of a paragraph that appears at the top of a page or column (see Figure 7-1). An **orphan** is the first line of a paragraph left at the bottom of a page or column (see Figure 7-2). Widows and orphans can be removed by adding a **hard return** (by pressing the Enter key) or by adjusting the column.

Figure 7-1
A widow is the final line of a paragraph that appears at the top of a page or column.

allows text to be saved in a format that can be loaded and used by other programs. Graphics can be created with a paint or draw program, or clip art can be used. Another art alternative is to use a scanner to record photographs or drawings on disk electronically. Text and graphics are loaded into a page layout

publishing system.

Widow

How It All Began

Today's printing industry is huge. But how did it all begin? In the fifteenth century, a man named Johannes Gutenburg created a printing press with movable type. This allowed printers to make one copy of a publication, such as a book

- *Don't overlook the details that are necessary to some documents.* For example, if you are designing a mailer—a document sent through the mail to promote and advertise a business—for a babysitting service, don't forget to include a phone number.

- *Decide on a completion time and budget for the document.* To determine a completion time, decide the date the document must be in the hands of its audience and work backward. This will give you an idea of the time you have for designing, editing, and printing the document. The budget is affected by the number of copies you will need and the type of paper you will use. Call various commercial printers to compare prices.

Figure 7-2
An orphan is the first line of a paragraph left at the bottom of a page or column.

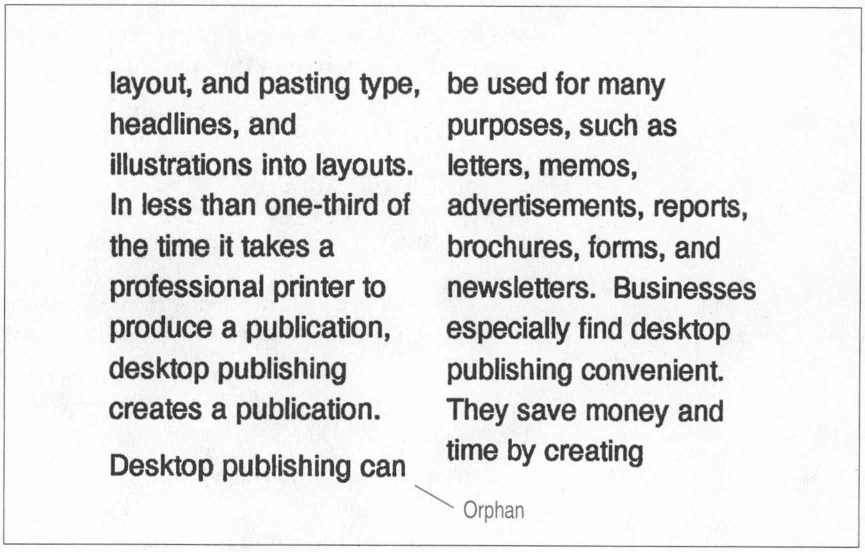

layout, and pasting type, headlines, and illustrations into layouts. In less than one-third of the time it takes a professional printer to produce a publication, desktop publishing creates a publication.

Desktop publishing can be used for many purposes, such as letters, memos, advertisements, reports, brochures, forms, and newsletters. Businesses especially find desktop publishing convenient. They save money and time by creating

Orphan

WORKING WITH MULTIPAGE DOCUMENTS

Many documents have multiple pages. For example, newsletters and reports typically have several pages. Even a brochure consists of two pages, one on the front and one on the back side of the paper. When documents contain more than one page, the pages typically are bound together. When pages are bound, additional margin space is needed to allow room for the binding.

Types of Binding

Documents can be bound in several ways. An inexpensive binding method is to staple the pages of a document together in the top corner. Another method is to punch holes along the binding edge of a document and place it in a three-ring binder. Three-ring binders allow pages to be replaced easily and are, therefore, useful for binding documents that need to be updated periodically.

Saddle stitching and mechanical binding are commonly used binding methods for documents needing a professional appearance. **Saddle stitching** is the process of stapling the pages of a document down the middle fold and is suitable for binding booklets and magazines. For example, a telephone directory for a student organization could be prepared in booklet form and then saddle stitched. **Mechanical binding** is the process of punching a series of holes in the binding edge of a document and running a plastic or wire spiral coil through the holes. Mechanical binding, which is provided by a commercial printer, is useful for documents that need to lie flat, such as a procedure manual for a chemistry lab class.

Planning the Margins

Before determining the margins of a multipage document, you should consider how the document will be bound and whether the text will be printed on one side of the paper, **single-sided**, or on both sides of the paper, **double-sided**. For example, a single-sided document that will be mechanically bound should have a large left margin to allow room for the binding. Because every page will be bound on the left side, the left margin on each page should be larger than the right margin. For a double-sided document that will be mechanically bound, the text on the front side of the paper should have a larger left margin, while the text on the back side of the paper should have a larger right margin. With a double-sided document, the front side of the paper is bound at the left of the text, but the back side of the paper is bound at the right of the text.

Adding Pages

When creating a multipage document, you will need to add pages to accommodate the length of your document. You can add pages to a document using one of these three methods:

1. The **Add one page command** in the Page menu adds one blank page after the page currently displayed on the screen.

2. If the last page of your document is displayed, you can add a page by clicking on the right page turning Arrow in the Page Icon, as shown in Figure 7-3.

3. The **Add pages command** in the Page menu displays the Add Pages dialog box, shown in Figure 7-4. The Add Pages dialog box enables you to specify the number of pages to add to a document and to choose whether the pages will be added before or after the current page.

Figure 7-3
The Page Icon displays the current page number and the page turning arrows, which allow you to move between pages in a document.

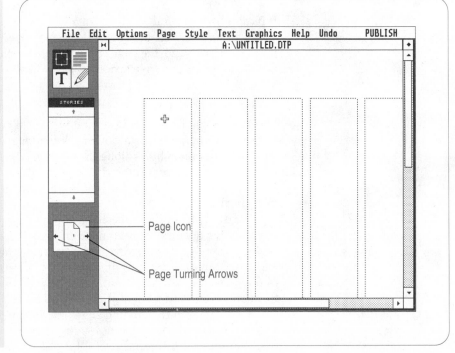

Inserting Pages

As with adding pages, inserting pages increases the number of pages in a document. However, the **Insert one page command** inserts a page *before* the current page while the Add one page command inserts a page *after* the current page. Publish It! automatically renumbers the pages of a document when a page is inserted.

Changing Pages

You will need to move from page to page in a document in order to proofread, edit, and review the document. There are two methods of moving among pages in a document. The first method is to click on the left and right page turning arrows, which turn the pages forward or backward one at a time. The second method is to choose the Go to page command from the Page menu. The **Go to page command** displays the Go to Page dialog box, shown in Figure 7-5. It lets you go to the master page or specify a page number to go to. Master pages are discussed later in this chapter. If the first page of a 20-page document is displayed and you want to review the closing or summary, the second method is the most efficient way to get there.

Figure 7-4
The Add pages command allows you to add more than one page to a document.

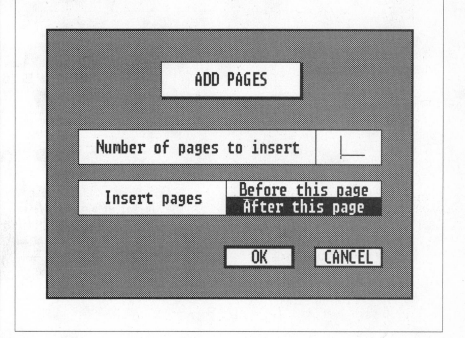

Figure 7-5
The Go to page command is the most efficient way to move to a page that is more than two pages away from the current page.

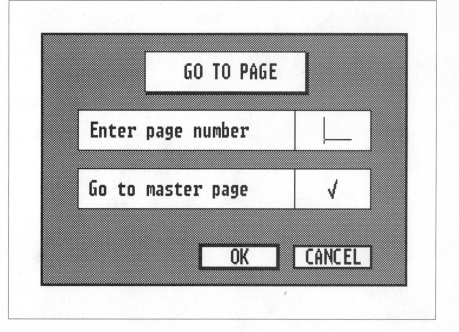

Deleting Pages

The **Delete pages command** in the Page menu enables you to delete pages from a document. When you choose the Delete pages command, the Delete Pages dialog box appears, as shown in Figure 7-6. The Delete Pages dialog box lets you specify the page number that you want to begin deleting from and the number of pages to delete. For example, if you want to delete pages 2 through 4 in a document, you would key 2 for the Delete from page option and 3 for the Number of pages to delete option. Before Publish It! deletes a page, a warning box appears telling you which pages will be deleted and giving you the opportunity to cancel the command.

Figure 7-6
The Delete Pages dialog box allows you to delete one or several pages from a document.

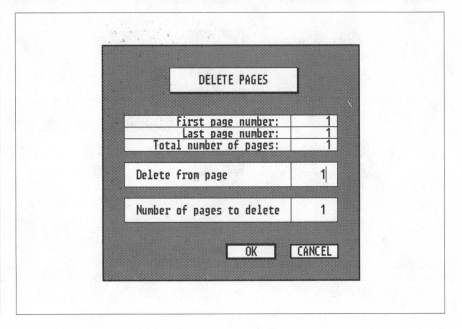

ACTIVITY 7-1 • Adding, Inserting, Changing, and Deleting Pages

In this activity you will add, insert, change, and delete pages.

1. Open a new untitled document.
2. Choose **Add one page** from the **Page** menu. Notice that the Page Icon displays page 2.
3. Choose **Insert one page** from the **Page** menu. Notice that the Page Icon continues to display page 2 even though a new page was inserted.
4. Click on the right page turning arrow. Page 3 is displayed.

1. Open a new untitled document.
2. Choose **Add one page** from the **Page** menu. Notice that the Page Icon displays page 2.
3. Choose **Insert one page** from the **Page** menu. Notice that the Page Icon continues to display page 2 even though a new page was inserted.
4. Position the pointer on the right page turning arrow. Press **Home**. Page 3 is displayed.

Continued

5. Click on the right page turning arrow again. A dialog box appears asking if you want to add a page. Click on **Yes**.

6. Choose **Add pages** from the **Page** menu. The Add Pages dialog box appears.

7. Key **5** for the Number of pages to insert. Click on **OK**. The Page Icon displays page 9.

8. Choose **Go to page** from the Page menu. The Go to Page dialog box appears.

9. Key **6** for the page number. Click on **OK**.

10. Choose **Delete pages** from the **Page** menu. The Delete Pages dialog box appears.

11. Key **5** for Delete from page. Key **4** for Number of pages to delete. Click on **OK**. The warning box appears. Click on **OK**. Pages 5 through 8 are deleted. You do not need to save this file.

5. Position the pointer on the right page turning arrow. Press **Home**. A dialog box appears asking if you want to add a page. Choose **Yes**.

6. Choose **Add pages** from the **Page** menu. The Add Pages dialog box appears.

7. Key **5** for the Number of pages to insert. Press **Enter**. The Page Icon displays page 9.

8. Choose **Go to page** from the **Page** menu. The Go to Page dialog box appears.

9. Key **6** for the page number. Press **Enter**.

10. Choose **Delete pages** from the **Page** menu. The Delete Pages dialog box appears.

11. Key **5** for Delete from page. Key **4** for Number of pages to delete. Press **Enter**. The warning box appears. Press **Enter**. Pages 5 through 8 are deleted. You do not need to save this file.

MASTER PAGES

A **master page** is a single- or double-sided page that acts as a template for all pages of a document. The master page ensures that each page in a document has the same basic layout—the same number of columns, frame size and position, and headers and footers. For example, if you create a master page with a one-inch left margin and three frames, each succeeding page in the document will have a one-inch left margin and three frames. Although the master page will cause all of the pages to have three frames, you can always modify a page when necessary. For example, you may want to create a new frame to accommodate a graphic. When a master page is created for a particular document, it is saved and retrieved with that document. If a change is made to the master page, the change is reflected in the pages that are inserted after the change but not in those already created. Master pages are not printed.

Single-sided master pages ensure that every page in a document has the same basic layout, whereas double-sided master pages ensure that the left pages in a document have the same layout and the right pages in a document have the same layout. Imagine a textbook opened at the middle. The page at the left is referred to as the **verso** (left) page, and the page at the right is the **recto** (right) page. The Page Icon below the library indicates whether the page is a left page or a right page by turning back the left or right corner of the page. For a double-sided master page, Publish It! automatically adjusts the inner margin to 1 inch and the outer margin to ½ inch. The inner margin is the margin where the document will be bound.

ACTIVITY 7-2 • Creating Master Pages

In this activity you will create a single- and double-sided master page.

1. Open a new untitled document.
2. Choose **Set column guides** from the **Options** menu.
3. Change the number of columns to **3**. Click on **OK**.
4. Choose **Go to page** from the **Page** menu.
5. Choose **Go to master page**.
6. Choose **Size to fit** from the **Page** menu.
7. Create a frame surrounding the first column.
8. Create one frame surrounding both the second and third columns.
9. Click on the right page turning arrow. Page 1 is displayed and the frames you created appear on the page.
10. Add three pages to the document.
11. Click on the left page turning arrow three times. Notice that every page has the same layout.
12. Choose **New** from the **File** menu. You do not need to save the current document.
13. Choose **No** when asked if you want to load a style sheet. The Page Format dialog box appears.
14. Choose **Left & right** for the Master pages option. Click on **OK**.
15. Choose **Go to page** from the **Page** menu. Notice that the Go to master page option now has a left and right arrow instead of a checkmark.
16. Click on the left arrow. You can now create the left master page.
17. Create frames similar in size and position to those shown in Figure 7-7.
18. Click the right page turning arrow. You can now create the right master page.
19. Create frames similar in size and position to those shown in Figure 7-8.
20. Click on the right page turning arrow. Page 1 appears and reflects the layout of the right master page.

1. Open a new untitled document.
2. Choose **Set column guides** from the **Options** menu.
3. Change the number of columns to **3**. Press **Enter**.
4. Choose **Go to page** from the **Page** menu.
5. Choose **Go to master page**.
6. Choose **Size to fit** from the **Page** menu.
7. Create a frame surrounding the first column.
8. Create one frame surrounding both the second and third columns.
9. Position the pointer on the right page turning arrow. Press **Home**. Page 1 is displayed and the frames you created appear on the page.
10. Add three pages to the document.
11. Position the pointer on the left page turning arrow. Press **Home** three times. Notice that every page has the same layout.
12. Choose **New** from the **File** menu. You do not need to save the current document.
13. Choose **No** when asked if you want to load a style sheet. The Page Format dialog box appears.
14. Choose **Left & right** for the Master pages option. Press **Enter**.
15. Choose **Go to page** from the **Page** menu. Notice that the Go to master page option now has a left and right arrow instead of a checkmark.
16. Choose the left arrow. You can now create the left master page.
17. Create frames similar in size and position to those shown in Figure 7-7.
18. Position the pointer on the right page turning arrow. Press **Home**. You can now create the right master page.
19. Create frames similar in size and position to those shown in Figure 7-8.

Continued

21. Add five pages to the document.

22. Click on the left page turning arrow five times. Notice that all right pages have the same layout and all left pages have the same layout.

23. Choose **Actual size** from the **Page** menu. You do not need to save this document.

20. Position the pointer on the right page turning arrow. Press **Home**. Page 1 appears and reflects the layout of the right master page.

21. Add five pages to the document.

22. Position the pointer on the left page turning arrow. Press **Home** five times. Notice that all right pages have the same layout and all left pages have the same layout.

23. Choose **Actual size** from the **Page** menu. You do not need to save this document.

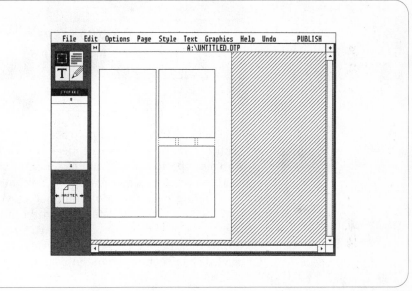

Figure 7-7
The left master page controls the layout of all left pages of a document.

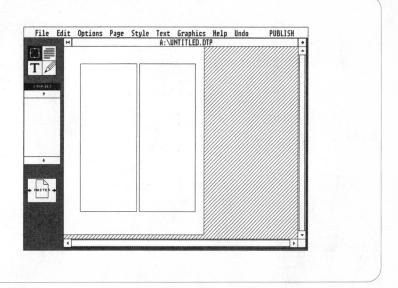

Figure 7-8
The right master page controls the layout of all right pages of a document.

HEADERS AND FOOTERS

A **header** is text that appears at the top of every page or alternate pages. A **footer** is text that appears at the bottom of every page or alternate pages. Headers and footers usually contain information such as the document title, author, or page number. The **Headers & footers command** is located in the Text menu and displays the Headers and Footers dialog box, shown in Figure 7-9.

Figure 7-9
Headers and footers can be positioned at the left, center, or right of a page; different headers and footers can be created for right and left pages.

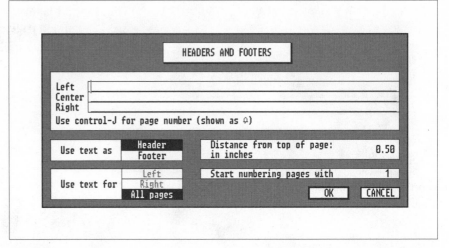

Headers and footers can be placed at the left, center, or right of each page. You can create different headers and footers for right and left pages. You can also specify the amount of space from the top of the page to the header and the amount of space from the bottom of the page to the footer. The Start numbering pages with option enables you to change the page number if you do not want the first page to be numbered 1. If you do not want a header or footer to appear on a particular page, you can turn the command off for that page by choosing the **Header on this page command** or **Footer on this page command** in the Text menu.

ACTIVITY 7-3 • Creating Headers and Footers

In this activity you will create a header and a footer for a document.

<div style="text-align:center">🖱</div>	<div style="text-align:center">⌨</div>
1. Open *ACT7-3.DTP* from your template disk.	1. Open *ACT7-3.DTP* from your template disk.
2. Choose **Size to fit** from the **Page** menu.	2. Press **Alt + 0** to choose **Size to fit** from the Page menu.
3. Choose **Headers & footers** from the **Text** menu. The Headers and Footers dialog box appears.	3. Choose **Headers & footers** from the **Text** menu. The Headers and Footers dialog box appears.
4. Key **Desktop Publishing** on the Right header line. Click on	4. Key **Desktop Publishing** on the Right header line. Press

Continued

OK. The header appears in the top right corner of the page.

5. Choose **Headers & footers** from the **Text** menu.

6. Change the Use text as option to **Footer**.

7. Key **Introduction** on the Center footer line. Change the Distance from the bottom of page option to **1.00**. Click on **OK**. The footer appears at the bottom center of the page.

8. Click on the right page turning arrow two times. The header and footer appear on every page.

9. Go to page 1.

10. Choose **Header on this page** from the **Text** menu. The header no longer appears on page 1.

11. Choose **Footer on this page** from the **Text** menu. The footer no longer appears on page 1.

12. Click on the right page turning arrow two times. The header and footer remain on pages 2 and 3.

13. Choose **Actual size** from the **Page** menu.

14. Save this document as *ARTI-CLE.DTP* on your data disk.

Enter. The header appears in the top right corner of the page.

5. Choose **Headers & footers** from the **Text** menu.

6. Change the Use text as option to **Footer**.

7. Key **Introduction** on the Center footer line. Change the Distance from the bottom of page option to **1.00**. Press **Enter**. The footer appears at the bottom center of the page.

8. Position the pointer on the right page turning arrow. Press **Home** twice. The header and footer appear on every page.

9. Go to page 1.

10. Choose **Header on this page** from the **Text** menu. The header no longer appears on page 1.

11. Choose **Footer on this page** from the **Text** menu. The footer no longer appears on page 1.

12. Position the pointer on the right page turning arrow. Press **Home** twice. The header and footer remain on pages 2 and 3.

13. Press **Alt + 3** to choose **Actual size** from the Page menu.

14. Save this document as *ARTI-CLE.DTP* on your data disk.

PAGE NUMBERS

Keying Ctrl + J in a header or footer displays the current page number. You can also display the total number of pages in a document by keying %(percent sign) in a header or footer. Suppose you have a three-page document and you want to create a header or footer that will display the current page number as well as the total number of pages in the document. For example, keying "Page (Ctrl + J) of %" as the header or footer displays "Page 1 of 3" on page 1. The Headers & footers command controls the position of the page number on a page, while the Page numbers command lets you change the page number format.

The **Page numbers command** displays the Page Number Format dialog box, which offers five number formats, as shown in Figure 7-10. Roman numerals (i, ii, iii) are commonly used to number the introductory pages of books; arabic numerals (1, 2, 3) are used to number the main text of books. You can change the format of the page numbers before or after you create the header or footer.

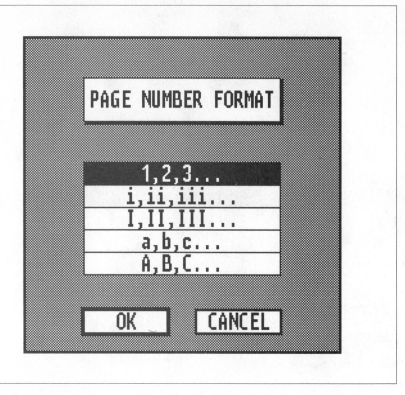

Figure 7-10
The Page Number Format dialog box displays five types of number formats.

ACTIVITY 7-4 • Numbering Pages

In this activity you will number the pages of a document and change the page number format. *ARTICLE.DTP* should be on your screen.

1. Choose **Headers & footers** from the **Text** menu.	1. Choose **Headers & footers** from the **Text** menu.
2. If the Footer is displayed, choose **Header** from the **Use text as** option.	2. If the Footer is displayed, choose **Header** from the **Use text as** option.
3. Position the cursor immediately after the header Desktop Publishing in the Right header line. Press the Space Bar 5 times. Key **Page**. Key **Ctrl + J** to insert the page number. The Right header line should appear as shown in Figure 7-11. Click on **OK**.	3. Position the cursor immediately after the header Desktop Publishing in the Right header line. Press the **Space Bar** 5 times. Key **Page**. Key **Ctrl + J** to insert a page number. The Right header line should appear as shown in Figure 7-11. Press **Enter**.
4. Go to page 2. Use the scroll bar in the bottom right corner of the work area to move the	4. Go to page 2. Use the scroll bar in the bottom right corner of the work area to move the

Continued

Text
Find...	✦F
Find & replace...	✦R
Find again	✦A
Soft hyphen	^-
Paragraph style...	
Kern...	✦K
Page numbers...	
Headers & footers...	
▶ Header on this page	
▶ Footer on this page	
Name text...	
Autoflow text...	

page until the page number is visible.

5. Choose **Page numbers** from the **Text** menu. The Page Number Format dialog box appears.

6. Choose **A, B, C** for the page number format. Click on **OK**. Notice the new page number format.

7. Change the page number format to **1, 2, 3**. Click on **OK**.

8. Choose **Headers & footers** from the **Text** menu.

9. Position the cursor immediately after the bell shape in the Right header line. Press the **Space Bar**. Key of %. Click **OK**. Notice the page number.

10. Save this document as *PGNUMBER.DTP* on your data disk.

page until the page number is visible.

5. Choose **Page numbers** from the **Text** menu. The Page Number Format dialog box appears.

6. Choose **A, B, C** for the page number format. Press **Enter**. Notice the new page number format.

7. Change the page number format to **1, 2, 3**. Press **Enter**.

8. Choose **Headers & footers** from the **Text** menu.

9. Position the cursor immediately after the bell shape in the Right header line. Press the **Space Bar**. Key of %. Press **Enter**. Notice the page number.

10. Save this document as *PGNUMBER.DTP* on your data disk.

Figure 7-11
When you press Ctrl + J, a bell shape appears in place of the page number.

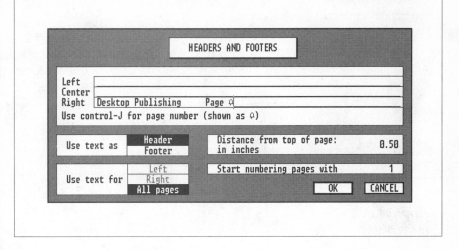

HEADERS AND FOOTERS

Left
Center
Right | Desktop Publishing   Page ♫
Use control-J for page number (shown as ♫)

Use text as | **Header** / Footer

Distance from top of page: in inches   0.50

Use text for | Left / **Right** / **All pages**

Start numbering pages with   1

OK   CANCEL

NAMING TEXT

The **Name text command** in the Text menu enables you to assign a name to text that you key or text that has been saved in a *.DTP* file. Publish It! automatically adds the *.ASC* extension to the name and the filename appears in the library. After text is named and the filename appears in the library, you can link frames to position the text in the appropriate place in the document. The text must be exported before Publish It! gives you the opportunity to save the text so that it can be imported later. For a review of exporting text, refer to Chapter 2.

ACTIVITY 7-5 • Naming Text

In this activity you will name text.

Mouse

1. Choose **New** from the **File** menu. Abandon the current document.

2. Create a frame approximately 1 inch high by 2 inches wide.

3. Key the following sentence in the frame: **Desktop publishing is a process that utilizes a computer to create a publication.**

4. Select the frame containing the text.

5. Choose **Name text** from the **Text** menu. The Name Text dialog box appears, as shown in Figure 7-12.

6. Key **Desktop**. Click on **OK**. The filename Desktop appears in the library.

7. Press **Delete**. The frame and text disappear.

8. Create a frame approximately 1 inch high by 2 inches wide.

9. Click on **Desktop** in the library. The text flows into the frame. You do not need to save this document.

Keyboard

1. Choose **New** from the **File** menu. Abandon the current document.

2. Create a frame approximately 1 inch high by 2 inches wide.

3. Key the following sentence in the frame: **Desktop publishing is a process that utilizes a computer to create a publication.**

4. Select the frame containing the text.

5. Choose **Name text** from the **Text** menu. The Name Text dialog box appears, as shown in Figure 7-12.

6. Key **Desktop**. Press **Enter**. The filename Desktop appears in the library.

7. Press **Delete**. The frame and text disappear.

8. Create a frame approximately 1 inch high by 2 inches wide.

9. Select **Desktop** in the library. The text flows into the frame. You do not need to save this document.

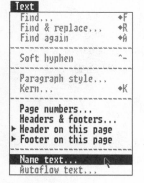

Figure 7-12
When you name text, Publish It! automatically assigns the .*ASC* extension to the name.

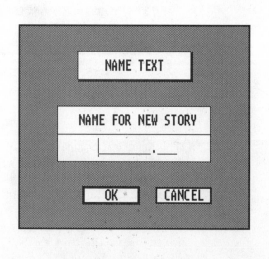

AUTOFLOWING TEXT

The **Autoflow text command** in the Text menu simplifies the process of creating multipage documents. When you select the Autoflow text command, Publish It! automatically adds the number of pages and frames necessary to accommodate the entire text file. If you want all the pages to have a multi-frame layout, the first page should have the desired number of frames and each of the frames should be filled with text. For example, if you have five frames on page one, but only two of them contain text, then only two frames will be created on the remaining pages. The Autoflow text command is helpful for creating documents with multiple columns, such as a newsletter. The Autoflow text command can be chosen only when the dashed line appears at the bottom of a frame.

ACTIVITY 7-6 • Autoflowing Text

In this activity you will import a multipage document and use the Autoflow text command to accommodate the text.

Mouse	Keyboard
1. Open a new untitled document.	1. Open a new untitled document.
2. Create three frames of approximately the same size and position as those shown in Figure 7-13.	2. Create three frames of approximately the same size and position as those shown in Figure 7-13.
3. Select the top frame.	3. Select the top frame.
4. Choose **Import text** from the **File** menu. The Import Text dialog box appears.	4. Choose **Import text** from the **File** menu. The Import Text dialog box appears.
5. Choose **WordPerfect 4** for the text format. Click on **OK**.	5. Choose **WordPerfect 4** for the text format. Press **Enter**.
6. Change the directory to **A:*.WPD**.	6. Change the directory to **A:*.WPD**.
7. Choose *ACT7-6.WPD*. Click on **OK**. Notice the dashed line at the bottom of the frame.	7. Choose *ACT7-6.WPD*. Press **Enter**. Notice the dashed line at the bottom of the frame.
8. Select the frame at the bottom left. Click *ACT7-6.WPD* in the library. Another dashed line appears at the bottom of the frame.	8. Select the frame at the bottom left. Position the pointer on *ACT7-6.WPD* in the library. Press **Home**. Another dashed line appears at the bottom of the frame.
9. Select the frame at the bottom right. Click *ACT7-6.WPD* in the library. The dashed line appears again.	9. Select the frame at the bottom right. Position the pointer on *ACT7-6.WPD* in the library. Press **Home**. The dashed line appears again.
10. Choose **Autoflow text** from the **Text** menu. Another page is created with the same three	

Text

Find...	◆F
Find & replace...	◆R
Find again	◆A
Soft hyphen	^~
Paragraph style...	
Kern...	◆K
Page numbers...	
Headers & footers...	
▶ Header on this page	
▶ Footer on this page	
Name text...	
Autoflow text...	

Continued

frames, and the text is flowed into each of the frames until all of the text is accommodated.

11. Save this document as *TEXTFLOW.DTP* on your data disk.

10. Choose **Autoflow text** from the **Text** menu. Another page is created with the same three frames, and the text is flowed into each of the frames until all of the text is accommodated.

11. Save this document as *TEXTFLOW.DTP* on your data disk.

Figure 7-13
Only frames that contain text are re-created on succeeding pages when the Autoflow text command is chosen.

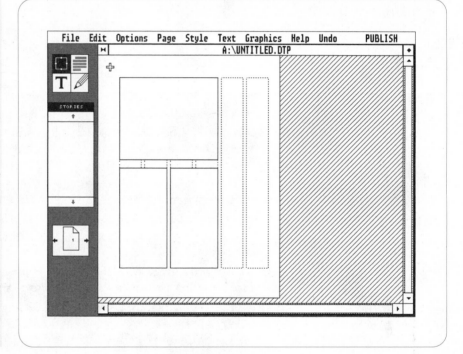

FRAME OPTIONS

Three frame options are available to help you capture the reader's interest or call attention to a particular item in a multipage document. These options include the Frame border command, the Frame tint command, and the Size & position command, all located in the Options menu.

Frame Border

Borders can be used to call the reader's attention to various parts of a document, to isolate certain information from the other text in a document, or simply for eye appeal. The **Frame border command** in the Options menu displays the Frame Border dialog box, shown in Figure 7-14. The Frame Border dialog box offers four border styles and lets you choose on which side or sides of the frame you want the border to appear.

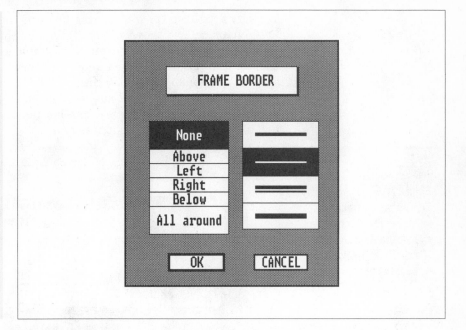

Figure 7-14
The Frame Border dialog box offers four border styles that can be placed around a frame.

Frame Tint

The **Frame tint command** in the Options menu displays the Frame Tint dialog box, shown in Figure 7-15. The Frame Tint dialog box lets you select a background shade for a frame and choose whether the background will be clear or **opaque**. A clear background allows you to see underlying frames and the column guides through the tinted frame. Column guides and frames cannot be seen through an opaque background. When selecting a frame tint, be sure that the tint does not affect the readability of the text. For example, lighter frame tints should be used with black text and darker frame tints should be used with white text. White text is text that appears white and is not visible unless a frame is tinted.

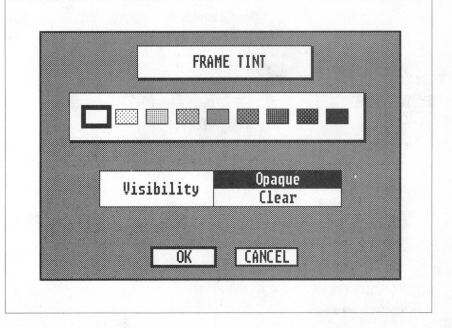

Figure 7-15
Light frame tints should be chosen when you are using black text and dark frame tints should be chosen when you are using white text.

Size and Position

The **Size & position command** in the Options menu displays the Size and Position dialog box, shown in Figure 7-16. The Size and Position dialog box shows you the width and height of the frame and the X and Y (horizontal and vertical) positions of the frame on the page. The X and Y values represent the position of the top left corner of the frame. You can change the size and position of a frame by changing the values in this dialog box. The unit of measurement used in the Size and Position dialog box is the same as the unit of measurement chosen for the rulers.

Figure 7-16
The Size and Position dialog box enables you to change the width, height, X position, and Y position of a selected frame.

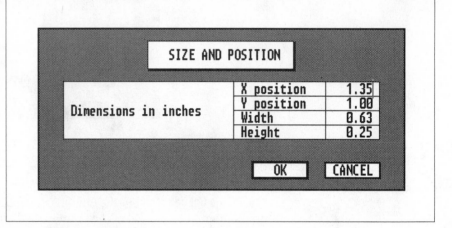

SIZE AND POSITION		
Dimensions in inches	X position	1.35
	Y position	1.00
	Width	0.63
	Height	0.25

OK   CANCEL

ACTIVITY 7-7 • Using the Frame Border, Frame Tint, and Size & Position Commands

In this activity you will use the Frame border, Frame tint, and Size & position commands.

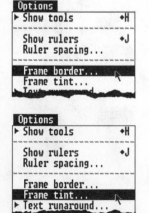	Mouse	Keyboard
	1. Open a new untitled document.	1. Open a new untitled document.
	2. Create a frame approximately 2 by 2 inches in the top left corner of the work area. Hint: Use the rulers.	2. Create a frame approximately 2 by 2 inches in the top left corner of the work area. Hint: Use the rulers.
	3. Choose **Frame border** from the **Options** menu.	3. Choose **Frame border** from the **Options** menu.
	4. Choose the border with the thickest black line (the last option). Click on **OK**.	4. Choose the border with the thickest black line (the last option). Press **Enter**.
	5. Choose **Frame tint** from the **Options** menu.	5. Choose **Frame tint** from the **Options** menu.
	6. Choose the tint that is third from the right. Click on **OK**.	6. Choose the tint that is third from the right. Press **Enter**.
	7. Click on the **Text tool** in the tool box.	7. Select the **Text tool** in the tool box.

Continued

8. Click inside the frame.

9. Change the Font size to **36** (or another large size that is less than 38 point).

10. Click on **White** in the library.

11. Key **Happy** and press **Enter**. Key **Birthday**.

12. Select the **Frame tool** from the tool box.

13. Select the frame.

14. Choose **Size & position** from the **Options** menu.

15. Change the X position to **2.00**. Change the Y position to **1.50**.

16. Change the Width and Height to **3.00**. Click on **OK**. Notice the new size and position of the frame on the page.

17. Save this file as *BIRTHDAY.DTP* on your data disk.

8. Position the pointer inside the frame. Press **Home**.

9. Change the Font size to **36** (or another large size that is less than 38 point).

10. Position the pointer on **White** in the library. Press **Home**.

11. Key **Happy** and press **Enter**. Key **Birthday**.

12. Select the **Frame tool** from the tool box.

13. Select the frame.

14. Choose **Size & position** from the **Options** menu.

15. Change the X position to **2.00**. Change the Y position to **1.50**.

16. Change the Width and Height to **3.00**. Press **Enter**. Notice the new size and position of the frame on the page.

17. Save this file as *BIRTHDAY.DTP* on your data disk.

SUMMARY

Whether you are creating a one–page document or a multipage document, designing an effective layout is important. A few of the guidelines to follow when designing the layout for a document are to determine the purpose of the document, to consider the type of image you want the document to project, and to analyze your audience.

Documents such as newsletters and reports often have multiple pages. Several methods are available for binding multipage documents, including staples, three-ring binders, saddle stitching, and mechanical binding. Adding, inserting, changing, and deleting pages are important features that allow you flexibility when you are working with multipage documents. Master pages assist you by ensuring that each page of a multipage document has the same basic layout. You can also create double-sided master pages, which enable you to have different layouts for right and left pages. Headers and footers often appear in multipage documents and can be part of the master page.

Headers and footers usually contain information such as the document title, author, and page number. The location of page numbers on the page is specified with the Headers & footers command. The page number format can be changed using the Page numbers command.

Naming text that you key gives the text the features of an imported text file. Named text can be exported and saved so that you can import it at a later time. If an imported text file is long, you can create the desired number of frames on the first page, flow text into each of the frames, then choose the Autoflow text command. This command adds the number of pages and frames necessary to accommodate the entire text file.

The Frame border and Frame tint commands are used to gain the reader's interest or to call attention to a particular item in a document.

The Size & position command is used to change the size and position of a frame on a page. This allows you to make a frame larger or smaller without having to recreate the frame, its border and tint, and the text that is in the frame.

CHAPTER

Review

Name _____ Date _____

TRUE OR FALSE

The following statements are either true or false. Circle T or F to indicate your answer.

1. The typeface, paper quality, and paper color you use contribute to a document's character. (Obj. 1)   1. T F

2. The most inexpensive binding method is mechanical binding. (Obj. 2)   2. T F

3. The only way to change pages in a document is to use the page turning arrows. (Obj. 3)   3. T F

4. You can delete more than one page at a time. (Obj. 3)   4. T F

5. Master pages can be single or double sided. (Obj. 4)   5. T F

6. Headers and footers can be positioned at the left, right, or center of the page. (Obj. 5)   6. T F

7. The Page numbers command is used to change the page number format. (Obj. 6)   7. T F

8. When text is named, Publish It! assigns the text a .DTP extension. (Obj. 7)   8. T F

9. A dashed line must appear at the bottom of the frame before you can choose the Autoflow text command. (Obj. 8)   9. T F

10. An opaque background is one that can be seen through. (Obj. 9)   10. T F

COMPLETION

Write your answers in the space provided.

11. Explain the difference between a widow and an orphan. (Obj. 1)

_____

_____

_____

12. Define saddle stitching. (Obj. 2)

_____

_____

13. What is the difference between the Add one page command and the Insert one page command? (Obj. 3)

_____

_____

_____

14. What is the purpose of a master page? (Obj. 4)

_____

_____

15. Define footer. (Obj. 5)

_____

_____

16. Which command causes a header not to appear on the current page? (Obj. 5)

_____

_____

17. What combination of keys should you press to display the page number in the Headers and Footers dialog box? (Obj. 6)

_____

18. What is the purpose of naming text? (Obj. 7)

_____

_____

_____

19. What does the Autoflow text command do? (Obj. 8)

_____

_____

_____

20. What is the purpose of the Size & position command? (Obj. 9)

_____

_____

APPLICATION 7-1

In this application you will create a master page, create a header, display the page number, change the page number format, add pages, and delete pages.

1. Open a new untitled document.
2. Go to the master page.
3. Create a frame surrounding the first three columns.
4. Create a frame surrounding the last three columns.
5. Choose Headers & footers from the Text menu.
6. For the left header, key Wego High Times.
7. Display the page number for the right header.
8. Change the page number format to I,II,III.
9. Go to page I.
10. Add five pages to the document.
11. Delete pages II through IV.
12. Save this document as _WEGOHIGH.DTP_ on your data disk.

APPLICATION 7-2

In this application you will name text, use the Autoflow text command, and change pages.

1. Open _APP7-2.DTP_ from your template disk. Abandon the current document.
2. Select the frame.
3. Name the text _PUBLISH_.
4. Delete the frame.
5. Create a frame surrounding the first two columns.
6. Select Publish from the library.
7. Choose Autoflow text from the Text menu.
8. Go to page 1.
9. Save this document as _PUBLISH.DTP_ on your data disk.

APPLICATION 7-3

In this application you will use the Frame border, Frame tint, and Size & position commands.

1. Open a new untitled document.
2. Create a frame approximately 2 by 2 inches in the top left corner of the work area.
3. Frame the border with the double line.

4. Tint the frame with the second option (white with black dots).

5. Select the Text tool.

6. Change the Body Text paragraph style to Centered justification.

7. Change the font size to 20.

8. Key: The student of the month is Danielle Brucker.

9. Select the Frame tool.

10. Select the frame.

11. Change the size and position of the frame as follows:
    X position   2.00
    Y position   2.50
    Width   2.50
    Height   2.50

12. Insert hard returns above the text to center the text vertically in the frame.

13. Save this document as *STUDENT.DTP* on your data disk.

APPLICATION 7-4

Using what you have learned, design and produce a two-page newsletter. Write a story or article for your newsletter. Using what you know about exporting text, share your story or article with other members of your class. Import text from other students' newsletters to complete your own newsletter. Use clip-art that relates to the stories to make the newsletter more interesting.

CHAPTER

Working with Template Files

LEARNING OBJECTIVES

When you complete this chapter, you will be able to:

1. Use templates.
2. Create your own templates.

TEMPLATES

A **template** is a predesigned layout for a document. Templates are convenient for documents that are published on a regular basis—such as newsletters, mailers, or flyers. Imagine how useful a template would be for a monthly newsletter. Instead of being designed from scratch every month, the layout of the newsletter would already be designed. You would need only to insert the articles and graphics for that month's news.

A template includes text frames, graphics frames, graphics, and any default settings. Templates can also include text that is repeated every time the template is used, for example, the name and the masthead of a publication. A **masthead** is a portion of text appearing in every issue of a publication, which provides the name of the publication and other information, such as address, personnel, and so on. Mastheads are often used in newsletters, magazines, and newspapers.

Do not confuse a template document with the template disk that comes with this text–workbook. The templates used in creating documents are simply Publish It! files that include a layout that can be used as a foundation for other documents. The template disk is a data disk that consists of text and graphics files to use with the exercises in this text–workbook.

USING TEMPLATES

Using a template is just like creating your own document, except that the page layout has already been specified. To use a template, open the template document and add the desired text and graphics. When you are ready to save the new document, use the Save as command so that you do not save over the template document. Be careful not to save the newly created document by the same name as the template document. In the activity that follows, you will use a template to create an insert for a cassette tape case.

ACTIVITY 8-1 • Using Templates

In this activity you will use a template to create a paper label insert for a cassette tape case.

1. Open *ACT8-1.DTP* from your template disk. A frame with two horizontal lines appears.

2. Create a frame approximately 1 by 1 inch in the upper left corner of the frame, as shown in Figure 8-1. Hint: Use the rulers.

3. Import *NOTES.PCX* into the frame. Choose **PC PaintBrush**.

4. Crop the graphic to remove the white space.

5. Position the text cursor to the right of the frame containing the graphic.

6. Choose a large font size. Space over toward the right margin and key **LHS**, as shown in Figure 8-2.

7. Choose a smaller font size and key **Lincoln High Band** below the graphic, as shown in Figure 8-2. Press **Enter**. Key **Spring Concert**.

8. Create a frame between the two horizontal lines.

9. Choose a small font. Key **Lincoln High Band Spring Concert** in the frame.

10. Save the document as *CAS-SETTE.DTP* on your data disk.

11. Print the document.

12. Cut the label along the outside edges. Fold the label along the two horizontal lines. Place it into a cassette case.

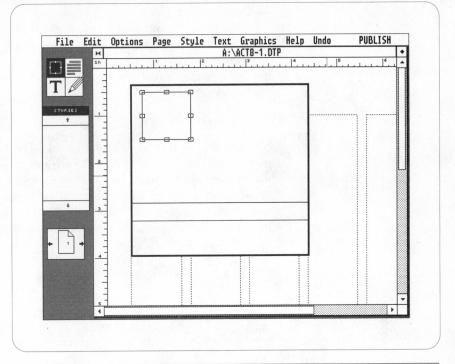

Figure 8-1
Templates provide a page layout on which to add text and graphics.

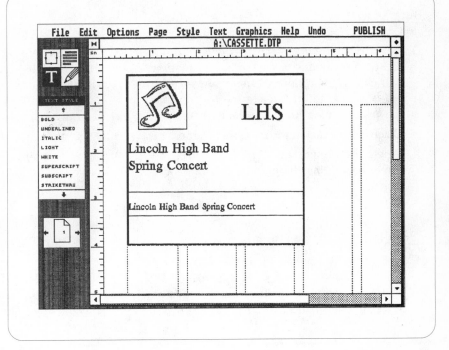

Figure 8-2
Font styles and sizes different from those shown here may cause your document to look slightly different.

CREATING TEMPLATES

Publish It! does not provide special features for creating and using templates. However, templates can be used with any desktop publishing program because a template is simply a document with a layout that can be used to create other documents. When creating a template, you should consider the guidelines for designing a layout discussed in Chapter 6. There are two ways to create a template. Templates can be made from existing documents or you can create a new template.

There are advantages to each method of creating templates. Creating a template from an existing document gives you the option of including text or graphics as part of the template. Creating new templates means you do not have to delete text and graphics that you do not want to appear in future documents.

Creating a Template from an Existing Document

You will find from time to time that you have created a desktop publishing masterpiece, and you will want to preserve the format of the document for use in future documents. To create a template from an existing document, delete all text and graphics that will be replaced in future editions. Then, save what is left as a *.DTP* file. When saving documents to be used as templates, be sure to assign the template document a name that's different from the existing document's name.

ACTIVITY 8-2 • Creating a Template from an Existing Document

In this activity you will open a document that already exists and create a template from the document. You will include part of the text in the template.

1. Open *ACT8-2.DTP* from your template disk.
2. Delete **September 27** and the issue number **(218)** from the document—this information will change each time the template is used. Use the Text tool to delete the text so that the frame remains in the document.
3. Delete all the text in the two large frames.
4. Delete the camera graphic. Hint: Select the frame containing the graphic and press the Delete key.
5. Delete the text in the scroll at the bottom of the page.
6. Choose **Save as** from the **File** menu.
7. Save this document as LHSTIMES.DTP on your data disk. This document can now be used as a template for upcoming issues of "Lincoln High Times."

Creating a New Template

There may be times when it is more appropriate to create a template from scratch. Suppose that you are chosen to create a school handbook to be given to each student and that you are to be responsible for keeping it updated. This is a perfect situation for creating a template.

A common handbook size is 5½ by 8½ inches. A handbook with these dimensions consists of landscape-oriented 8½-by-11-inch pages folded in half and stapled along the fold to form the pages of the handbook. The pages of a handbook are printed on both sides of the paper. To number the pages in the correct sequence, it is helpful to create a dummy copy. Several landscape-oriented pages can be folded in half and the page numbers penciled in on each half. When the pages are separated, you can see how scrambled the page number sequence seems, but once the document is printed double sided, the order makes sense.

Creating a template from scratch is the same as creating a document for regular use, except that you save only the information that will be used regularly. For example, in creating a school handbook, you would include the title of the handbook and the headings, such as Table of Contents, but the date and contents would not be included in the template because they change from year to year. Templates created from scratch, like templates created from existing documents, are saved as *.DTP* files.

ACTIVITY 8-3 • Creating a Template from Scratch

In this activity you will create a template for an eight-page handbook.

1. Open a new untitled document. Change the Orientation to **Landscape**.

2. Choose **Set column guides** from the **Options** menu. Change the following settings:
   Number of columns   2
   Top margin   1.00
   Bottom margin   1.00
   Left margin   1.00
   Right margin   1.00
   Gap between columns   2.00

3. Create a frame surrounding the second column. Key **COVER** in a large font size in the frame. Remember that the page will be folded in half so that each half forms a page. The second half of the page, where column two is located, will be the cover of the handbook.

4. Add one page to the document.

5. Create a frame surrounding the second column. Key **Table of Contents** in a medium font size in the frame, as shown in Figure 8-3.

6. Create a small frame immediately below the first column, as shown in Figure 8-3. Key **8** in the center of the frame. Hint: Create a new paragraph style with centered as the justification.

7. Add a third page to the document.

8. Create a small frame immediately below each of the columns, as you did in step 6.

1. Open a new, untitled document. Change the Orientation to **Landscape**.

2. Choose **Set column guides** from the **Options** menu. Change the following settings.
   Number of columns   2
   Top margin   1.00
   Bottom margin   1.00
   Left margin   1.00
   Right margin   1.00
   Gap between columns   2.00

3. Create a frame surrounding the second column. Key **COVER** in a large font size in the frame. Remember that the page will be folded in half so that each half forms a page. The second half of the page, where column two is located, will be the cover of the handbook.

4. Add one page to the document.

5. Create a frame surrounding the second column. Key **Table of Contents** in a medium font size in the frame, as shown in Figure 8-3.

6. Create a small frame immediately below the first column, as shown in Figure 8-3. Key **8** in the center of the frame. Hint: Create a new paragraph style with centered as the justification.

7. Add a third page to the document.

8. Create a small frame immediately below each of the columns, as you did in step 6.

Continued

Key **2** in the center of the first frame. Key **7** in the center of the second frame. This page will be printed on the opposite side of the Table of Contents page.

9. Add a fourth page to the document.

10. Create a frame immediately below each of the columns. Key **6** in the center of the first frame. Key **3** in the center of the second frame.

11. Add a fifth page to the document.

12. Create a frame immediately below each of the columns. Key **4** in the center of the first frame. Key **5** in the center of the second frame. This page will be printed on the back of page numbers 6 and 3.

13. Save the document as *HANDBOOK.DTP* on your data disk.

14. Print the document. Fold the pages in half and place the page numbers in order. Remember that pages will be printed double sided. If it helps you to visualize the finished design, tape the pages that should be printed double sided back-to-back. See Figure 8-4. Once you have folded and creased the pages, open the pages and lay them flat with the fold pointed down. Staple the document in the crease three times with approximately 2 inches between each staple. (You will need a special stapler to reach the crease.) The staples should be parallel to the crease.

Key **2** in the center of the first frame. Key **7** in the center of the second frame. This page will be printed on the opposite side of the Table of Contents page.

9. Add a fourth page to the document.

10. Create a small frame immediately below each of the columns. Key **6** in the center of the first frame. Key **3** in the center of the second frame.

11. Add a fifth page to the document.

12. Create a small frame immediately below each of the columns. Key **4** in the center of the first frame. Key **5** in the center of the second frame. This page will be printed on the back of page numbers 6 and 3.

13. Save the document as *HANDBOOK.DTP* on your data disk.

14. Print the document. Fold the pages in half and place the page numbers in order. Remember that pages will be printed double sided. If it helps you to visualize the finished design, tape the pages that should be printed double sided back-to-back. See Figure 8-4. Once you have folded and creased the pages, open the pages and lay them flat with the fold pointed down. Staple the document in the crease three times with approximately 2 inches between each staple. (You will need a special stapler to reach the crease.) The staples should be parallel to the crease.

Figure 8-3

In a handbook the last page of the document appears on the same page as one of the first pages of the document.

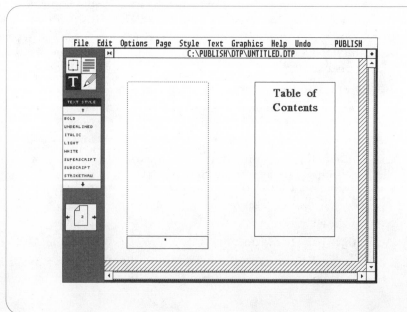

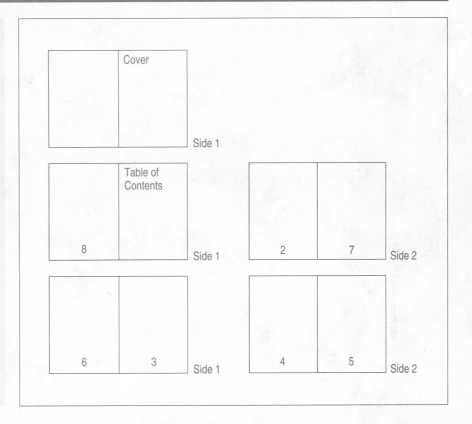

Figure 8-4
Double-sided pages and
the number of pages used
both make numbering
pages for a handbook
confusing.

SUMMARY

Templates are predesigned layouts that can be used with documents produced on a regular basis. A template eliminates the effort of redesigning a document every time a new version of a routine document is needed. Once a template is made, text and graphics are inserted into designated places in the template.

You can create your own templates by removing text and graphics from an existing document or by creating a new template. Each method has its advantages, but no matter which method you use, templates will save you time and improve the quality of your documents.

CHAPTER

Review

Name _____ Date _____

TRUE OR FALSE

The following statements are either true or false. Circle T or F to indicate your answer.

1. A template is a predesigned layout for a document. (Obj. 1)   1. T   F

2. A template document is the same as a template disk. (Obj. 1)   2. T   F

3. A template never includes graphics of any kind. (Obj. 1)   3. T   F

4. A template would be convenient for a newsletter. (Obj. 1)   4. T   F

5. All desktop publishing programs provide special features for creating and using templates. (Obj. 2)   5. T   F

6. Templates can be used with any desktop publishing program. (Obj. 2)   6. T   F

7. Guidelines for designing a layout do not apply to templates. (Obj. 2.)   7. T   F

8. When a template is created from an existing document, the template should be saved with a different name. (Obj. 2)   8. T   F

9. Creating a template from scratch is just the same as creating a document for regular use. (Obj. 2)   9. T   F

10. When you create a template, you save only the text that will be different with each use of the template. (Obj. 2)   10. T   F

COMPLETION

Write your answers in the space provided.

11. What does a finished document include that may not be found in a template? (Obj. 1)

_____

_____

12. What is a masthead? (Obj. 1)

_____

_____

13. What is the difference between using a template and creating your own document? (Obj. 1)

_____

_____

14. Think of two documents, in addition to the ones discussed in this chapter, that would be convenient to create from templates. (Obj. 1)

_____

15. How would you use a template that has already been created? (Obj. 2)

_____

_____

_____

16. In what two ways can you create a template? (Obj. 2)

_____

_____

17. How would you create a template from an existing document? (Obj. 2)

_____

_____

18. What is an advantage of creating a template from an existing document? (Obj. 2)

_____

_____

19. What is an advantage of creating a new template? (Obj. 2)

_____

_____

20. What are two advantages of using templates? (Obj. 2)

_____

_____

APPLICATION 8-1

In this application you will use a template to make a new disk jacket for a 5¼-inch disk.

1. Open *APP8-1.DTP* from your template disk.

2. Position the text cursor in the upper left corner of the large frame between the small frames.

3. Press Enter 3 times.

4. Key WORK IN PROGRESS DATA DISK.

5. Select the Paragraph tool from the tool box. Select the text in the frame.

6. Change the paragraph style to Headline.

7. Create a small graphics frame below the text.

8. Import *DISK.PCX* into the frame. Choose PC PaintBrush. Crop the graphic.

9. Save this document as *JACKET.DTP*.

10. Print the document.

11. Cut the document jacket along the outside edges.

12. Fold the jacket along the horizontal line beneath the graphic so the text and graphic are showing. The bottom part of the page now becomes the back of the disk jacket. The two smaller frames become flaps.

13. Fold each flap so they overlap the back of the disk jacket. Tape each flap to the back of the disk jacket. Place a 5¼-inch disk into the jacket.

APPLICATION 8-2

In this application you will create a template from an existing document.

1. Open *APP8-2.DTP* from your template disk. A list of things to do appears.

2. Delete all the text except for the headings.

3. Save the document as *TODO.DTP* on your data disk.

4. Print the document.

APPLICATION 8-3

In this application you will create a template for a greeting card from scratch.

1. Choose New from the File menu. Choose No when asked if you want to load a style sheet.

2. Change the Orientation to Landscape.

3. Create a frame surrounding the last three column guides. This will be the front of the greeting card.

4. Add one page to your document.

5. Create a frame surrounding the first three column guides. Create another frame surrounding the last three column guides. This will be the inside of the greeting card.

6. Save the document as *CARD.DTP* on your template disk.

APPLICATION 8-4

Using the template you created in Activity 8-2, design and produce a four-page newsletter. Like Application 7-4, share stories and articles with other members of your class.

CHAPTER

Desktop Publishing Center Simulation

LEARNING OBJECTIVES

In this desktop publishing center simulation, you will create publications necessary to operate the desktop publishing center.

A DESKTOP PUBLISHING CENTER SIMULATION

The previous chapters in this book have acquainted you with Publish It! In this chapter you will apply what you have learned to produce documents for the new Desktop Publishing Center (DtPC) to be started at your school. The DtPC is a business operated by students from the Advanced Desktop Publishing course. The business opens at the beginning of the last class hour, 2:50 p.m., and remains open until 5 p.m. Students work three days a week. The grade is based on the quality of the documents produced. One copy of each document produced is given to the teacher to be graded.

DtPC DOCUMENTS

As a DtPC worker, you will create business forms and advertisements to launch the new center. You will design a logo, a letterhead, posters, a business card, a weekly work schedule, a job order form, and a brochure.

Logo, Job 1

A logo for the DtPC is needed to place on many of the DtPC documents.

Job 1A. Copy the logo in Figure 9-1. Save the logo as *DTPCLOGO.DTP* on your data disk.

Job 1B. Design an original logo for the DtPC. Include your school's name as part of the logo. Save the logo as *NEWLOGO.DTP* on your data disk.

Figure 9-1
A logo can combine text and graphics to represent a business name.

———————— Desktop

———————————— Publishing

———————————————— Center

Letterhead, Job 2

The DtPC needs a letterhead. A letterhead combines an organization's logo, name, address, and telephone number to be used as stationery for business communication.

Job 2A.   Copy the letterhead in Figure 9-2. Begin the document using the logo from Job 1A. Save the letterhead as *LTRHD.DTP*. Print the letterhead.

Job 2B.   Create an original letterhead for the DtPC. Use the logo from Job 1B as a starting point. Save the letterhead as *NEWLTRHD.DTP*. Print the letterhead.

Figure 9-2
A letterhead includes an organization's logo, name, address, and phone number on a page to be used as stationery.

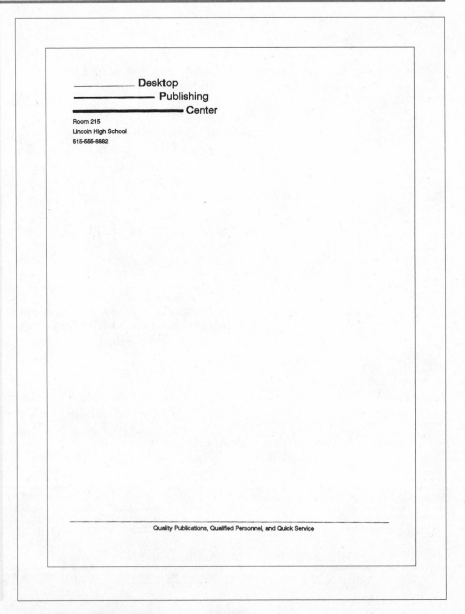

Advertisement Poster, Job 3

Posters should be designed to be read at a minimum distance of ten feet. A poster is needed to advertise the DtPC's grand opening to the school and will be displayed in the cafeteria, in the halls, and in classrooms.

Job 3A. Copy the poster in Figure 9-3. Save the poster as *ADPOSTR.DTP*. Print the poster.

Job 3B. Create an original poster for the DtPC. Include the following information:

Who: Desktop Publishing Center
What: Grand opening
When: Monday, September 12, at 2:50 p.m.
Where: A room number in your school
Why: The production of publications for students, teachers, staff
Save the poster as *NEWPOSTR.DTP*. Print the poster.

Figure 9-3
When designing a poster, include all the important information that will convey your message.

_____ **Desktop**
_____ **Publishing**
_____ **Center**

GRAND OPENING

Monday
September 12
2:50 p.m. - 5:00 p.m.

Room 215

Brochures
Business Cards
Invitations
Letterheads
Newsletters
Posters
Programs
Tickets...

and other publication needs...

for students, teachers, and staff.

Business Hours Poster, Job 4

The DtPC needs a sign displaying its business hours, which are 2:50 p.m. to 5 p.m, Monday through Friday. The sign will be placed on the door to the DtPC.

Job 4A. Copy the sign in Figure 9-4. Save the sign as *DTPCPOST.DTP*. Print the sign.

Job 4B. Design an original sign for the DtPC. Use landscape orientation to utilize the paper fully. Save the sign as *NEWPOST2.DTP*. Print the sign.

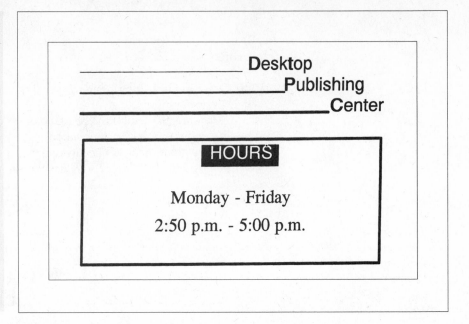

Figure 9-4
The DtPC needs a poster indicating its business hours.

Business Card, Job 5

Business cards are used to promote a business and the people who work in business. A standard business card is 2 inches high and 3½ inches wide (see Figure 9-5) and usually includes the following information:

> The business name and logo
> Employee's name
> Address of the business
> Phone number of the business

Job 5A. Copy the model in Figure 9-5. Save the business card as *BCARD.DTP*. Print the card.

Job 5B. Design an original business card for the DtPC. Save the business card as *NEWBCARD*.DTP. Print the card.

Figure 9-5
A business card should include the logo, name, address, and phone number of a business and the name of the business representative who uses the card.

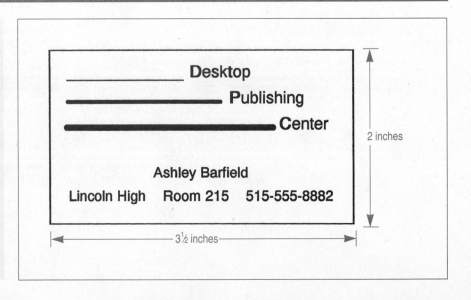

Weekly Work Schedule, Job 6

The desktop publishing teacher schedules DtPC students to work three days a week. Create a chart so the teacher can schedule work time for students. The schedule will be posted in the DtPC.

Job 6A. Copy the schedule in Figure 9-6. Save the work schedule as *SCHED.DTP*. Print the schedule.

Job 6B. Use the schedule in Figure 9-6 as a model, but include a space after each student's name for a signature. The student's signature will indicate agreement with that week's schedule. Save the work schedule as *NEWSCHED.DTP*. Print the schedule.

Figure 9-6
The weekly work schedule is a record of the days each student will work at the DtPC.

WEEKLY WORK SCHEDULE
Week of _____

Student	M	T	W	Th	F

Job Order Forms, Job 7

Business forms are necessary for recording and processing information in business. When designing forms, remember that form captions, which indicate the information needed on the form, should be placed in the order in which they are to be processed.

Job 7A.   Copy the form in Figure 9-7. Hint: Use the underscore symbol on your keyboard for the short blanks, but draw lines for the large blanks. Save the order form as *ORDER.DTP*. Print the form.

Job 7B.   Revise the form in Figure 9-7 to include a tear-off receipt for customers to present when they pick up the finished document. Include the following captions:

Date
Receipt No. (to match the Job No.)
Amount
Payment: Charge, Cash
Signature of DtPC Worker as Proof of Payment

Save the order form as *NEWORDER.DTP*. Print the form.

Figure 9-7
Arrange captions in the order in which they are to be processed.

JOB ORDER   Job No. _____

Desktop Publishing Center

Customer _____   Phone _____
              Last   First

Organization _____   Room No. _____

Publication Description _____
              _____

Sample Attached: Yes _____ No _____

Special Instructions   _____
              _____
              _____
              _____
              _____
              _____
              _____
              _____
              _____
              _____
              _____
              _____

Production Schedule:
   Order Taken By _____ Date _____
   Date Promised _____ Date Completed _____
   Produced By _____
   Cost Calculated By _____

Delivered To _____ Date _____
Payment: Charge _____ Cash _____

Brochure, Job 8

The layout of a brochure consists of two landscape-oriented pages printed double sided. The layout consists of three or four columns on each page, which fit inside panels. Brochures must be designed with care so that when the two pages are combined into one double-sided document, the text in the panels is centered attractively and reads in a logical order. Creating a dummy in pencil, as shown in Figure 9-8, will help you lay out the brochure.

Job 8A. Copy the three-panel brochure in Figure 9-9.

1. Open *DTPCLOGO.DTP*.
2. Choose **Select all** from the **Edit** menu. This selects all frames used to create the logo.
3. Choose **Cut** from the **Edit** menu.
4. Open a new untitled document. Change the Orientation to **Landscape**.
5. Paste the logo in the new document.
6. Choose **Size to fit** from the **Page** menu.
7. Duplicate side one of the brochure, as shown in Figure 9-9.
8. Add one page to the document.
9. Duplicate side two of the brochure, as shown in Figure 9-9.
10. Save the document as *BROCH.DTP* on your data disk.
11. Print the document.

Job 8B. Design a four-panel brochure to advertise the DtPC. Save the brochure as *NEWBROCH.DTP*. Print the brochure.

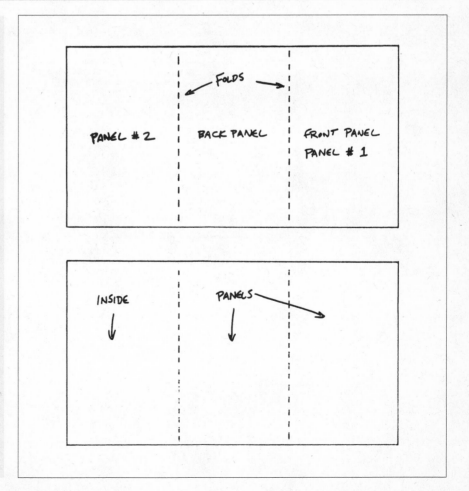

Figure 9-8
Sketching the layout of a brochure in pencil is helpful.

Figure 9-9
A brochure consists of two landscape-oriented pages with three columns on each page. Once a brochure is designed, a commercial printer can print the brochure on one double-sided page.

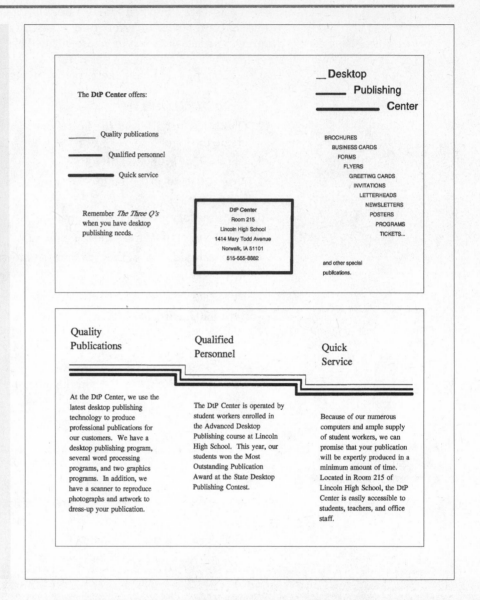

You have created the necessary forms to operate the DtPC. Your posters and the circulation of the business cards and brochures inform the students, teachers, and staff about the upcoming DtPC grand opening. Soon you will be overwhelmed with customers, so be prepared!

CHAPTER

Desktop Publishing Center Applications

LEARNING OBJECTIVE

In this chapter you will create documents for DtPC customers.

CUSTOMER DOCUMENTS

The posters advert sing the DtPC grand opening captivated students, teachers, and office staff. Eager to use the DtPC, customers arrive with publication needs. Students, teachers, student organizations, and the administrative staff provide work to keep the DtPC staff's desktop publishing skills sharpened. The following jobs are document orders for which you are responsible.

Ticket to a Musical, Job 1

Joe Schuman, who is a tenor in the student choir, is in charge of publicity for this year's musical, "The Harmonious Jangle of Sound." Performances will be in one month, so tickets must go on sale soon. Pondering his situation at lunch, Joe noticed the DtPC grand opening poster on the cafeteria wall. Relieved that he could get the DtPC workers to design a ticket, Joe was the first customer to appear at the DtPC counter.

Follow the job order form on page 190. You will design a ticket using *MUSICAL.PCX* from your template disk as part of the design. Save the document as *TICKET.DTP*. Print the ticket.

Senior Banquet Poster, Job 2

The senior banquet committee is already planning for the banquet scheduled in March. Kim Montoya, chairperson of the committee, likes to get a quick start on projects. Having recently learned of the DtPC, Kim became enthusiastic about using the center for the banquet publications. First, she decides, the DtPC can design a poster to advertise the banquet.

You will design a poster to promote the senior banquet. Follow the job order form on page 192. Save the document as *BQTPOSTR.DTP*. Print the poster.

Program to a Musical, Job 3

Joe Schuman arrives at the DtPC counter a second time. He was so pleased with the ticket design that he wants the DtPC to create a program for the musical. Joe sketches a sample program for you to use as an example.

Design a program for the musical, following the job order form on page 193 and the program sample that follows it. Substitute your school's name in place of Lincoln High School. Save the document as *PROGRAM.DTP*. Print the program.

Invitations to Open House, Job 4

Mrs. Washington, the consumer math teacher, is in charge of organizing the school's open house. She would like to send invitations in greeting card format to parents this year instead of the usual letter. The DtPC can prepare invitations economically.

Follow the job order form on page 196 to design the open house invitation. Use the greeting card template you created in Chapter 8. Save the document as *INVITE.DTP*. Print the invitation.

School Stationery, Job 5

The principal decides it is time to update the school's letterhead and sends her secretary, Ms. Norman, to the DtPC. Ms. Norman brings the old school stationery and requests a modern version. Along with the stationery, she includes a sketch of the desired letterhead.

Design an updated letterhead, following the job order form on page 197 and the attached samples. Replace Lincoln High School, the address, and date of establishment with the name of your school, your school's address, and your school's date of establishment. If you have access to a scanner, scan your school logo for the letterhead. Save the document as *LETTERHD.DTP*. Print the letterhead.

Perfect Attendance Certificate, Job 6

Mrs. Tims, the attendance office supervisor, would like to provide teachers with certificates of recognition to acknowledge students with perfect attendance.

Design a certificate, following the job order form on page 200. Think of an innovative way to draw a border. Key the text in an appropriate font. Save the document as *CERTIF.DTP*. Print the certificate.

Phone Message Notepad, Job 7

The principal's secretary was very impressed with the letterhead you designed. Now she wants to update her phone message notepad. She submits the old version with some ideas sketched for a new variation.

Design a notepad following the job order form on page 201 and the attached samples. Save the document as *NOTEPAD.DTP*. Print the notepad.

Personal Information Form, Job 8

Many teachers like to get acquainted with their students by obtaining personal information, such as their future goals and hobbies. Mr. Reddell, the sophomore English teacher, decides that a standardized form for this information would be helpful for him and other teachers.

Create the personal information form, following the job order form on page 204. Save the document as *PERSONAL.DTP*. Print the form.

DESKTOP PUBLISHING IN YOUR FUTURE

The simulation is over and you are now an experienced desktop publisher. You can design documents like newsletters, brochures, programs, handbooks, business forms, and flyers to communicate a message effectively. These new skills increase your ability to find jobs in the future. Organizations that use desktop publishing are diverse. They include government agencies, churches, newspapers, advertising agencies, colleges, volunteer services, publishing companies, and hospitals. Both small and large businesses use desktop publishing.

So, whether you become a federal employee, a church secretary, a newspaper layout artist, an advertising executive, a college recruiter, a volunteer service director, a book publisher, or publicity person for a hospital, your desktop publishing skills will be an asset.

JOB ORDER

Job No. _____1_____

Desktop Publishing Center

Customer __SCHUMAN__ , __JOE__   Phone _555 - 6828 (HOME)_

Last   First

Organization _MUSIC DEPARTMENT_   Room No. _113_

Publication Description __TICKET TO A MUSICAL__

Sample Attached: Yes _____ No __✓__

Special Instructions __2½ x 4½ INCHES__
__INCLUDE FOLLOWING INFORMATION:__
__WHAT- THE HARMONIOUS JANGLE OF SOUND__
__WHERE- SCHOOL AUDITORIUM__
__WHEN - OCTOBER 11, 12__
__TIME- 8:15 P.M.__
__PRICE- $2 A TICKET__

Production Schedule:

Order Taken By __MARY TYLER__   Date __9/12__

Date Promised __9/19__   Date Completed _____

Produced By __YOU__

Cost Calculated By _____

Delivered To _____   Date _____

Payment: Charge _____   Cash _____

JOB ORDER

Job No. __2__

Desktop Publishing Center

Customer __MONTOYA, KIM__   Phone __555-7169 (HOME)__
Last   First

Organization __SENIOR BANQUET COMMITTEE__   Room No. __—__

Publication Description __POSTER FOR THE SENIOR BANQUET__

Sample Attached: Yes _____   No __✓__

Special Instructions
__8½ X 11 INCHES__
__INCLUDE FOLLOWING INFORMATION:__
__WHAT - SENIOR HIGH BANQUET__
__WHERE - ELEGANT COW STEAKHOUSE__
__WHEN - MARCH 19__
__TIME - 6:30 P.M.__
__PRICE - $9 A TICKET__
__OTHER - TICKETS GO ON SALE JANUARY 10.__

Production Schedule:
Order Taken By __SAMMY KING__   Date __9/13__
Date Promised __9/20__   Date Completed _____
Produced By __YOU__
Cost Calculated By _____

Delivered To _____   Date _____
Payment: Charge _____   Cash _____

JOB ORDER   Job No. __3__

Desktop Publishing Center

Customer ___Schuman___, ___Joe___   Phone __555-6828 (Home)__
           Last   First

Organization __Music Department__   Room No. __113__

Publication Description __Program to a Musical__

Sample Attached: Yes __✓__ No _____

Special Instructions ___See Sample, Include Following Information___
Cover - The Choir and Drama Students Present Mark
White's The Harmonious Jangle of Sound
Page Two - The Harmonious Jangle of Sound, Friday, October 11,
Saturday, October 12, 19--, 8:15 p.m., Lincoln High School;
Cast - Whole Note... Leigh Welch, Half Note... Bruce Gott,
Eighth Note:... Chris Sivo, Kristen Lynam, Sharp... Tracy Phipps
Page Three - Director - Billy Toman, Stage Crew-Lights... Roy
Drexer, Props... Missy Harmon, Makeup... Tommy Eppler.
Page Four - Program Designed and Created by Students
in the Advanced Desktop Publishing Class, Desktop Publishing
Center, Room 215, 515-555-3233

Production Schedule:
Order Taken By __Toby Tomlinson__ Date __9/19__
Date Promised __9/26__ Date Completed _____
Produced By __You__
Cost Calculated By _____

Delivered To _____ Date _____
Payment: Charge _____ Cash _____

THE HARMONIOUS JANGLE
OF SOUND
FRIDAY, OCTOBER 11,
SATURDAY, OCTOBER 12
19 - -
8:15 P.M.

CAST
←

DIRECTOR

STAGE CREW
←

PROGRAM DESIGNED
AND CREATED BY STUDENTS
IN THE ADVANCED DESKTOP
PUBLISHING CLASS

Desktop Publishing Center
Room 215
515 555-3233

The Choir and Drama
Students present
Mark White's

The
Harmonious
Jangle
of
Sound

JOB ORDER   Job No. _4_

Desktop Publishing Center

Customer _WASHINGTON , IRMA_   Phone _551-2000 (Home)_
           Last   First

Organization _OPEN HOUSE PROGRAM COMMITTEE_ Room No. _105_

Publication Description _OPEN HOUSE INVITATION_

Sample Attached: Yes _____   No _✓_

Special Instructions
INCLUDE FOLLOWING INFORMATION:
COVER - EXPLORE YOUR CHILDREN'S TERRITORY...
INSIDE - FOLLOW THEIR DAILY TRAIL FROM CLASS
TO CLASS
ATTEND OPEN HOUSE — MEET YOUR CHILDREN'S
TEACHERS AND SIT IN YOUR CHILDREN'S DESKS.
WHEN - NOVEMBER 11
TIME - 7 P.M.
MEET IN THE CAFETERIA TO RECEIVE YOUR
"SCHOOL SCHEDULE" FOR THE EVENING
"CLASS" BEGINS AT 7:30! DON'T BE TARDY!

Production Schedule:
Order Taken By _DAWN STEWART_ Date _9/16_
Date Promised _10/1_ Date Completed _____
Produced By _YOU_
Cost Calculated By _____

Delivered To _____ Date _____
Payment: Charge _____ Cash _____

JOB ORDER

Job No. *5*

Desktop Publishing Center

Customer ___NORMAN , JOAN___   Phone _555 - 7623 (OFFICE)_
           Last   First

Organization ___PRINCIPAL'S OFFICE___   Room No. _101_

Publication Description ___UPDATED LETTERHEAD___

Sample Attached: Yes ___✓___   No _____

Special Instructions ___SEE SAMPLE___

Production Schedule:
Order Taken By ___NORA CORTEZ___   Date ___9/25___
Date Promised ___10/2___   Date Completed _____
Produced By ___YOU___
Cost Calculated By _____

Delivered To _____   Date _____
Payment: Charge _____   Cash _____

Lincoln High School

1414 Mary Todd Avenue   Norwalk, IA 51101   515-555-3335

Established in 1921

LINCOLN
HIGH
SCHOOL

1414 Mary Todd Ave.

Norwalk, IA 51101

515-555-3335

JOB ORDER   Job No. _6_

Desktop Publishing Center

Customer ___TIMS___ , ___NORMA___   Phone _555-7621 (OFFICE)_
       Last   First

Organization ___ATTENDANCE OFFICE___   Room No. _102_

Publication Description _CERTIFICATE OF RECOGNITION FOR_
PERFECT ATTENDANCE

Sample Attached: Yes _____ No _✓_

Special Instructions
    INCLUDE FOLLOWING:
    CERTIFICATE OF RECOGNITION
        PRESENTED TO
        (BLANK LINE)
        FOR
    PERFECT ATTENDANCE
    FROM (BLANK LINE) TO (BLANK LINE)
  (BLANK LINE)   _(BLANK LINE)_
    TEACHER   _DATE_
    (BLANK LINE)
    SCHOOL

Production Schedule:
Order Taken By _BILLY RHINEHART_ Date _9/26_
Date Promised _10/3_ Date Completed _____
Produced By _YOU_
Cost Calculated By _____

Delivered To _____ Date _____
Payment: Charge _____ Cash _____

JOB ORDER   Job No. __7__

Desktop Publishing Center

Customer ____NORMAN____ , ____JOAN____   Phone __555-7623 (OFFICE)__
                Last   First

Organization __PRINCIPAL'S   OFFICE__   Room No. __101__

Publication Description ___PHONE MESSAGE NOTEPAD___

Sample Attached: Yes ___✓___ No _____

Special Instructions ___4 x 5 INCHES , SEE SAMPLE___

_____
_____
_____
_____
_____
_____
_____
_____
_____
_____
_____
_____

Production Schedule:

Order Taken By __YOU__   Date __10/5__
Date Promised __10/12__   Date Completed _____
Produced By __YOU__
Cost Calculated By _____

Delivered To _____   Date _____
Payment: Charge _____   Cash _____

PHONE MESSAGES

For

_____

From

_____

Phone No.

_____

Message

_____

_____

_____

_____

Operator

_____

PHONE MESSAGE

For _____

Date _____   Time _____

Caller _____

From _____

Phone No. _____

Area Code Number Extension

☐ Telephoned   ☐ URGENT

☐ Please Call   ☐ Came To See You

☐ Will Call Back   ☐ Wants To See You

☐ Returned Your Call

Message _____

_____

_____

_____

_____ Initials _____

JOB ORDER   Job No. _8_

Desktop Publishing Center

Customer ___REDDELL___ , ___HARLAN___   Phone _555-9876 (HOME)_
           Last   First

Organization _SOPHOMORE ENGLISH TEACHER_   Room No. _241_

Publication Description _PERSONAL INFORMATION FORM FOR STUDENTS_

Sample Attached: Yes _____ No __✓__

Special Instructions _TITLE — PERSONAL INFORMATION FORM_
INCLUDE FOLLOWING CAPTIONS (LEAVE ENOUGH
SPACE AFTER EACH CAPTION FOR STUDENT'S ANSWER):
NAME; COURSE; HOUR; CLASS (CIRCLE ONE):
FRESHMAN, SOPHOMORE, JUNIOR, SENIOR;
SHORT TERM GOALS; LONG TERM GOALS;
CAREER PLANS; FAVORITE SUBJECT;
SCHOOL ACTIVITIES AND/OR HONORS; FAVORITE
BOOK; HOBBIES.

Production Schedule:

Order Taken By ___TAMMY ROBINSON___ Date __9/24__

Date Promised __10/10__   Date Completed _____

Produced By __YOU__

Cost Calculated By _____

Delivered To _____   Date _____

Payment: Charge _____   Cash _____

APPENDIX A

Quick Keys

Quick keys are shortcuts to menu commands and other functions. For your convenience, this appendix summarizes the quick keys first alphabetically, then by function.

GROUPED ALPHABETICALLY

Keystroke	Action
Alt + A	Repeat last Find
Alt + B	Bold text
Alt + C	Copy frame, text, or graphic
Alt + E	Show/hide column guides
Alt + F	Find a string of text
Alt + G	Go to page
Alt + H	Show/hide tool box
Alt + I	Italic text
Alt + J	Show/hide rulers
Alt + K	Kern two characters by 0.5 point
Alt + L	Light text
Alt + M	Switch between frame/text/paragraph/graphics modes.
Alt + N	Normal text
Alt + O	Open document
Alt + P	Print a document
Alt + Q	Quit the program
Alt + R	Find and replace text
Alt + S	Save file
Alt + T	Open font/size dialog box
Alt + U	Underlined text
Alt + V	Paste frame, text, or graphic
Alt + W	White text
Alt + X	Cut out a frame, text, or graphic
Alt + Z	Hide all pictures
Alt + 0 (zero)	Size to fit
Alt + 1	Half size
Alt + 2	¾ size
Alt + 3	Actual size
Alt + 4	Double size
Alt + 5	Two pages
Alt + 6	Bring frame/graphic to front
Alt + 7	Send frame/graphic to back

Alt + +	Superscript
Alt + −	Subscript
Home	Move insertion point to beginning of current line
End	Move insertion point to end of current line
Shift + Home	Highlight a range of text from the insertion point to the beginning of the current line
Shift + End	Highlight a range of text from the insertion point to the end of the current line
Page Up	Move to the previous page
Page Down	Move to the next page
Ctrl + Page Up	Move to first page
Ctrl + Page Down	Move to last page
Ctrl + -	Soft hyphen
Ctrl + Space Bar	Fixed space

SHORTCUTS FOR TEXT

Alt + A	Repeat last Find
Alt + B	Bold text
Alt + C	Copy text
Alt + F	Find a string of text
Alt + I	Italic text
Alt + K	Kern two characters by 0.5 point
Alt + L	Light text
Alt + M	Switch between frame/text/paragraph/graphics modes
Alt + N	Normal text
Alt + R	Find and replace text
Alt + T	Open font/size dialog box
Alt + U	Underlined text
Alt + V	Paste text
Alt + W	White text
Alt + X	Cut out text
Alt + +	Superscript
Alt + −	Subscript
Home	Move insertion point to beginning of current line
End	Move insertion point to end of current line
Shift + Home	Highlight a range of text from the insertion point to the beginning of the current line
Shift + End	Highlight a range of text from the insertion point to the end of the current line
Ctrl + -	Soft hyphen
Ctrl + Space Bar	Fixed space

SHORTCUTS FOR GRAPHICS

Alt + C	Copy graphic
Alt + M	Switch between frame/text/paragraph/graphics modes
Alt + V	Paste graphic
Alt + X	Cut out graphic
Alt + Z	Hide all pictures
Alt + 6	Bring graphic to front
Alt + 7	Send graphic to back

SHORTCUTS FOR FRAMES

Alt + C	Copy frame
Alt + M	Switch between frame/text/paragraph/graphics modes
Alt + V	Paste frame
Alt + X	Cut out frame
Alt + 6	Bring frame to front
Alt + 7	Send frame to back

MOUSE/KEYBOARD EQUIVALENTS

Home	Same as clicking the mouse button
End	Same as pressing and holding the mouse button
Up Arrow	Moves pointer up one line
Down Arrow	Moves pointer down one line
Right Arrow	Moves pointer right one space
Left Arrow	Moves pointer left one space
Shift + arrow keys	Moves pointer one pixel up, down, right, or left

APPENDIX B

●

Desktop Publishing Technology

THE DESKTOP PUBLISHING SYMPHONY

A desktop publishing system is an extraordinary tool that increases the power of the printed page. To students, it may seem as though desktop publishing has always been a part of the printing process. Actually, desktop publishing technology had its beginnings in the 1980s and is evolving rapidly. In most instances, you can use a desktop publishing system without understanding the underlying technology. In fact, the goal of a desktop publishing system is to free you from technological concerns. However, some knowledge of what happens "behind the scenes" helps you understand the possibilities and the limitations of your system. Inside your computer millions of electrical signals and dozens of devices each have a small part in the production of your documents. Let's look at how these devices work in harmony to create a "desktop publishing symphony."

This appendix is not intended to cover all technological issues related to desktop publishing. Some topics not mentioned here are covered in chapters throughout the book.

BITS, BYTES, AND ASCII—THE SHEET MUSIC

Members of an orchestra follow a special form of communication, known as sheet music. To the untrained eye, the written symbols look like dots, lines, and bars. To the musician, the symbols are special codes that communicate a musical score.

Computers also have a special code by which instructions and data are represented. Because computers are electronic machines, this code is based on electrical signals. Inside a computer, a piece of data is represented by groups of electrical signals. A single signal, called a **bit**, is either on or off. Bits are usually in groups of eight, called a **byte**.

Imagine bits in a computer as lightbulbs. Like a bit, a lightbulb can be either on or off. A group of two lightbulbs can be lit in four combinations (see Figure B-1). If you expand the group to four lightbulbs, sixteen combinations are possible. With eight lightbulbs, there are 256 possible combinations. A byte (eight bits) therefore, has 256 combinations of bits.

Each of the 256 combinations is assigned a meaning. Some represent characters; some represent codes. Not all computers assign the same meaning to each combination. Most personal computers assign meanings based on the American Standard Code for Information Interchange (**ASCII**). Each character keyed represents one byte in the computer. Figure B-2 gives a sample of four ASCII equivalents. All data in a computer are represented in a number system of ones and zeros, called the **binary number system**. Zeros represent the bits that are off. Ones represent the bits that are on.

Figure B-1
The bits in a computer can be thought of as light-bulbs which are either on or off. Two bits can produce four possible combinations.

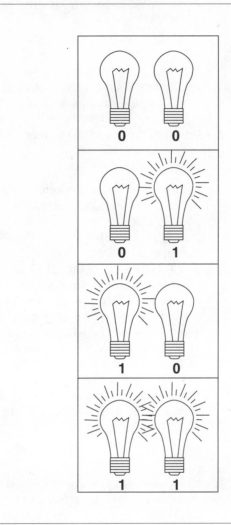

Figure B-2
In the ASCII code, each character is represented by a number that corresponds to a combination of bits in the computer.

Character	Bit Combination	ASCII Code
A	○ ● ○ ○ ○ ○ ○ ● 0 1 0 0 0 0 0 1	65
B	○ ● ○ ○ ○ ○ ● ○ 0 1 0 0 0 0 1 0	66
C	○ ● ○ ○ ○ ○ ● ● 0 1 0 0 0 0 1 1	67
D	○ ● ○ ○ ○ ● ○ ○ 0 1 0 0 0 1 0 0	68

Publish It! accepts text saved in an ASCII-formatted text file. Publish It!, however, imports from word processors better than from ASCII files.

HARDWARE—THE SYMPHONY'S INSTRUMENTS

When you think of an orchestra, you probably think of the musical instruments. In the same way, when you think of a computer system, you probably think of a monitor and keyboard. These physical parts of a computer system are called **hardware**. Hardware also includes the main system unit, the disk drives, and the printer.

Microprocessors

All microcomputers include a **microprocessor**, often called a **central processing unit (CPU)**. A microprocessor processes instructions and moves data from place to place.

Although IBM invented the PC, other companies produced computers that operated like an IBM PC, basing them on the same Intel microprocessor. These copies of the IBM PC became known as **IBM compatible computers** or **clones**. As Intel introduced new microprocessors, IBM and other manufacturers built computers that incorporated improvements in speed and capacity. Some of the microprocessors used to build more powerful IBM compatibles are the 8086, 80286, 80386, and 80486. These last three are often referred to as the 286, 386, and 486. When people say they have a 386, they mean they have a computer with an 80386 microprocessor.

Although the later models of these microprocessors give better desktop publishing performance, Publish It! is made to work with older models as well. A computer with an 8088 microprocessor can take full advantage of Publish It! features.

Memory

Computers store instructions and data in memory. **Random Access Memory (RAM)** is a temporary storage area that is erased when a computer is turned off. While you are working with Publish It!, the program and the document you are working on are stored in RAM. RAM is measured in thousands of bytes, using the abbreviation **K** (from the prefix kilo) to represent approximately 1,000 bytes of memory. For instance, 640K of RAM is approximately 640,000 bytes of memory. Publish It! requires a large amount of RAM to operate. Even with 640K of RAM, you may have to make room for it by removing other items that compete for memory. Publish It! Version 2.0 and later can make use of extended or expanded memory beyond 640K.

Disk Storage

Because RAM is erased when the computer is turned off, a more permanent means of storing programs and data is necessary. Disk storage is the most popular means of long-term storage.

Floppy Disks.   **Floppy disks** are an inexpensive way to store data. They consist of a magnetic disk in a cover. The computer's disk drive spins the disk and reads and writes data through an access slot in the diskette cover. Floppy disks are commonly found in two sizes: 5¼ inch and 3½ inch. The 3½-inch floppy disks are gaining in popularity because of their compact size and high reliability. A 5¼-inch floppy disk typically stores 360K (double density) or 1200K (high density) of data. A 3½-inch floppy disk typically stores 720K (double density) or 1440K (high density).

Hard Disks.   **Hard disks** are metal disks sealed in a case. Like a floppy disk, a hard disk spins while the computer magnetically records data on it. However, the computer is able to store much more on a hard disk than on a floppy disk. Hard disks commonly range in size from 20 megabytes (20 million bytes) to hundreds of megabytes.

Publish It! Version 2.0 and later requires a hard disk. However, earlier versions of Publish It! can run on a computer with two floppy drives and no hard disk.

Monitors

The quality of **monitors**, sometimes called **display screens**, has improved remarkably in recent years. What you see on a computer's screen is actually a product of the monitor and the graphics adapter. A **graphics adapter** is what creates the image the monitor displays. A graphics adapter is usually a card that plugs into an expansion slot in the computer. The most commonly used graphics adapters are known by **acronyms**, such as CGA, EGA, and VGA. Other graphics adapters include Hercules and Super VGA. The VGA and Super VGA provide the highest-quality image of the adapters mentioned.

Because desktop publishing involves the use of graphics, the higher quality graphics adapters and monitors are generally desired. However, Publish It! does not require an expensive monitor and graphics adapter. Publish It! supports Hercules, CGA, EGA, VGA and more.

Ports

A **port** is an **interface** through which external devices such as printers, mice, and modems can be attached to a computer. These devices are sometimes called **peripherals**. Ports are either parallel or serial.

Parallel Ports.   A **parallel port** provides high-speed communication with a peripheral, such as a printer. A parallel port can send and receive data quickly by sending 8 bits (1 byte) simultaneously, in rapid succession over a group of wires.

Serial Ports.   A **serial port** transmits and receives data one bit at a time. Serial transmission is much slower than parallel transmission. Although a serial port is slower, the wires can be run greater distances, giving serial ports an advantage in applications where speed is not critical.

Printers

Printers play a key role in desktop publishing. The quality of your finished document depends on your printer's capabilities. Many people find that cost is the biggest factor in printer selection. Chapter 4 gives a summary of the popular printer technologies and features of each.

The most affordable printers use a dot pattern, called a **bit map**, to print graphics. In a bitmapped image, graphics are drawn using dots, the same way your computer's monitor draws graphics.

More expensive printers use a page description language. A **page description language** is a computer language that a printer understands. The most widely known page description language is **PostScript** by Adobe Systems. A page description language instructs the printer to draw lines, text, patterns, and other images using commands. Because the image is created in the printer using commands from the computer, the image can be created at the highest quality available from the printer. With a page description language, the same publication can be printed at 300 dots per inch (dpi) on a laser printer, or at more than 1000 dpi on a typesetting printer.

Mice

A **mouse** is a small hand-operated tool that allows the user to improve the speed of work with text and graphics. The mouse looks like its name, with a small body and a wire like a tail running to the computer. Most mice have rollers on their undersides that enable the computer to interpret your instructions by what direction you are rolling the mouse. The computer transforms this movement into action on the screen. Mice have at least one button that is clicked to communicate with the computer. IBM compatibles use either a serial mouse or a bus mouse.

A **serial mouse** is attached to the computer through a serial port. Installation involves simply plugging the mouse connector into the serial port connector and installing a **mouse driver** program to make the mouse available to programs like Publish It!

A **bus mouse** functions like a serial mouse. Instead of connecting to a serial port, a bus mouse occupies one of the expansion slots inside the computer.

Publish It! will run without a mouse, but it is highly recommended that you have a mouse.

Scanners

Scanners are becoming increasingly popular and affordable. A **scanner** allows you to bring an image, such as a logo or photograph, into the computer as if it were created on a computer, as shown in Figure B-3. Typical uses for a scanner in desktop publishing include entering logos or photographs.

Figure B-3
A scanner electronically copies an existing image into a computer. This allows the image to be integrated into an existing file.

There are three widely used types of scanners. The first is what is known as a flatbed scanner. With a **flatbed scanner**, you place a photograph or other image that is on paper onto a window much like that on a photocopier. **Hand-held scanners** allow you to roll a hand-held device over the image to be scanned. Some scanners work with video cameras. With **video scanners**, anything that can be captured on videotape can be scanned into the computer.

SOFTWARE—INTRODUCING HARMONY

A concert hall filled with musical instruments does not make an orchestra. An orchestra needs musicians following specific directions from a conductor to give the instruments life and produce the music. A computer also needs an extra ingredient to give it life. That ingredient is known as software. **Software** provides the instructions that orchestrate the desktop publishing symphony. There are two types of software: application and system.

Application Software—The Musicians

Application software is the reason you have a computer. It is the **application software** that directs the parts of the system to perform a useful task, such as desktop publishing. Therefore, Publish It! is application software. It provides the instructions that the computer needs to carry out desktop publishing functions. Other examples of application software include games, word processors, spreadsheets, and database programs.

System Software—The Conductor

System software conducts the basic functions of the computer, such as organizing memory, loading programs, operating the disks and keyboard, and many other tasks. The system software that you are most likely to deal with is the operating system. On an IBM compatible computer, the operating system is commonly called **DOS**. DOS is an acronym for **disk operating system**. If your computer has a hard disk, DOS automatically loads when the computer is turned on. If your computer has floppy drives only, a DOS disk, sometimes called a **boot disk**, must be loaded when the computer is turned on.

CONCLUSION—THE NEXT VERSE

Desktop publishing technology is still advancing by leaps and bounds. The future will bring higher quality, faster speeds, and lower prices. Compact disks for computers will soon be common, providing volumes of graphics ready to import into your documents. Improved scanners will allow the desktop publisher to capture high-quality color images. Scanners will be used to read text off a printed page to minimize the time spent keying. Printers will produce full-color output.

The future is bright for desktop publishing. Having some understanding of what happens behind the scenes will help you take full advantage of the improvements to come in desktop publishing technology.

APPENDIX C

●

Capstone Projects

Think of a capstone as the top stone of a pyramid. It is the final stone, necessary to complete the structure. Capstone projects have a similar purpose. These realistic, useful applications will give you a chance to demonstrate and refine your desktop publishing skills.

PERSONAL PROJECTS

The following projects are publications that apply to your personal life.

Personal Stationery, Project 1

Design a letterhead for personal stationery. On this stationery, you can write letters to family and friends or job application letters to companies. For a professional look, which is desirable for letters of application, you could have a commercial printer print the letterhead on high-quality bond paper. Save as *MYLTTRHD.DTP*.

Family Newsletter, Project 2

Correspond with family members in other locations to find out family news. Once you are updated, create a two-page newsletter and send it to family members. Save as *FAMILY.DTP*.

SCHOOL PROJECTS

The following projects are publications that can be used at your school.

Current Events Newsletter, Project 3

Create a four-page newsletter summarizing local current events for classmates. Save as *EVENTS.DTP*.

Student Rules Handbook, Project 4

Determine the student rules at your school. Create a student rules handbook using the handbook template you created in Chapter 8. Save as *RULES.DTP*.

Brochure for the School Library, Project 5

Many students do not use the school library's resources because they are not aware of them. Confer with the library staff to determine which resources need to be promoted. Design a brochure for your school library publicizing and explaining these resources. Save as *LIBRARY.DTP*.

Administrative Forms, Project 6

Interview the school's office staff to find out what type of form, such as an office inventory form, is needed. Design the form. Save as *ADMFORM.DTP*.

BUSINESS PROJECTS

The following projects are publications for business use.

Newspaper Ad, Project 7

Find a newspaper ad that you believe needs improvement. Redo the ad and list the changes you made. Explain why your changes improve the ad's design. Save as *BETTERAD.DTP*.

Real Client, Project 8

Locate an organization with a desktop publishing need, such as a restaurant that needs a new menu. Before you confirm that you will create this organization's publication, get your teacher's approval. Before you begin the publication, plan a publication schedule listing the following dates:

- Date draft will be completed
- Date draft will be submitted to the organization for approval
- Date draft should be returned to you by organization with suggestions
- Time period for draft alterations
- Date final copy will be completed
- Due date for teacher
- Date publication will be submitted to organization

Plan the publication budget and design the publication. Save as *CLIENT.DTP*.

APPENDIX D

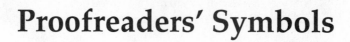

Proofreaders' Symbols

Sometimes you must proofread a publication after it has been printed. Proofreaders' symbols, such as those below, are used to show where corrections will be made on the next draft of the publication.

Revision	Symbol	Edited Copy	Corrected Copy
Align text	⊔	Matt *and* Terri	Matt and Terri
	⊓	Matt *and* Terri	Matt and Terri
	⊏	⌈Matt and Terri	Matt and Terri
	⊐	Matt and Terri⌉	Matt and Terri
Case		Matt and terri	Matt and Terri
uppercase (capitalize)	☰ *or* cap	Matt and terri	Matt and Terri
lowercase	*lc or* /	Matt and TErri	Matt and Terri
		Matt and TErri	Matt and Terri
Close up horizontal space	⌣	Matt and Te rri	Matt and Terri
vertical space	( )	Matt and Terri ( ) Bryan and Stacy	Matt and Terri Bryan and Stacy
Delete	℘	Matt and Terri Neal	Matt and Terri
Delete and add	— *or* /	Matt and Lisa *Terri*	Matt and Terri
		Matt and Ti*e*ri	Matt and Terri
Delete and close up	(/)	Matt and Tee͡rri	Matt and Terri

216

Revision	Symbol	Edited Copy	Corrected Copy
Insert			
apostrophe	ˇ	Terri purse	Terri's purse
comma	⌃	Matt Terri and John	Matt, Terri, and John
dash	⌃—	Put it down now!	Put it down—now!
hyphen	⌃	One page ad	One-page ad
letter or number	⌃s	Purse and hats	Purses and hats
period	⌃•	Mr Matt Neal	Mr. Matt Neal
quotation marks	ˇ ˇ	Matt said, Hello.	Matt said, "Hello."
word	⟲→	Matt Terri	Matt and Terri

| Ignore correction | … or stet | Matt and Terri | Matt and Terri |
| | stet | Matt and Terri | Matt and Terri |

| Italicize | ital | It must be here. | It *must* be here. |

| Move text | ⟲→ | Matt Terri and Neal | Terri and Matt Neal |

| Paragraph, new | ¶ | ¶Matt and Terri came today. | Matt and Terri came today. |

Spacing horizontal	#	Matt andTerri	Matt and Terri
vertical double space	DS⟩	A proofreader must be alert.	A proofreader must be alert.
single space	SS⟩	A proofreader must be alert.	A proofreader must be alert.

| Spell out word or number | sp | Ash St. | Ash Street |
| | | 4th Street | Fourth Street |

Revision	Symbol	Edited Copy	Corrected Copy
Transpose letters	∼	M/ht a/lt	Matt
words		Please carefully read	Please read carefully.
Verify accuracy	?	The play begins at 7 a.m. ?	The play begins at 7 p.m.

USING PROOFREADERS' SYMBOLS

Instructions

Refer to the proofreaders' symbols on pages 216-218. Using these symbols, revise the following sentences as directed. Sentence 0 is given as an example.

0. Move text. Jean and Scott left for school early this morning.

1. Align text. Suzy and Pam are studying.

2. Insert commas. Denise Kim and Jill studied together.

3. Insert periods. J T Smith jogs two miles everyday.

4. Add italics for emphasis Be there at five o'clock sharp!

5. Move *today* to the beginning of the sentence and revise the punctuation. Dan and Scott ran a mile today.

6. Spell out the word. Washington St

7. Add quotation marks. Yankee Doodle Dandy is a folk song.

8. Correct the typographical error. Mike and Linda ride bices for exercise.

9. Transpose letters. Beth and Rhonda wlak to school.

10. Do not delete *and Dwayne*. Angela and Dwayne went to school.

11. Verify the accuracy of the meeting time. The SADD meeting was at 10 p.m.

12. Capitalize. Amy and Mr. evans talked about the test.

13. Add a hyphen. Time saving habits save money.

14. Delete and close up. Leslie and Jeff are gooing to class.

15. Delete the extra word. Leslie and Jeff are going to to class.

16. Change to lowercase. Pam started her Work.

17. Insert a dash for emphasis. Close the door now!

18. Close up the space. Jill sta rted work today.

19. Insert an apostrophe. Scotts car won't start.

20. Delete *Travis* and add *Darren*. Travis and Kelly study together.

APPENDIX E

●

Hyphen Rules

The hyphen is used:

1. to divide a word between syllables at the end of a line.
   Example: The traffic near my sister's apartment was heavy yesterday afternoon.

2. to join compound numbers from twenty-one to ninety-nine when they are keyed as words.
   Example: Forty-four students are in this group.

3. to join compound adjectives before a noun they modify as a unit.
   Example: The wash-and-wear blouse was made of a purple synthetic.

4. after each word or figure in a series that modifies the same noun.
   Example: We need to process the first-, second-, and third-class mail.

5. to form certain compound nouns.
   Example: She is my sister-in-law.
   Frances Martin-Jones is our group leader.

6. to spell out a word or name.
   Example: d-e-l-i-v-e-r-y
   S-c-h-u-l-t-z

7. to show consecutive numbers or the passage of time.
   Example: The pages are number 1-500.
   I'll be gone from 1-4 p.m.

GLOSSARY

acronym Word made from the first letters of a phrase or group of words.

application software Computer program used for a specific application, such as word processing or desktop publishing.

ascender Portion of a character above the x-height.

ASCII Acronym for American Standard Code for Information Interchange. ASCII was developed to provide a standard for communication among programs and computers.

asymmetrical When designs do not mirror or balance on each side of a dividing point.

baseline Invisible line on which characters sit. Baselines are used for aligning characters.

binary number system Number system based on two states, represented electronically as on and off.

bit Shortened term for binary digits in computing.

bit map Graphic formed by a pattern of dots.

boot disk Disk that is the source of the operating system for the computer.

bus mouse Mouse that attaches to a card plugged into an expansion slot in the computer.

byte Unit of storage made up of eight bits. A byte is roughly equivalent to one character.

camera-ready masters Final copies of a document used by commercial printers to create printing plates.

cap height Height from the baseline to the top of a capital letter.

central processing unit Component of a computer that controls computer operations and processes instructions. Often abbreviated CPU.

character Each letter, number, and symbol in a typeface.

click Press and release of the mouse button to perform a function. Keyboard users press the Home key.

clip art Art that is stored magnetically on disk as graphics files.

Clipboard Area in the computer's memory where text or a picture can be held temporarily. The Clipboard is used for cutting, copying, and pasting.

clone Computer that is a functional equivalent to an IBM microcomputer.

close box Small square to the left of the title bar that allows you to stop work on the current document without saving the changes.

collate Arrange pages in their proper order.

column guides Dotted lines that appear on the screen to help you position frames.

commercial printing Mass production of a document by a printing press or copier.

continuous paper Printer paper that is stacked in a fan-fold fashion.

cropping Cutting off parts of a graphic to include only waht you need. Removes unwanted blank space and readjusts the graphic to fill the frame.

CPU See central processing unit.

daisy-wheel printer Letter-quality impact printer that uses a daisy print wheel that strikes characters against an ink ribbon, which in turn impacts the paper to create printed characters.

default setting Setting used by Publish It! unless it is changed by the user.

descender Portion of a character below the baseline.

desktop publishing Production of professional-quality documents, such as newsletters, pamphlets, journals, or business reports, using a personal computer.

dialog box Box that appears on the screen when most commands are chosen. A dialog box can contain choices that will enable you to complete a task.

Directory line Specifies the directory in which the Item Selector is to look.

disk operating system Program that manages the operation of a computer. Often abbreviated DOS.

display screen See monitor.

DOS See disk operating system.

dot-matrix printer Printer that impacts the paper using pins that are pushed against an ink ribbon to create an image of text or graphics.

double-click Press and release the mouse button twice quickly to perform some function. Keyboard users press the Home key twice quickly.

double sided Document that is printed on both sides of the paper.

drag Hold the mouse button down while moving the mouse across the desk. Keyboard users press the End key and move using the arrow keys.

editing In Publish It! graphics, magnifying a graphic to four times its original size so that you can work with the individual pixels.

fixed space Holds related text together so that it is not split between lines.

flatbed scanner Scanner that has a window on which images are placed, much like a photocopier.

floppy disk Thin disk coated with magnetic material used as storage for microcomputers.

font All characters that appear in one size, style, and typeface. Includes upper-case and lower-case characters, figures, and punctuation marks.

footer Text that appears at the bottom of every page or alternate pages.

Frame tool Creates boxes to hold text or graphics.

full box Small square to the right of the title bar that expands the work area to fill the entire screen.

graphics Art that is used to illustrate the message of text, to provide a path for the eye to travel, and to help the reader of a publication find specific information.

graphics adapter Circuitry that provides an interface between the computer and the monitor.

gutter Vertical strip of white space between columns.

hand-held scanner Scanner that is hand held and rolled over a printed image.

handles Small boxes that appear on the perimeter of a frame that can be used to resize frames.

hard disk Storage device consisting of metal disks (platters) coated with magnetic material.

hard return Code at the end of a paragraph of text that tells the computer to start a new line. Inserted with the Enter key.

hardware Computer equipment.

header Text that appears at the top of every page or alternate pages.

hiding Replaces all imported graphic images with an X and displays the graphic filename in the middle of the frame.

hyphenation hot zone Invisible area at the end of every line of ragged text. If a word is too long to fit on a line and is in the hot zone, Publish It! will hyphenate the word.

IBM compatible computer Microcomputer that runs the same software as an IBM microcomputer.

image files Graphics files created with a paint program or a scanner.

imported graphics Graphics loaded into Publish It! from files created in other programs.

importing Process by which text or graphics are brought into Publish It! from another source.

ink-jet printer Nonimpact printer that uses tiny jets to spray ink on the page in the form of a character or graphic image.

interface Means of connecting devices to computers.

Item Selector Dialog box that allows you to choose a file from any available disk and directory.

K Abbreviation for kilobyte.

kerning Adjusts the spacing between two characters.

landscape orientation Page that is positioned with the longest sides at the top and bottom.

laser printer Printer that works like a photocopier except that it gets an image from the computer and uses a laser instead of the reflected light.

layout Blueprint of a document that includes margin settings, paper size, and page orientation, as well as columns and their arrangement on a page.

leaders Characters, usually dots, that precede a tab stop. Used to guide the reader's eye across the page.

leading Space between baselines of text, measured in points. Pronounced "ledding."

library Contains a list of text and graphics files that have been imported and displays paragraph styles and graphics tools.

line art files Graphics files created with a drawing program.

logo   Design using a combination of text and graphics.

mailer   A document sent through the mail to promote and advertise a business.

master page   Single- or double-sided page that acts as a template for all pages of a document. The master page ensures that each page has the same basic layout.

masthead   Portion of text in a periodical publication, providing name, address, and other information about the publication.

mechanical binding   Process, performed by a commercial printer, of punching a series of holes in the binding edge of a document. The pages are held together by a plastic or wire spiral coil that runs through the holes.

menu bar   Bar across the top of the screen that contains ten names representing pull-down menus.

microprocessor   Integrated circuit that makes up the CPU of a computer.

monitor   Output device that consists of an image on a video display device.

mouse   Small hand-operated tool with which the user communicates with the computer. It improves the speed of work with text and graphics.

mouse driver   Program installed in the computer that makes the mouse available to programs like Publish It!

opaque   Frame that you cannot see through.

orientation   How the page is positioned; can be landscape or portrait.

orphan   First line of a paragraph left at the bottom of a page or column.

page description language   Computer language that a printer understands. It instructs the printer to draw lines, text, patterns, and other images using commands.

page dimensions   Size of the page on which your document will be printed. The most common page dimensions are letter, note, and legal.

page format   Includes the page dimensions, orientation, and master pages.

page icon   Tells you the page number of the page that is currently displayed in the work area.

parallel port   Interface that sends and receives 8 bits (1 byte) of data simultaneously through a group of wires.

path   Specifies the directory where files are located on a disk.

path name   (See path)

peripherals   External devices such as printers, mice, and modems.

picas   Measurement used in typography. There are 6 picas per inch.

pixels   Dots that make up a pattern or image.

placing   Putting graphics down on the page.

point   Unit of measurement for typefaces. There are 72 points per inch.

pointer   Indicates on the screen where the current action will take place.

port   Interface through which external devices such as printers, mice, and modems are attached to a computer.

portrait orientation   Position of a page when the shortest sides are at the top and bottom.

PostScript   Most widely known page description language.

print resolution   Measure of the density of the dots that a printer creates on paper.

printing   Process that creates a document on paper.

pull-down menus   Menus that reveal commands below each menu title at the top of the screen.

quick keys   Keyboard shortcuts.

RAM   See random access memory.

random access memory   Memory in a computer that is used to hold programs and data while they are in use. Often abbreviated RAM.

range   Span of pages in a document. For example, if you print pages 5 through 8 in a document, pages 5 through 8 would be called a range.

recto   Right page of a multipage document.

resizing   Changing the size of an entire graphic or individual parts of a graphic.

rulers   Displayed at the top and right sides of the work area. Used to create appropriately sized frames and to align the frames in your document.

saddle stitching   Binding pages by stapling them down the middle fold, suitable for booklets and magazines.

sans serif typeface   Typeface that does not have small lines added to the ends of characters.

scaling   Ensures that a graphic that has been modified is proportionally correct.

scanner   Machine that electronically converts graphics such as hand-drawn pictures and photographs into graphics that can be used by a computer program.

scroll bars   Partially shaded columns along the right and bottom edges of the screen that are used to move the document on the screen either horizontally or vertically.

serial mouse   Mouse that attaches to a computer's serial port.

serial port   Interface that sends and receives data one bit at a time.

serif typeface   Typeface that has small lines added to the ends of characters.

serifs   Small lines added to the ends of characters in a typeface.

sharpness   Visual appearance of a clearly printed document that includes well-defined characters and graphics.

sidebar   Box of related information set apart from the main body of text to add visual interest.

single sheet paper   Type of paper found in photocopiers, also used in some printers.

single sided   Multipage document printed on one side of the paper.

size   Height of a typeface measured in points.

slider   Rectangular box located in the scroll bars. Used to view quickly different parts of the page on the screen.

soft hyphen   Hyphen that you insert into text where you would prefer a word to be broken. Soft hyphens override the Publish It! automatic hyphenation.

software   Computer programs.

style   How typeface appears. Common styles are bold, italic, and normal.

style sheet   Set of format specifications for a document.

symmetrical   Designs that mirror or balance on each side of a dividing point.

system software   Programs that manage the operation of a computer.

tab stop   Marker set at a specified position that is used for aligning text in columns.

template   Predesigned layout for a document that includes graphics and text that are common to each document. Templates are convenient for documents that are published on a regular basis.

text cursor   Thin solid vertical bar that shows where text is to be inserted next.

text frame   Box that holds text in your document.

Text tool   Tool used to work with text within a text frame.

title bar   Contains the name of the current document; located directly under the menu bar.

tool box   Contains tools used to create and alter graphics and text.

typeface   Set of characters that have been designed with a consistent appearance.

typographer   Person who produces type.

typography   Process of producing type.

verso   Left page of a multipage document.

video scanner   Scanner that scans images input from a video source rather than a printed image.

widow   Final line of a paragraph that appears at the top of a page or column.

word wrap   Feature that moves any word that will not fit on the current line to the next line of text during keying. With this feature the user does not need to key a return after each line of keyed text.

work area   Where a document is displayed.

x-height   Invisible line drawn across a typeface at the level of the top of a lower-case *x*.

INDEX

A

Acronym, 38, 212
Adobe Systems, 212. *See also*
    PostScript.
Aldus PageMaker, 8
Apple Computer, Inc., 4-5
Apple LaserWriter, 5,
Application software, 214
Arrow pointer, 10
Art. *See* Graphic(s).
Ascenders, 45
ASCII (American Standard Code for
    Information Interchange)
    format, 38, 42-43, 209, 210
Aspect ratio options, 66
Asymmetrical layout, 121
Audience, analysis of, 145-146
Autoflowing, of text, 159

B

Background color, 161
Baseline, 45
Binary number system, 209
Binding, types of, 147
Bit, 209, 210
Bitmap, 212
Byte, 209

C

Camera-ready copy (masters), 7, 95
Cap height, 45
Capstone projects, 215-216
    Administrative forms, 216
    brochure for school library, 215
    current events newsletter, 215
    family newsletter, 215
    newspaper ad, 216
    personal stationery, 215
    real client, 216
    student rules handbook, 215
Centimeters. *See* Measurement,
    units of.
Central processing unit (CPU), 211
Clicking, 11
Clip art, iv, 8, 58
Clipboard, 34, 35, 78
Close box, 9

Collate print option, 93
Column guides, 10, 39-40, 124-127
    aligning frames to, 126-127
    dialog box for, 125
        column dimensions option, 125
        default settings, 125
        number of columns option, 124
        page offset option, 125
    hiding, 94
    setting, 124-126
Commands
    3/4 size, 16
    Actual size, 16
    Add one page, 148
    Add pages, 148
    Autoflow text, 159
    Bring to front, 76, 77-78
    Copy, 35, 77-78
    Crop picture, 63-64
    Cut, 34, 77-78
    Delete page, 150
    Double size, 16
    Edit picture, 65
    Erase, 18
    Fill style, 72, 74
    Find, 39, 40-41
    Find again, 39, 40
    Find and replace, 39, 41-42
    Footer on this page, 154
    Frame border, 160, 162
    Frame tint, 161, 162
    Go to page, 149, 152
    Half size, 16
    Header on this page, 154
    Headers and footers, 154
    Hide all pictures, 67-68
    Import picture, 58
    Import text, 39, 157, 159
    Kern, 134-135
    Line style, 72, 74
    Name text, 157
    New, 25-27
    Open, 14, 15
    Page numbers, 155
    Paragraph style, 105
    Paste, 34, 35, 77
    Preview, 94-95
    Print, 91, 92, 95

    Quit, 20
    Revert to last, 37
    Ruler spacing, 56
    Save, 17
    Save as, 17
    Save style sheet, 114, 115
    Send to back, 76, 77
    Set column guides, 124, 152
    Show frames and columns, 94-95
    Show grid, 69, 70
    Show rulers, 56
    Show tools, 94-95
    Size and position, 162-163
    Size to fit, 16, 78, 152
    Snap to grid, 69
    Snap to guides, 126
    Soft hyphen, 134
    Status, 29-30
    Text runaround, 129
    Undo, 3
Commercial printing, 5, 6, 87
    preparing for, 95
Copying
    of graphics, 77-79
    of text, 35
CPU (central processing unit), 211
Cropping, of graphics, 63-64

D

Daisy-wheel printers, 87, 88
Data disk, 7, 19, 169
Delete
    text, 33-34
    graphics, 78
Descenders, 45
Desktop publishing
    in your future, 190
    overview of, iii, 3-6,
    terminology, 209-214
Desktop Publishing Center docu-
    ments, 181-188
    advertisement poster, 182-183
    attendance certificate, 190
    banquet poster, 189, 192
    brochure, 186-188
    business card, 184
    business hours poster, 183-184
    invitation, 189-190, 196

job order forms, 185-186
letterhead, 182, 197-199
logo, 181
musical program, 189, 193-195
personal information form, 190, 204
phone message note pad, 190-203
stationery, 190
ticket, 189, 191
weekly work schedule, 185
Dialog boxes
Add pages, 148
defined, 13
Delete pages, 150
Fill style, 72
Find, 40
Find and replace, 42
Frame border, 160, 161
Frame tint, 161
Go to page, 149
Headers and footers, 154, 157
Import picture, 58
Item selector, 14-16, 115
Kern two characters, 135
Line style, 72
Name text, 158
Page format, 103
Page number format, 155
Paragraph options, 106
Paragraph style, 106
Print document, 91, 92
Ruler spacing, 57
Scale picture, 66
Set column guides, 125
Set tab points, 111-112
Size and position, 162
Status, 30, 62
Text runaround, 130
Directory line, 14-16
Disk operating system (DOS), 13
Disk(s)
data, 7, 19, 169
floppy, 211
hard, 212
template, 7, 15, 169
Document(s)
erasing, 18
headers and footers for, 154
master pages for, 150-153
multipage, 147-150
opening, 14-16
previewing, 94-95
saving, 17-18
view, changing, 16-17
DOS (disk operating system), 13
Dot-matrix printers, 88, 89
Double clicking, 11
Double-sided, 147, 151
dpi (dots per inch), 90-91, 212
Dragging, 11, 73, 76, 77
Drawing (graphics) tools, 56, 68
box, 68, 70, 71, 74
circle, 69
ellipse, 69

freehand, 69
graphics pointer, 68, 73, 75
polygon, 69
rounded rectangle, 68, 70
straight line, 68

E

Editing
of graphics, 64-65
of text, 32-36
Exiting Publish It!, 19-20
Exporting text, 42-43, 157

F

File(s)
ASCII, 38, 42-43
erasing, 18
formats, 14, 58
image, 61, 63
line art, 61-62
opening, 15-16
printing to, 95
saving, 17-18
template, 169-175
File management, 14, 18
Filenames, 13-14, 157
extensions to, 14, 157
Fixed space, 134, 135-136
Font, *See also* Typeface.
changing, 47-48, 107
explained, 43-44
selecting, 46-47
Frame(s)
aligning, 69, 126
deleting, 127
linking, 127-129
options, 160-163
resizing, 127
running text around, 129-134
using snap to guides command
with, 127
Frame border, hiding 94
Frame mode, 27, 72, 78
Frame tool, 10, 25-26, 27, 76
Full box, 10, 16
Function key, assigning to paragraph
style, 109

G

Graphic(s), 55-79
adding to layout, 121, 146
aligning, 69
altering, 63-68
aspect ratio options for, 66
categories of,
copying, 77-79
cropping, 63-64
cutting, 77-79
deleting, 62
dragging, 76
drawing, 68-71
editing, 64-65

enhancing, 71-75
fill style in, 72
formats, 58
frame(s), 56, 68
hiding, 67-68
importing, 56, 58-61
layers, 76
line style in, 72
moving, 76-77
objects,
pasting, 77-79
placing, 60
positioning, 75-76
purposes of, 55
resizing, 72, 73-75
restoring, 63
scaling, 65-67
Graphics adapters (cards), 9, 212
CGA, 9, 212
EGA, 9, 212
Hercules, 9, 212
VGA and Super VGA, 9, 212
Graphics mode, 69, 72, 78
Grid, 69
Gutter, 121

H

Handles, 27, 68, 73
Hard return, 38, 146
Hardware, 211
Headers and footers, 154-155
Help, using, 18-19
Hourglass pointer, 10
Hyphen rules, 221
Hyphen, soft, 134, 135-136
Hyphenation, automatic, 106
hot zone for, 108, 134

I

I-beam pointer, 10, 26
IBM PC (personal computer), 11, 211
IBM-compatible computer (clone),
11, 211
Image files, 61, 63
Importing
of graphics, 58-61
of text, 38-39, 157, 159
Inches. *See* Measurement, units of.
Insert key, 79
used to paste graphics, 78
Inserting text, 32
Ink-jet printers, 88, 89

J

Justification options, 106, 108
automatic hyphenation, 106
bullet style, 107, 109
centered, 106-107
fixed spaces and, 134
flushed left, 106-107
flushed right, 106-107
justified, 106-107
letter spacing, 106-107

line spacing (leading), 107
table, 107, 111

K

Kerning, 134-136
Keyboard equivalents, 12
Keyboard shortcuts, 11. *See also* Quick keys.
Kilobyte (K), 211

L

Landscape (horizontal) orientation, 103
Laser printers, 4, 5, 7, 88, 90, 95
Layering, of graphics, 76
Layout, page, 121-136
   adding graphics to, 121, 146
   advanced strategies for, 145-147
   asymmetrical, 121
   basic guidelines for, 121-124
   column spacing and, 121
   designing for visual appeal, 121-124
   fonts and, 107, 123
   graphic placement and, 122
   margins and spacing in, 121, 147-148
   multicolumn, 121
   multiframe, 159
   single-column, 121
   symmetrical, 121
   in template, 169
   type style and, 123
   white space and, 121, 122
Leaders. *See* Tab leaders.
Leading, 107
Letter-quality impact printers, 4, 87
Library, 10, 47, 61-62, 63, 68-69, 94, 105, 106, 109, 110, 151
Line art files, 61-62
Linking, of text frames, 127-129, 157

M

Macintosh computer, 3-4
Margins
   in multipage documents, 147-148
   page, 147, 151
Master pages, 150-153
   recto (right), 151, 153
   verso (left), 151, 153
Masthead, 169
Measurement, units of, 56-57
   default setting, 56
   selecting, 56-57
Mechanical binding, 147
Menu(s), 12
   Edit, 34, 35, 77
   File, 14, 15, 17, 20, 29, 30, 43, 61, 92, 95, 114, 152
   Graphics, 63, 65, 69, 70
   Help, 18-19
   Options, 10, 56, 94, 124, 126, 127, 152, 163
   Page, 16, 77, 94, 148, 152
   pulling down, 12-13

Style, 46
   Text, 41, 106, 108, 109 134, 154, 157
   Undo, 37
Menu bar, 9, 18
Microcomputers. *See* Computers.
Microprocessors, 211
Modes
   frame, 27, 72, 75-76, 78
   graphics, 69, 72, 76, 78
   normal, 31
   pointer, 31
Monitors (display screens), 212
Mouse, 11, 213
   bus, 213
   click, 11
   double click, 11
   drag, 11
   driver, 213
   serial, 213
Moving
   around in text, 30-31
   text frames, 27
MS-DOS (Microsoft disk operating system), 13
Multipage document(s),
   adding and inserting pages into, 148-151
   adding page numbers to, 155-157
   binding for, 147
   deleting pages from, 150-151
   margins in, 147-148
   moving around in, 149, 152

O

Objects, graphic. *See* Graphic(s).
Open cross pointer, 10, 27
Orphan, 146

P

Page(s)
   adding, 148, 149, 150-151
   deleting, 150-151
   inserting, 148, 150-151
   moving between, 148-149
Page description language, 212
Page format, 101-103
   dialog box, 103
   dimensions, 101
      legal, 101
      letter, 101
      master, 101, 151-153
   orientation, 101
      landscape (horizontal), 101, 102, 125
      portrait (vertical), 101, 102, 125
Page icon, 10, 94, 148, 151
Page margin(s), 147, 151
Page number(s), 155-157
   aligning in table of contents, 111
   changing format of, 155
   displaying on screen, 155
   location of, 155
Page size, setting, 101

Page turning arrow, 148
Paragraph options dialog box, 106. *See also* Justification.
Paragraph style(s), 106-108
   assigning function key to, 109
   automatic hyphenation, 106
   Body text, 104-105
   Bullet, 104-105, 106
   creating, 109-110
   deleting, 110-111
   dialog box for, 106
   dimensions, 107, 108
   font and size, 107
   Headline, 104-105
   letter spacing, 106-107
   line spacing (leading), 107
   modifying, 105-106, 108-109
   set tabs option, 107, 111-112
   Subhead, 104-105
   word spacing, 108
Paragraph tool, 10, 108, 113
Path, pathname, 14
PC Paintbrush (.PCX), 59, 170
Pencil tool, 10, 68, 70, 76, 78
Peripherals, 212
Pica(s), 56. *See also* Measurement, units of.
Pixels, 64, 66
Point(s), 56. *See also* Measurement, units of.
Pointer, 10
   arrow, 10
   hour glass, 10
   I-beam, 10, 26
   open cross, 10
   scissors, 63
   spinning wheel, 10
Pointer mode, 31
Port (interface), 212
   parallel, 212
   serial, 212
   specifying, 94
Portrait (vertical) orientation, 101-103
PostScript format, 212
Previewing, 94-95
Print document dialog box options, 92-94
Print options, 92-94
   collate, 93
   copies, 93
   default, 91
   left pages, 93
   output destination, 94
   page range, 92-93
   paper type, 93
      continuous, 93
      single sheet, 93
   pause between pages, 93
   print images, 93-94
   print line art, 93-94
   reverse order, 93
   right pages, 93
   start page, 92

Print quality, 90. *See also* dpi.
    resolution and, 90
    sharpness and, 90-91
Printer(s),
    daisy-wheel, 87, 88
    dot-matrix, 88, 89
    impact, letter-quality, 87
    ink-jet, 88, 89
    laser, 88, 90
    setup for, 91-94
Printer port, selecting, 94
Printing, 87-96. *See also* Printer(s).
    commercial, 5, 6, 87
    to disk, 94, 95-96
Programs. *See* Software.
Proofreader's symbols, 217-219
Publish It!
    desktop publishing with, iv, 6-7
    exiting from, 19-20
    features and capabilities of, 8
    screen elements, 9
        close box, 9
        column guides, 10, 39-40, 94,
            124-127
        full box, 10, 16
        library, 10, 94
        menu bar, 9
        page icon, 10, 94
        pointer, 10
        rulers, 10
        scroll bars, 10
        slider, 10
        text cursor, 10, 26
        title bar, 9
        tool box, 10, 94
        work area, 9
    starting, 7
Pull-down menus, 9

Q

Quick keys, 11, 205-207
    frame shortcuts, 206
    graphics shortcuts, 206
    mouse/keyboard equivalents, 207
    text shortcuts, 206
Quit command, 20

R

Random Access Memory (RAM), 211
Redrawing screen, 66
    with hidden graphic, 66
Resizing
    of graphics, 72-75
    of text frames, 27
Resolution, 90
Reverting to last saved copy, 37-38
Rulers, 10
    using, 56-57

S

Sans serif (sans) typeface, 45
Saving
    in ASCII format, 42-43

document as template, 169
    files, 17-18
Scanner, 213
    flatbed, 213
    hand-held, 213
    video, 214
Scroll bars, 9, 10
Selecting text, 32-33
Serif typeface, 45
Set tab points dialog box options,
        111-112
    copy tab settings?, 112
    leader spacing, 112
    tab #, 112
    tab position, 112
Sharpness, 91
Sidebars, 146
Single-sided, 147, 151
Slider, 10
Soft hyphen, 134
Software, 214. *See also* Aldus
        PageMaker; PC Paintbrush;
        Publish It!; Ventura Publisher.
    application, 214
    system, 214
Spacing options
    letter, 106-107
    line (leading), 108
    word, 108
Spinning wheel pointer, 10
Status box, 30, 62-63, 128
Storage. *See* Disk(s).
Stories (imported text files), 127
    renaming, 128
Style, of typeface, 44
Style sheet, 101-116
    creating, 101-110
    deleting, 110-111
    loading, 115-116
        .STY extension for 115
    saving, 114-115
Symmetrical layout, 121
System software, 214

T

Tab key, 111
Tab leaders, 112
    changing leader characters, 112
Tab stops, 111
Table of contents, 111
Tables, creating, 113-114
Template(s), 169-175
    creating, 171-174
    defined, 169
    from existing document, 172
    saving, 169
    from scratch, 172-174
    using, 169-171
Template disk, 7
Text
    autoflowing, 159-160
    copying, 35
    creating, 27-29

cutting, 34-35
    deleting, 33-34
    editing, 32-36
    exporting, 42-43
    font, changing, 47
    importing, 38-39, 154, 157
    inserting, 32
    keying, 28-29
    moving around in, 30-31
    naming, 157-158
    pasting, 34-35
    selecting, 32-33
Text cursor, 10, 26
Text frame(s), 27
    imported text in, 127
    linking, 127-129
    moving and resizing, 27
Text runaround dialog box options,
        130-134
    choose runaround, 130
    define border, 130, 132-134
    defining odd-shaped frames,
        130-131
    frame padding, 130
Text tool, 10, 25-26, 114
Title bar, 9
Tool box, 10, 25
    drawing graphics with, 68-71
    hiding, 94
    tools in, 10
Typeface, 44-45. *See also* Font.
    ascenders of, 45
    baseline of, 45
    cap height of, 45
    characters of, 45
    descenders of, 45
    sans serif, 45
    serif, 45
    size, 44, 107
    style, 44, 47
    terminology, 45
    x-height of, 45
Typographer, typography, 3, 56

U

Undo command and menu, 37

W

White space, 121, 123
Widow, 146
Word wrap, 27-28
Work area, 9
WYSIWYG (what you see is what
        you get), 94

X

x-Height, 45
Xerox Ventura Publisher, 8

Z

Zooming in and out, 16-17